WORLD POVERTY

ISSN 1930-3300

WORLD POVERTY

Nancy Dziedzic

INFORMATION PLUS® REFERENCE SERIES
Formerly Published by Information Plus, Wylie, Texas

Detroit • New York • San Francisco • New Haven, Conn. • Waterville, Maine • London

World Poverty

Nancy Dziedzic
Paula Kepos, Series Editor

Project Editor
John McCoy

Permissions
Shalice Caldwell-Shah, Edna Hedblad,
Emma Hull

Composition and Electronic Prepress
Evi Seoud

Manufacturing
Cynthia Bishop, Drew Kalasky

ISBN-13: 978-0-7876-5103-9 (set)
ISBN-10: 0-7876-5103-6 (set)
ISBN-13: 978-1-4144-0984-9
ISBN-10: 1-4144-0984-2
ISSN 1930-3300

This title is also available as an e-book.
ISBN-13: 978-1-4144-1045-6 (set)
ISBN-10: 1-4144-1045-X (set)
Contact your Thomson Gale sales representative for ordering information.

Printed in the United States of America
10 9 8 7 6 5 4 3 2 1

TABLE OF CONTENTS

PREFACE

World Poverty is part of the *Information Plus Reference Series*. The purpose of each volume of the series is to present the latest facts on a topic of pressing concern in modern American life. These topics include today's most controversial and most studied social issues: abortion, capital punishment, care for the elderly, crime, health care, the environment, immigration, minorities, social welfare, women, youth, and many more. Although written especially for the high school and undergraduate student, this series is an excellent resource for anyone in need of factual information on current affairs.

By presenting the facts, it is Thomson Gale's intention to provide its readers with everything they need to reach an informed opinion on current issues. To that end, there is a particular emphasis in this series on the presentation of scientific studies, surveys, and statistics. These data are generally presented in the form of tables, charts, and other graphics placed within the text of each book. Every graphic is directly referred to and carefully explained in the text. The source of each graphic is presented within the graphic itself. The data used in these graphics are drawn from the most reputable and reliable sources, in particular from the various branches of the U.S. government and from major independent polling organizations. Every effort has been made to secure the most recent information available. The reader should bear in mind that many major studies take years to conduct and that additional years often pass before the data from these studies are made available to the public. Therefore, in many cases the most recent information available in 2006 dated from 2003 or 2004. Older statistics are sometimes presented as well, if they are of particular interest and no more recent information exists.

Although statistics are a major focus of the *Information Plus Reference Series*, they are by no means its only content. Each book also presents the widely held positions and important ideas that shape how the book's subject is discussed in the United States. These positions are explained in detail and, where possible, in the words of their proponents. Some of the other material to be found in these books includes: historical background; descriptions of major events related to the subject; relevant laws and court cases; and examples of how these issues play out in American life. Some books also feature primary documents, or have pro and con debate sections giving the words and opinions of prominent Americans on both sides of a controversial topic. All material is presented in an even-handed and unbiased manner; the reader will never be encouraged to accept one view of an issue over another.

HOW TO USE THIS BOOK

It can be argued that poverty is the most widespread and serious problem confronting the modern world. Billions of people are so poor that they struggle, and sometimes fail, to meet their needs for sustenance, shelter, and security. Even among those who can meet these basic needs, there are many who cannot afford adequate medical care, a good education, and other aspects of a decent standard of living. The problems posed by poverty are especially acute in what is sometimes called the undeveloped world. When judged in relative terms, however, poverty afflicts substantial numbers of people in even the richest nations on Earth. This book examines the forms that poverty takes around the world, its many causes, the serious negative consequences that it has for individuals and societies, and the effort to eliminate it.

World Poverty consists of ten chapters and three appendices. Each of the chapters is devoted to a particular aspect of poverty around the world. For a summary of the information covered in each chapter, please see the synopses provided in the Table of Contents at the front of the book. Chapters generally begin with an overview of the basic facts and background information on the chapter's topic, then proceed to examine subtopics of particular interest. For example, Chapter 1: What is Poverty? begins by explaining the concepts of absolute poverty and relative poverty. It then discusses the controversies surrounding attempts to establish absolute and relative poverty standards. The most widely used worldwide poverty standards are examined, as are the poverty standards in use in the United States. The chapter concludes by explaining the concept of identifying counties in terms of their development and how this is one way in which poor and rich nations are commonly distinguished from each other. Readers can find their way through a chapter by looking for the section and subsection headings, which are clearly set off from the text. Or, they can refer to the book's extensive Index if they already know what they are looking for.

Statistical Information

The tables and figures featured throughout *World Poverty* will be of particular use to the reader in learning about this issue. These tables and figures represent an extensive collection of the most recent and important statistics on poverty, hunger, and related issues—for example, graphics in the book cover progress toward the elimination of world hunger; the link between illiteracy and poverty; living standards in India; links between poverty and school attendance; and the impact of war on Iraq's poverty levels. Thomson Gale believes that making this information available to the reader is the most important way in which we fulfill the goal of this book: to help readers understand the issues and controversies surrounding poverty around the world and reach their own conclusions.

Each table or figure has a unique identifier appearing above it for ease of identification and reference. Titles for the tables and figures explain their purpose. At the end of each table or figure, the original source of the data is provided.

In order to help readers understand these often complicated statistics, all tables and figures are explained in the text. References in the text direct the reader to the relevant statistics. Furthermore, the contents of all tables and figures are fully indexed. Please see the opening section of the index at the back of this volume for a description of how to find tables and figures within it.

Appendices

In addition to the main body text and images, *World Poverty* has three appendices. The first is the Important Names and Addresses directory. Here the reader will find contact information for a number of government and private organizations that can provide further information on aspects of world poverty. The second appendix is the Resources section, which can also assist the reader in conducting his or her own research. In this section the author and editors of *World Poverty* describe some of the sources that were most useful during the compilation of this book. The final appendix is the Index.

ADVISORY BOARD CONTRIBUTIONS

The staff of Information Plus would like to extend its heartfelt appreciation to the Information Plus Advisory Board. This dedicated group of media professionals provides feedback on the series on an ongoing basis. Their comments allow the editorial staff who work on the project to continually make the series better and more user-friendly. Our top priorities are to produce the highest-quality and most useful books possible, and the Advisory Board's contributions to this process are invaluable.

The members of the Information Plus Advisory Board are:

- Kathleen R. Bonn, Librarian, Newbury Park High School, Newbury Park, California

- Madelyn Garner, Librarian, San Jacinto College—North Campus, Houston, Texas

- Anne Oxenrider, Media Specialist, Dundee High School, Dundee, Michigan

- Charles R. Rodgers, Director of Libraries, Pasco-Hernando Community College, Dade City, Florida

- James N. Zitzelsberger, Library Media Department Chairman, Oshkosh West High School, Oshkosh, Wisconsin

COMMENTS AND SUGGESTIONS

The editors of the *Information Plus Reference Series* welcome your feedback on *World Poverty*. Please direct all correspondence to:

Editors
Information Plus Reference Series
27500 Drake Rd.
Farmington Hills, MI 48331-3535

CHAPTER 1
WHAT IS POVERTY?

Most people have an idea of what it means to be poor. We think of conditions like hunger, homelessness, preventable diseases, unemployment, and illiteracy as elements of poverty. Those and other issues will be covered later in this book. However, from a social and economic standpoint, poverty is a complex topic that can be difficult to describe in objective terms. Most governments and social service agencies have their own definitions of poverty, including how it is measured and who is considered poor. This chapter will explain the means used by the United States and the international community to define and measure poverty.

DEFINING AND MEASURING POVERTY INTERNATIONALLY

Because being poor differs dramatically across countries, experts have had a difficult time establishing concrete terms to discuss it. Since the publication of its *Human Development Report* (1997), the United Nations has defined poverty as the "denial of choices and opportunities most basic to human development—to lead a long, healthy, creative life and enjoy a decent standard of living, freedom, self-esteem, and the respect of others." This definition takes into account nearly all aspects of human experience—personal, political, social, and financial. Not all attempts to define the condition of being poor are as inclusive. More typically, the focus has been on the economic side of poverty—how much money people make compared with other people. Since the mid-1990s agencies have recognized that poverty affects more than a person's income and consumption habits, leading to expanded definitions—also called composite indicators—used by the United Nations, the World Bank, and others.

Absolute and Relative Poverty

The most common way for governments and organizations to explain poverty is to break it down into two facets: absolute poverty and relative poverty. In general, absolute poverty means that a person's basic subsistence needs (for food, clothing, and shelter) are not being met. Relative poverty, on the other hand, typically means that a person's needs are not being met in comparison to the rest of his or her society. Gordon M. Fisher, in "Is There Such a Thing as an Absolute Poverty Line over Time?" (http://www.census.gov/hhes/poverty/povmeas/papers/elastap4.html), offers this explanation of the two terms:

> an absolute poverty line is one which is constructed as an estimate of families' minimum consumption needs; this is done without reference to the income or consumption levels of the general population. In the same context, a relative poverty line is one which is set as a fraction of the median or mean income or consumption of the population as a whole (generally with appropriate adjustments for family size).

In other words, the measurement of absolute poverty considers whether a family can afford a specified amount of goods and services that are necessary for basic living in the country, city, or village in which they live. The measurement of relative poverty compares a family's financial situation with that of the rest of the population group to which they belong.

At the United Nations World Summit for Social Development in 1995, the governments of 117 countries signed the Copenhagen Declaration, which defined absolute poverty in these terms:

> Absolute poverty is a condition characterised by severe deprivation of basic human needs, including food, safe drinking water, sanitation facilities, health, shelter, education, and information. It depends not only on income but also on access to social services.

In 1979 researcher Peter Townsend defined relative poverty as "the absence or inadequacy of those diets, amenities, standards, services, and activities which are common or customary in society" (*Poverty in the United Kingdom*).

But as David Gordon and Paul Spicker, editors of *The International Glossary on Poverty* (Comparative Research Program on Poverty of the International Social Science Council, 1999), point out, much of the discussion of absolute versus relative poverty is a matter of semantics—people's interpretations of the meanings of words—when in reality the two concepts are more similar than different.

PROBLEMS WITH ABSOLUTE AND RELATIVE POVERTY DEFINITIONS. Critics say that the concepts of absolute and relative poverty are not objective and depend too heavily on individual judgments of what it means to be poor. Ivan P. Felligi, Chief Statistician of Canada, argued in *On Poverty and Low Income* (1997, http://www.statcan.ca/english/research/13F0027XIE/13F0027XIE.htm) that there really is no "internationally accepted" definition of poverty, largely because the international community has yet to agree on whether poverty should be defined and measured across countries or within them. Felligi noted that the idea of absolute poverty is particularly problematic: "Before anyone can calculate the minimum income needed to purchase the 'necessities' of life, they must decide what constitutes a 'necessity' in food, clothing, shelter, and a multitude of other purchases, from transportation to reading material." For example, a donkey might be a necessity for a family living in a remote village in Africa but would be useless to a family in an American inner city; a tent might be the ideal shelter for a nomadic family, whereas those who live in one place require a more permanent structure. In a city with adequate public transportation, a person would not necessarily need a car, but those living in rural areas might not have any other options for transportation.

Additionally, Felligi pointed out that definitions of poverty can change over time within a single country. Living conditions that were acceptable in previous centuries and even decades are now considered inhumane; everyone in the United States agrees that indoor plumbing and electricity are basic necessities, yet as recently as the mid-twentieth century these things were luxuries to many Americans. Similarly, according to Felligi, a person who is considered rich in one country might be seen as abysmally poor in a wealthier country.

Composite Poverty Indicators

Composite poverty indicators allow for a broader explanation and measurement of poverty because they take into account factors not directly related to a family's income or larger economic forces such as a country's gross domestic product (GDP; a country's total income and economic output). Although GDP is often used to measure a nation's standard of living (the availability of goods and services to a country's citizens), many experts contend that it is not an adequate way to explain poverty because it measures only the consumption of material goods.

Using composite poverty indicators allows those who study and track poverty to consider factors other than income and possessions, instead examining a person's overall quality of life.

THE HUMAN POVERTY INDEX. In its *Human Development Report 1997* the United Nations Development Program added another element to the standard definitions of poverty: the Human Poverty Index (HPI). Rather than relying solely on the terms absolute and relative poverty, the UN Development Program uses the concepts of "income poverty" and "human poverty." Under income poverty fall the terms "extreme poverty" and "overall poverty." Extreme poverty is the inability to meet basic food needs, which are defined by minimum calorie requirements. Overall poverty is the inability to afford basic needs other than food, such as shelter, clothing, and energy, along with food. The concept of human poverty is further broken down into direct and indirect effects of poverty on human life. Direct effects of poverty on people include illiteracy, hunger and malnutrition, shortened life spans, illness or death from preventable diseases, and poor health of pregnant women and mothers. Indirect effects include a compromised or total lack of access to essentials such as energy, sanitation, clean drinking water, health care, transportation, and communication services.

The Human Poverty Index frequently is divided into two measures. HPI-1 is used to measure absolute poverty in less developed countries. Its variables are: the percentage of a population likely to die before the age of forty; the percentage of people over age fifteen who are illiterate; the percentage of children under age five who are underweight; and the percentage of people without access to public and private services such as health care and clean water.

HPI-2 is used to measure relative poverty in industrialized (more developed) countries. It focuses on the same variables as HPI-1, but with adjustments to the conditions of the poor living in wealthier countries. HPI-2 measures: the percentage of people likely to die before the age of sixty; the percentage of adults living with functional illiteracy (a degree of illiteracy that does not allow people to function at a basic level in reading and writing); and the proportion of people living with long-term unemployment and below the poverty line, which is set at 50% of the median disposable household income. Additionally, HPI-2 examines the social alienation that can accompany persistent unemployment and poverty.

OTHER COMPOSITE INDICATORS. Other commonly used composite poverty indicators are:

- The Human Suffering Index (HSI) ranks the levels of suffering experienced by poor people in the areas of life expectancy; calorie intake; supply of clean water; child immunization; enrollment in secondary school; per capita gross domestic product; inflation rate; access to communications systems; technological development; civil rights; and political freedoms.

- The Physical Quality of Life Index (PQLI) combines measurements of life expectancy, infant mortality, and literacy rates.

- The Human Development Index (HDI) measures poverty using a combination of life expectancy, literacy, and amount of education, along with the domestic purchasing power of GDP (how much citizens of a country are able to buy based on the country's gross domestic product). Like the Human Poverty Index, the Human Development Index was devised by the United Nations Development Program, but its purpose is to measure how well a country is progressing toward development, whereas the Human Poverty Index measures the level of poverty and suffering experienced in a country at any given time.

Poverty Measurements Used by the World Bank

The World Bank is an international organization of member nations whose goal is to reduce poverty and increase development in poor countries. It is divided into two distinct groups: the International Bank for Reconstruction and Development, which focuses on middle-income countries and those with good credit, and the International Development Association, with a focus on the very poorest countries, which may be deeply in debt to other nations. The World Bank provides lines of credit, loans, and grants so that poor countries can improve infrastructure (roads, bridges, waterways, etc.), communications, health care, and education.

Like many international institutions, the World Bank uses its own terminology to define and measure poverty:

- *Incidence of poverty*: The percentage of a country's population that cannot afford basic necessities (a "basket of goods and services"). This is also known as living below the poverty line—an income level below which a person is unable to meet basic needs (see below for more information on poverty lines).

- *Depth of poverty*: How far below the poverty line the poor population lives; also called the poverty gap.

- *Poverty severity*: Measures how poor the poor are. In other words, poverty severity (also called the squared poverty gap) measures how far below the poverty line individuals and households are, with more consequence given to those at the very bottom.

VULNERABILITY TO POVERTY. An important facet of the World Bank's measurements is tracking how likely people are to fall into poverty or to fall deeper into poverty today. The World Bank Web site explains why keeping track of vulnerability to poverty matters: "Vulnerability may influence household behavior and coping strategies and is thus an important consideration for poverty reduction policies." For example, if a farmer and his or her family lives on the brink of poverty at any time, "The fear of bad weather conditions or the fear of being expelled from the land they cultivate can deter households from investing in more risky but higher productivity crops and affect their capacity to generate income." This fear and its resultant behaviors can influence the wider economy of the community and the nation, as a farmer who avoids planting high-yield crops might affect prices, consumers' buying habits, and the market overall.

According the World Bank, a number of incidents can trigger a descent into poverty, and these incidents can occur at several socioeconomic levels. At the individual level are unexpected events like major illnesses or deaths within the household, which can lead to financial ruin when medical bills cannot be paid or if it is the main breadwinner who becomes ill or dies. At the community level are things like environmental damage due to pollution that causes unsuitable working conditions or local social problems like rioting and crime. Larger trends at the macroeconomic level include national or international incidents like natural disasters and war, which also effect people's level of vulnerability to poverty. A family that is already experiencing financial instability can easily fall into poverty under any of these circumstances, and the more people there are living on the brink of poverty, the less stable the local, national, and international economies will be.

While vulnerability to poverty is difficult to measure and track, the World Bank uses such monetary indicators as income and consumption, as well as nonmonetary indicators like health status, weight (to determine whether minimum calorie requirements are being met), and how many financial and nonmonetary assets a person or family has.

POVERTY LINES AND THE DOLLAR-A-DAY STANDARD

A poverty line is a level of income below which a person cannot afford the bare minimum to exist: an amount of food sufficient to fuel the human body, clothing appropriate to a person's living and working conditions, and suitable shelter to protect from the elements. Governments determine their countries' poverty lines by calculating the annual average cost of basic necessities for an adult to function. Because these costs differ substantially across countries, it is impossible to set a single international poverty line. Additionally, measurements of poverty depend in part on household surveys that are issued and analyzed by government agencies. According to Don Sillers of the U.S. Agency for International Development (USAID), many governments fail to take poverty surveys regularly and use inadequate survey methodologies, and there can be problems with the way the data are analyzed and presented ("National and International Poverty Lines: An Overview," 2005, http://www.povertytools.org/Project_Documents/Poverty_lines___An_Overview_1_4_06.pdf). Therefore, in order to measure poverty at the international level, the World Bank developed the dollar-a-day standard in 1990, which assumes an income for those living in "extreme poverty" of $370 per year, or about a dollar per day.

National Poverty Lines

According to Sillers, national poverty lines are defined by "identifying a minimally acceptable diet," meaning the most basic number of calories on which the human body can function. Once that number is determined, analysts calculate the cost of obtaining this minimum amount of food at the current market price. The cost of necessary items other than food is then added to the equation, the total of which forms the poverty line.

However, as Sillers pointed out, several factors complicate measurements using poverty lines. It is difficult to compare poverty in different nations because wealthy, middle-income, and low-income countries have varying notions of what percentage of income is or should be spent on food and nonfood items. Also, what constitutes an "adequate diet" is a subject of debate. People living in poor countries tend to exist on a much less varied diet than those living in richer countries, where a reliance on more expensive prepackaged food is usually assumed.

The second problem with measurements using poverty lines is that countries may estimate two separate lines, one for urban and one for rural households, which may skew measurements because of assumptions about how much each group spends on necessities. Other problems include disparities that result from countries basing their household surveys on income rather than on expenditures (income—how much people make—is considered more difficult to measure than expenditures—how much people spend), and adjustments for price changes are not always correctly applied to poverty lines, causing them to drift over time, which makes it more difficult to track changes in poverty.

One Dollar per Day

The international dollar-per-day poverty standard was developed by the World Bank for its 1990 *World Development Report* in order to provide a single global measurement. To account for exchange rates and differences in prices and gross domestic product (GDP), the World Bank had to set a level that would be relevant in underdeveloped, developing, and developed countries despite immense differences in the meaning of poverty around the world.

Generally speaking, earning a dollar per day or less means that a person in any country is living in "extreme poverty," which means that that person cannot afford to buy even the most basic human necessities. However, "one dollar a day" is not a literal amount of money. Rather, it means a dollar a day at purchasing power parity in 1985 prices. Purchasing power parity (PPP) is a way to measure the value of currency that allows economists and poverty researchers to compare the standards of living in different countries while accounting for differences in both wages and costs of living. In general, PPP refers to the goods and services that a currency has the power to buy, typically expressed as a "basket" or "bundle" of necessary items. PPP measures how much the same basket or bundle of goods and services costs around the world; allowing for exchange rates, the PPP number in each country should allow people to purchase the same basket of goods and services that a U.S. dollar can purchase in the United States. As with absolute poverty (see above), critics of PPP point out that one problem with the measure lies in the notion of what is and is not a necessity: a product or service considered a staple in one culture may be a luxury in others. Nevertheless, most researchers agree that purchasing power parity is, to date, the best way to examine poverty at the global level.

Because the dollar-a-day standard was conceived in 1990, currency values of 1985 were used as a baseline. By 1993 the value of the U.S. dollar had changed, so that "one dollar a day" was actually equal to $1.08 per day. Nevertheless, the term "dollar a day" is still used because it is simpler and easier to remember. To measure "poverty"—as distinguished from "extreme poverty"—the World Bank uses a two-dollars-per-day standard, meaning that anyone earning less than two dollars per day is living in poverty. In this measurement the concept of purchasing power parity is the same, but the two-dollars-per-day standard allows researchers to study the poor in slightly less impoverished countries while still using the PPP standard.

POVERTY THRESHOLDS AND GUIDELINES IN THE UNITED STATES

Governmental agencies in the United States tend to avoid using the term "poverty line" because they consider it ambiguous. Instead, U.S. officials divide poverty measurement tools into two categories: thresholds and guidelines. The U.S. Census Bureau issues poverty thresholds, which are statistical measurements used to track the total number of people living in poverty in the

United States. Poverty guidelines, on the other hand, are issued by the U.S. Department of Health and Human Services (HHS) and are used for the administrative purpose of determining eligibility for certain federal social programs and services, including Head Start, Medicare, AIDS Drug Assistance Program, the National School Lunch Program, and the Special Supplemental Nutrition Program for Women, Infants, and Children (WIC), among many others.

Poverty thresholds are calculated and issued by the Census Bureau in September or October of the year following the year that they measure. This is because they are based on the Consumer Price Index (CPI) and the Current Population Survey (CPS), the results of which are not known until the end of the year in question or the beginning of the following year. Poverty guidelines are published early in the year in the *Federal Register* by the Department of Health and Human Services. They are based on price changes over the preceding year. The guidelines are a simplified version of the thresholds, although at the time of their respective publications thresholds and guidelines are considered equally accurate.

History of the Poverty Threshold

In 1961 the U.S. Department of Agriculture (USDA) created four food plans that could be applied to the food buying patterns of American families. The Economy, Low-cost, Moderate-cost, and Liberal food plans were based on the food spending habits of U.S. households. They were developed by estimating the least amount of food necessary to meet nutritional requirements at specified prices. The Economy plan, now called the Thrifty food plan, has been updated several times over the years—most recently in 1999 by the USDA's Center for Nutrition Policy and Promotion—to allow for revisions in nutritional guidelines and changing food prices. These food categories are used to determine where households fall on the poverty threshold.

The poverty threshold was developed in 1963 Mollie Orshansky of the U.S. Social Security Administration. Orshansky's measurement was based on the USDA's Economy food plan. According to the USDA, the Economy plan was "designed for temporary or emergency use when funds are low" because it was based on the least amount of food at the lowest possible cost. Orshansky formulated calculations for families based on their size (how many people living in a household), the sex of the head of the household, how many family members were children, whether the families were farmers or not, and the age of the head of the household (specifically, over sixty-five or under). At the time, it was assumed that American families spent about one-third of their income on food, so Orshansky multiplied the numbers on the Economy food plan by three to come up with the poverty thresholds. Orshansky's calculations resulted in a matrix containing 124 different poverty thresholds for each different household variable.

In 1981 the matrix was reduced from 124 thresholds to forty-eight when some of the distinctions were eliminated or revised. For example, the farm and nonfarm categories were changed so that all households were measured by the criteria of nonfarms. Gender differences were cut by averaging male- and female-headed households together, and the size of the largest households considered was increased from seven people to nine.

CONTROVERSIES OVER U.S. POVERTY MEASUREMENTS

In the paper "Reconsidering the Federal Poverty Measure" (University of Maryland School of Public Policy, Welfare Reform Academy, June 14, 2004), Douglas J. Besharov and Peter Germanis discuss problems with the use of thresholds and guidelines, noting two commonly cited failures of the measurements:

1. The method of measuring poverty in the United States does not take into account all forms of income—specifically, the federal poverty threshold does not count noncash forms of aid, such as food stamps, Medicaid, school lunch programs, housing assistance, and the State Children's Health Insurance Program. Nor does it recognize the Earned Income Tax Credit, the monetary value of assets such as houses, or income brought into a household by non-family members, such as a mother's boyfriend.

2. The current poverty threshold calculation that assumes spending on food accounts for one-third of a household's budget most likely fails to reflect more contemporary household spending patterns. In the early 2000s food spending was estimated to be one-seventh of a household's income. Additionally, the calculation has not been accurately updated to reflect the costs of other current needs such as child care and higher taxes.

Besharov and Germanis write that many commentators believe a more accurate picture of poverty could be gained by measuring household consumption of certain goods and services rather than household income, while others argue that neither income nor consumption measurements can provide insight into the physical and emotional aspects of living in poverty and that, instead, "well-being" indicators—similar to the composite indicators discussed above—should be used.

In 2002 the Census Bureau began including "alternative estimates" in its publications on poverty, largely in response to the 1995 National Academy of Sciences/Committee on National Statistics' (NAS/CNSTAT) Panel on Poverty and Family Assistance, which concluded that the U.S. method of measuring poverty "no longer provides an accurate picture of the differences in the extent of economic poverty among population groups or geographic areas of the country, nor an accurate picture of trends over time" (*Measuring Poverty: A New Approach*, National Research Council, 1995). The Census Bureau's 2003 report *Alternative Poverty Estimates in the United States: 2003* examined the new measures of income and, more specifically, the recommendations of the NAS/CNSTAT panel report, in comparison with the old measures. In June 2004 the National Academy of Sciences hosted a Workshop on Experimental Poverty Measures, which examined issues including the role of childcare and medical expenses, home ownership, and demographic and geographic differences in assessing poverty. As of 2005, U.S. government agencies still relied heavily on the traditional poverty measures, although some, such as the Census Bureau, included alternative measures in their research to gain a broader view of poverty in the United States.

CLASSIFYING COUNTRIES BY LEVEL OF ECONOMIC DEVELOPMENT

In addition to the above definitions and measurements of poverty, countries are classified by how "developed" they are economically. During the cold war—the period of escalating tensions between the United States and the Soviet Union that lasted from the 1950s until the Berlin Wall was dismantled in 1989—the terms "first world," "second world," and "third world" came into use. Originally, third-world countries were those that did not align themselves with either the first-world United States and its Western allies or the second-world Soviet Union and other Eastern bloc countries. Over time, however, the term "first world" came to refer to those countries that were industrialized and relatively wealthy, while "third world" was used to describe countries that were poor, indebted to other nations, and not industrialized.

With the end of the cold war and the dissolution of the Soviet Union in the late 1980s and early 1990s, the term "second world," which was rarely used to begin with, was abandoned. "First world" came to refer to all countries that are industrially and technologically developed, while "third world" described poor countries that are largely undeveloped. However, the idea of a third world was considered derogatory—as if poor countries were hopelessly removed from the rest of the world when in fact their people make up at least two-thirds of the planet's population.

Instead, academics and researchers began using the terms "developed," "developing," and "underdeveloped" to describe rich, industrialized countries, countries whose economies are expanding, and those that remain poor and without large-scale industry or technology, respectively. Still others prefer "least developed countries," "majority world" or "two-thirds world" when discussing countries that belong to the poorest segment of the global economy. The term "fourth world" is sometimes used to describe either the very poorest social or economic groups within underdeveloped countries or indigenous or marginalized people within any country.

As there is still no widespread consensus about which terms to use, this book will give preference to "developed," "developing," and "underdeveloped" to discuss the three main categories of world economic development.

CHAPTER 2
THE CAUSES OF POVERTY AND THE SEARCH FOR SOLUTIONS

Massive poverty and obscene inequality are such terrible scourges of our times—times in which the world boasts breathtaking advances in science, technology, industry and wealth accumulation—that they have to rank alongside slavery and apartheid as social evils.

—Nelson Mandela, 2005

THE MYTHS AND REALITIES OF POVERTY

Poverty is a multidimensional problem, with numerous causes and contributing factors. Because of its complexity and subtleties, misconceptions abound about the poor. One common belief is that poverty is caused by overpopulation; many people think that if the poor would only stop having children they could rise out of poverty. Another belief is that poor people must have made wrong choices that led to their poverty. While these explanations might seem to make sense on the surface, they are in fact extremely simplistic. In the United States and other developed nations, beliefs about the poor frequently are based on stereotypes: many people think the poor are lazy; that the majority of poor people are immigrants or ethnic minorities; that the poor are single parents who should never have had children to begin with; or that the poor are dangerous, criminals, or mentally ill.

Poverty is not the result of personal failings, nor is it only a matter of income. Poverty is directly related to health, education, housing, political opportunities, and other factors. Likewise, poverty worsens people's social status and diminishes their involvement in their communities and in the larger sphere. These human development factors are critical to understanding poverty. They are also critical to solving the immense problem of poverty. Additionally, there are political and economic policies that can contribute to impoverishment. Most of the explanations are, however, as problematic as poverty itself.

Globalization and Fair Trade

Globalization—the growing economic interdependence of nations—is extremely controversial, with strong supporters and bitter detractors. Meetings of the World Trade Organization (WTO) and the G8 summits, which bring together leaders of the world's eight largest economies (Canada, France, Germany, Italy, Japan, Russia, United States, and the United Kingdom)—regularly draw large, sometimes violent, anti-globalization demonstrations and protests.

The proponents of globalization maintain that opening markets across national borders will allow for freer exchange of money and technology, which has the potential to develop the world's smaller and poorer economies and therefore help alleviate poverty in developing regions while increasing the wealth of developed ones. Theoretically, at least, globalization should work for everyone. The World Bank, the International Monetary Fund (IMF), the World Trade Organization, and the G8 countries are all proponents of globalization. A major facet of globalization is the forging of free trade agreements (FTAs). FTAs are agreements between countries that allow the exchange of goods and labor across borders without the imposition by governments of tariffs (a tax on imported goods) or other trade barriers. Two of the best-known FTAs are the North American Free Trade Agreement (NAFTA), among Canada, Mexico, and the United States, and the Central American Free Trade Agreement (CAFTA), among the United States, Costa Rica, El Salvador, Guatemala, Honduras, and Nicaragua. Other FTAs exist throughout the world. As of early 2006, thirty-four countries from North, Central, and South America were negotiating the details of a Free Trade Area of the Americas (FTAA).

Opponents of globalization argue that it puts the welfare of multinational corporations above the welfare of poor and indigenous people. According to the International

Forum on Globalization (IFG), the greatest danger of globalization is that it allows corporations to act without accountability, thus enabling them to victimize the poor. In "How to End Poverty: Making Poverty History and the History of Poverty" (http://www. navdanya.org/articles/end-poverty.htm, March 28, 2005), Vandana Shiva contends that the concept of poverty embodied by the globalization movement is mistaken because it is based on the notion that "simple, sustainable living" is the same as "dispossession and deprivation." According to Shiva, the globalization movement's focus on consumerism (selling products to people through international trade) denies people in traditional cultures the ability to support themselves by growing their own food, making their own clothing, and otherwise providing for themselves. Shiva further maintains that when corporations and industries take land from self-sustaining cultures, they actually push those people into poverty by depriving them of the resources they need to survive.

Other critics of globalization claim that it increases instances of unjust labor practices that take advantage of the poor, such as sweatshops and child labor. In addition, despite the increasing number of free trade agreements, poor countries are often subject to higher import tariffs when they export goods to developed countries. According to the report *Rigged Rules and Double Standards: Trade, Globalisation, and the Fight against Poverty* (Oxfam, Make Trade Fair, 2002), these tariffs cost developing countries about $1 billion per year, despite the fact that developing countries account for just 3% of the world's trade. However, the report does not attempt to discredit trade as a means of poverty reduction. Rather, it focuses on the importance of fair trade: eliminating trade barriers to poor countries and developing healthy, sustainable, trade-based employment opportunities within them. As low-income countries gain access to markets, investment is stimulated, which in turn promotes employment opportunities at the local level and economic growth at the national level.

International Debt

Lending and debt relief to underdeveloped and developing nations is another controversial issue. Many low-income countries became heavily indebted to wealthy nations in the 1970s, when banks around the world began lending money to developing countries that were rich in resources such as oil. The money, however, was often mismanaged by corrupt governments—particularly in the countries of sub-Saharan Africa—and spent on "pet" projects to expand the wealth of the upper classes rather than on infrastructure and social investments such as roadways, safe water, education, and health care. When interest rates on the loans rose and the prices of natural materials dropped in the 1980s, the indebted countries were left unable to repay the loans. Many of these nations turned

to the World Bank or the International Monetary Fund for help. These organizations underwrote more loans, but required that the poor countries agree to undergo "structural adjustment programs" (SAPs).

In essence, the World Bank and IMF demanded that poor countries restructure their economies by cutting spending and revaluing their currency so that they could begin to repay their loans and emerge from debt. Most low-income countries met the restructuring criteria by limiting their social spending (on education, health care, and social services, for example), lowering wages, cutting jobs, and taking land from subsistence farmers to grow crops for export. This focus on increasing trade has generated the most severe criticism from opponents of SAPs, who argue that the United States and other wealthy countries encourage such measures to improve their own trading opportunities, which destroys the ability of poor countries to support themselves because they become dependent on imports of food and other basic necessities. Supporters of SAPs, however, point out that this economic system allows poor countries to participate more fully in the global market, and that the benefits of restructuring will eventually "trickle down" to the poor.

In 1996 the World Bank and International Monetary Fund created the Debt Initiative for Heavily Indebted Poor Countries (HIPC), which was intended to provide debt relief to the poorest countries with the most debt. In June 2005 the G8 leaders met in Scotland, where they forged a massive debt relief agreement that was designed to go further than HIPC. The G8 proposal would effectively cancel the debt of eighteen countries (Benin, Bolivia, Burkina Faso, Ethiopia, Ghana, Guyana, Honduras, Madagascar, Mali, Mauritania, Mozambique, Nicaragua, Niger, Rwanda, Senegal, Tanzania, Uganda, and Zambia), with the possibility of adding or dropping countries and raising or lowering the amount cancelled. According to BBC News ("G8 Reaches Deal for World's Poor," June 11, 2005), a total of $40 billion in debt would be canceled, saving the poorest countries at least $1 billion a year in repayments. In December 2005 the IMF announced 100% debt relief for Benin, Bolivia, Burkina Faso, Cambodia, Ethiopia, Ghana, Guyana, Honduras, Madagascar, Mali, Mozambique, Nicaragua, Niger, Rwanda, Senegal, Tajikistan, Tanzania, Uganda, and Zambia. Because the World Bank and the IMF would essentially lose billions of dollars in capital if the total amount of debt was forgiven, the G8 finance ministers agreed to cover the loss in addition to paying the regular membership dues for both organizations. Early in the spring of 2006 the World Bank approved the debt cancellation plan—newly named the Multilateral Debt Relief Initiative (MDRI)—with relief for the world's poorest countries to begin on July 1, 2006.

THE MILLENNIUM DECLARATION

In September 2000, 189 member countries of the United Nations agreed to increase the state of human development, including reducing poverty, with the adoption of the Millennium Declaration. The Declaration itself includes a commitment to reducing the number of nuclear weapons, protecting the environment, and focusing attention on Africa. But the most significant section of the Declaration became known as the Millennium Development Goals (MDGs), a list of eight human development goals to be reached by 2015:

1. Eradicate extreme poverty and hunger.

2. Achieve universal primary education.

3. Promote gender equality and empower women.

4. Reduce child mortality.

5. Improve maternal health.

6. Combat HIV/AIDS, malaria, and other diseases.

7. Ensure environmental sustainability.

8. Develop a global partnership for development.

All eight MDGs involve poverty indicators directly or are linked to the problem of poverty in some way. The MDGs have become a standard way to gauge human development progress in all countries and regions of the world. Whether or not a country is "on target" to reach the goals by the 2015 deadline is a telling indicator in itself of the standard of living in that country. Since the adoption of the MDGs, some progress has been made toward achieving the goals. However, as the United Nations concedes, progress has been slow and uneven, with some regions moving forward and some actually falling behind.

HUNGER AND MALNUTRITION

Hunger's relation to poverty is reciprocal: poverty causes hunger, but hunger causes people to remain in poverty. As with every other aspect of global poverty, hunger is an immensely complicated problem, involving not just the lack of food but also the larger functions of macro- and microeconomics, national and international aid, weather and environmental changes, the availability of such social services as education and health care, use of arable land and equitable land distribution, and the healthy development of the agricultural sector. Figure 2.1 shows regional progress on the United Nations Millennium Development Goal of eliminating world hunger.

According to the report *The State of Food Insecurity in the World 2005* (Food and Agriculture Department of the United Nations, 2005), at least 842 million people (other sources cite 852 million) suffer from chronic hunger. The UN Food and Agriculture Organization (FAO) estimates that as many as two billion people suffer from periodic hunger and food insecurity (the condition of not knowing whether one will have enough food at any given time); 75% of the world's hungry people live in rural areas with few economic prospects. The FAO contends that hunger is a cause of poverty rather than a consequence. As Figure 2.2 shows, hunger causes disease, unemployment, high rates of child mortality, lack of

FIGURE 2.1

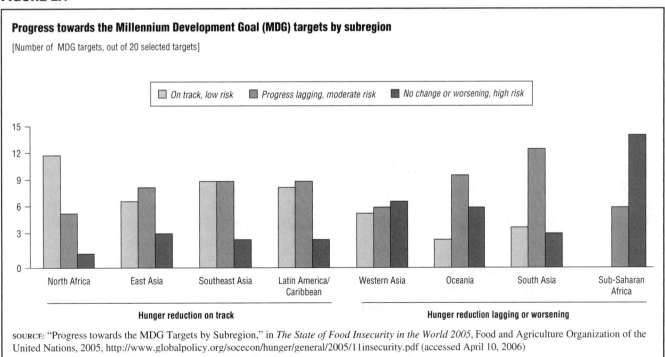

Progress towards the Millennium Development Goal (MDG) targets by subregion

[Number of MDG targets, out of 20 selected targets]

☐ On track, low risk   ☐ Progress lagging, moderate risk   ■ No change or worsening, high risk

Hunger reduction on track — North Africa, East Asia, Southeast Asia, Latin America/Caribbean

Hunger reduction lagging or worsening — Western Asia, Oceania, South Asia, Sub-Saharan Africa

SOURCE: "Progress towards the MDG Targets by Subregion," in *The State of Food Insecurity in the World 2005*, Food and Agriculture Organization of the United Nations, 2005, http://www.globalpolicy.org/socecon/hunger/general/2005/11insecurity.pdf (accessed April 10, 2006)

FIGURE 2.2

Relationship of hunger and malnutrition to other problems of poverty

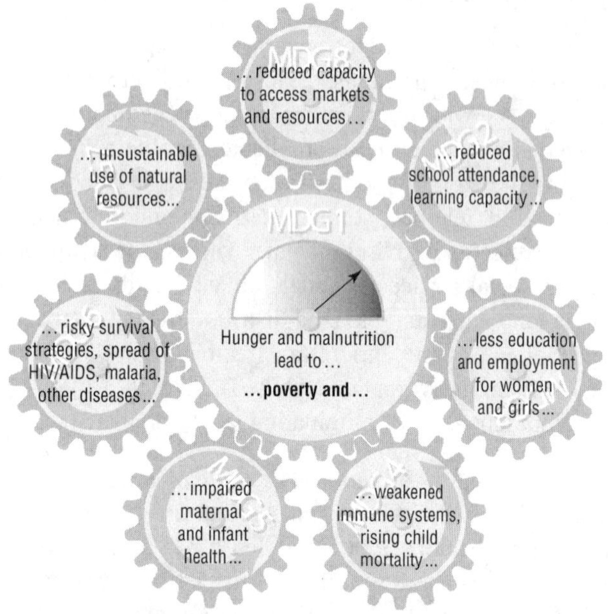

SOURCE: "Running in Reverse: Persistent Hunger Slows Progress towards Other Millennium Development Goals," in *The State of Food Insecurity in the World 2005*, Food and Agriculture Organization of the United Nations, 2005, http://www.globalpolicy.org/socecon/hunger/general/2005/11insecurity.pdf (accessed April 10, 2006)

TABLE 2.1

How investing in nutrition is critical to achieving the MDGs (Millennium Development Goals)

Goal	Nutrition effect
Goal 1: Eradicate extreme poverty and hunger.	Malnutrition erodes human capital through irreversible and intergenerational effects on cognitive and physical development.
Goal 2: Achieve universal primary education.	Malnutrition affects the chances that a child will go to school, stay in school, and perform well.
Goal 3: Promote gender equality and empower women.	Antifemale biases in access to food, health, and care resources may result in malnutrition, possibly reducing women's access to assets. Addressing malnutrition empowers women more than men.
Goal 4: Reduce child mortality.	Malnutrition is directly or indirectly associated with most child deaths, and it is the main contributor to the burden of disease in the developing world.
Goal 5: Improve maternal health.	Maternal health is compromised by malnutrition, which is associated with most major risk factors for maternal mortality. Maternal stunting and iron and iodine deficiencies particularly pose serious problems.
Goal 6: Combat HIV/AIDS, malaria, and other diseases.	Malnutrition may increase risk of HIV transmission, compromise antiretroviral therapy, and hasten the onset of full-blown AIDS and premature death. It increases the chances of tuberculosis infection, resulting in disease, and it also reduces malarial survival rates.

SOURCE: "Table 1.6. How Investing in Nutrition Is Critical to Achieving the MDGs," in *Repositioning Nutrition as Central to Development: A Strategy for Large-Scale Action*, The World Bank, The International Bank for Reconstruction and Development, 2006, http://siteresources.worldbank.org/NUTRITION/Resources/281846-1131636806329/NutritionStrategy.pdf (accessed April 10, 2006). Data adapted from Gillespie and Haddad (2003).

education, unsustainable use of natural resources, risky personal choices, and a lack of economic opportunities.

In *The World Food Situation: An Overview* (International Food Policy Research Institute, December 6, 2005), Joachim von Braun explained that hunger caused by the lack of adequate intake of calories is not the only type of food insecurity. Also on the rise are the incidence of underweight children (126 million), vitamin and mineral deficiencies (more than two billion people), and the prevalence of overweight and obese poor people (unknown number, but believed to be increasing). According to von Braun, the number of people in developing countries not getting enough food to sustain them (undernourished) dropped by nine million in the 1990s—just 1% of the total number of undernourished people in the world, despite the efforts of the Millennium Development Campaign, which are outlined in Table 2.1. Sub-Saharan Africa has experienced an increase of 20% in the number of undernourished people since 1990. Deficiencies in such micronutrients as iodine, vitamin A, iron, and zinc cause weakened immune systems, anemia, low IQs and learning disabilities, complications in pregnancy and childbirth, and numerous childhood diseases. These conditions result in poverty-causing problems such as absenteeism and poor performance at school and work,

unemployment, illiteracy, and the continuing cycle of poverty.

Every country has its share of hungry people. In the United States an estimated thirty-eight million Americans were food insecure, thirteen million families were at least periodically unable to afford food, and five million families had at least one member who regularly went hungry in 2004 (Vikki Valentine, "Q&A: The Causes behind Hunger in America," NPR.org, November 22, 2005).

What causes such widespread hunger? According to von Braun, world cereal production reached a record high of more than two billion tons in 2004, yet nearly a billion people worldwide suffered from hunger in 2005. (See Table 2.2 and Figure 2.3.) Most researchers agree that the Earth is capable of producing enough food to feed the entire world population; in fact, wealthy countries regularly subsidize (pay) some farmers to overproduce or underproduce certain crops to help control prices. The Institute for Food and Development Policy (known more informally as Food First) reported that the world's farmers produced enough to provide 4.3 pounds of food per person, per day, in 2002 (including cereals, grains, vegetables, meat, and fish). Anuradha Mittal of Food First commented in an interview in *The Sun* ("Anuradha Mittal on the True Cause of World Hunger,"

TABLE 2.2

Old and new global food and nutrition problems, 2005

Type	Causes	People affected
Hunger	Deficiency of calories and protein	0.9 billion
Underweight children	Inadequate intake of food and frequent disease	126 million
Micronutrient deficiency	Deficiency of vitamins and minerals	More than 2 billion
Overweight to chronic disease	Unhealthy diets; lifestyle	Increasing also among the poor

SOURCE: Joachim von Braun, "Figure 1. Old and New Global Food and Nutrition Problems," in *The World Food Situation: An Overview*, International Food Policy Research Institute, December 6, 2005, http://www.ifpri.org/pubs/agm05/jvb/jvbagm2005.pdf (accessed April 10, 2006). Based on data from the Food and Agriculture Organization (FAO) 2005a, United Nations Standing Committee on Nutrition (UN/SCN) 2004, Micronutrient Initiative and the United Nations Children's Fund (UNICEF) 2005.

FIGURE 2.3

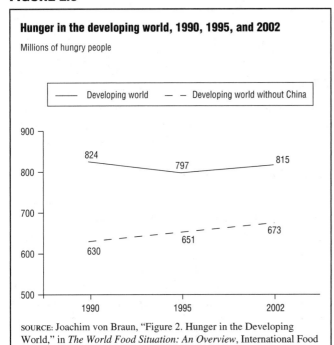

Hunger in the developing world, 1990, 1995, and 2002

Millions of hungry people

SOURCE: Joachim von Braun, "Figure 2. Hunger in the Developing World," in *The World Food Situation: An Overview*, International Food Policy Research Institute, December 6, 2005, http://www.ifpri.org/pubs/agm05/jvb/jvbagm2005.pdf (accessed April 10, 2006). Data from Food and Agriculture Organization (FAO) 2005a.

http://www.thesunmagazine.org/Mittal314.pdf, February 2002): "There is a shortage of purchasing power, not a shortage of food." So how is it possible that more than one-third of the human population goes hungry and 25,000 people die every day of starvation, malnutrition, and related diseases? As with other aspects of poverty, the answer involves global, regional, and local politics as well as economics.

Agricultural Subsidies, Trade, and Food Aid

Agricultural subsidies are often cited as a factor in either causing or exacerbating the problem of hunger. The governments of wealthy countries routinely pay farmers—mostly the owners of large agribusiness-type farms—billions of dollars each year to produce too much or not enough of certain crops in order to control prices of crops for export or import. In the United States, for example, farmers were paid $2 billion annually from 1995 to 2002 in "conservation subsidies," which means that these farmers were paid to not cultivate land for crops (Benjamin Powell, "It's Time to End Farm Subsidies," *Investor's Business Daily*, March 28, 2005).

These attempts to control crop and food prices are linked to the debate about fair trade discussed above. Farm subsidies in Europe, Japan, and the United States are designed to work in conjunction with trade barriers such as quotas and tariffs. As farmers in developed countries are paid to overproduce certain foods (for example, rice and corn), those countries export, or "dump," their surplus supplies to poor countries for extremely low prices or sometimes for free as "aid." At the same time, trade barriers prevent poor countries from exporting crops and other goods to wealthy countries (this is sometimes called "protectionism"). Food dumping from wealthy countries floods the markets, which drives down the value of crops in poor countries so low that it is often more economical for them to import the food or accept it as foreign aid than to invest in their own agricultural development. However, this also makes them more vulnerable to international economic factors and inhibits their ability to sustain themselves. According to "Farm Subsidies That Starve the World" (*New Statesman*, June 20, 2005), ending farm subsidies in the United States and Europe would cause the prices of African food exports to double, thus dramatically increasing the continent's economic growth.

International aid in the form of food seems like a straightforward way to deal with the worldwide crisis of hunger, yet many detractors claim that it actually makes the problem worse. Poverty researchers note that there is a difference between the kind of emergency aid that calls for the direct exportation of food to an area—such as occurs following a natural disaster like the Asian tsunami of December 2004 or the earthquake in Pakistan in 2005—and the practice of simply sending food to a poor region not experiencing an emergency situation. Very often, non-emergency food aid is actually just food dumping, as discussed above, which causes dependence on a foreign food source and prevents a poor country's farmers from competing in the international market.

In addition, when developed countries in North America, Europe, and elsewhere give aid in the form of food, they do not typically give it directly to hungry people (except in emergency cases, when food may be dropped from low-flying airplanes). Rather, they give it to the federal governments of poor countries, who distribute it to local governments, who in many cases sell it to the hungry at prices so low that local food producers, if any exist, cannot compete and may be forced out of business. Furthermore, an underdeveloped or developing country that depends on imports for food will often use its arable land to produce crops and goods, such as cut flowers or livestock feed, for export to developed countries rather than growing food for local consumption. When small farms shut down or are forced out of business, people often migrate to urban areas to work in manufacturing operations (typically sweatshops), leaving rural regions even more vulnerable to economic depression.

Access to Food

Food surpluses—whether subsidized or not—rarely make it to the hungry people of the world. Instead, they usually are sold as exports to wealthy countries for human or livestock consumption. The most fundamental reality of hunger is that poor people simply cannot afford food, even if it is available to them, but this is a simplification of a complex issue. According to J. W. Smith, author of *Economic Democracy: The Political Struggle of the Twenty-first Century* (Institute for Economic Democracy, 4th edition, 2005), the presence of excessive food imports from developed countries in poor countries inhibits the development of other industries in those poor countries because of the high cost of importing the food. Not only the agricultural but also other sectors of the economies of underdeveloped and developing countries suffer from the loss of financial and technological development. Smith and other economists argue that the high unemployment and lack of social services resulting from such economic underdevelopment are the real causes of poverty and widespread hunger.

Furthermore, arable land in developing countries often is sold to multinational corporations and agribusiness conglomerates, which use the land to grow crops and raise livestock for export to the developed countries in which their headquarters may be located. This inequitable distribution of land has been a serious problem in Latin America and the Caribbean for decades. In Guatemala, for example, large tracts of farmable land (called *latifundios*) are devoted to crops grown for export, while small plots of land (called *minifundios*) are allotted to the farmers who grow the food for the country's own population. This is a common situation throughout the Latin American–Caribbean region, where, according to the International Fund for Agricultural Development (IFAD), 64% of the rural population lives in poverty and the number of poor people—mostly indigenous groups—living in rural areas has increased since the 1980s. In all, small farmers account for 27% of the total rural poor population in Latin America and the Caribbean, and many argue this is largely due to the region's land distribution policies. The organization War on Want reports that just 1% of Brazil's farmers own two-thirds of the country's land, and 60% of all

arable land is left unused. ("Brazil's Landless Farmers Fight Back," 2006, http://www.waronwant.org/). Yet Brazil's small farmers cannot legally use the land. Like many other countries in the region, Brazil depends heavily on food exports from the multinational corporations that own most of the land to pay off its international debt of $223.6 billion (2003 estimate).

Critics of the system of subsidies, trade, and aid point out that even during such well-publicized events as the Ethiopian famine of the 1980s, enough food was available—but not to the people who needed it most. Anuradha Mittal notes that during several of the major food crises of the twentieth century (in Ethiopia, India, and Indonesia, for example), the countries involved were actually growing food for export; Ethiopia, Mittal says, was exporting green beans to Europe during its famine.

A report by the UN Food and Agriculture Organization (*The State of Food Insecurity in the World 2005*) finds a direct link between growth in a developing country's agricultural sector and a reduction in hunger and poverty; however, a growth in urban and industrial sectors or an overall growth in gross domestic product does not necessarily translate into a reduction in hunger and poverty. This finding suggests that economic growth itself is not enough to change patterns in hunger, but that the healthy development of farming, both for export and for in-country use, is essential.

Other Factors of Hunger

The FAO report lists a country's system of governance as chief among the factors affecting hunger rates. The World Bank has compiled as many as 350 variables to develop indicators to measure the overall status of a country's governance. Four governance indicators in particular—political stability, government effectiveness, rule of law, and control of corruption—are necessary to achieve hunger reduction in a country. For example, from 1991 to 2001 hunger worsened considerably in countries experiencing violent conflict and/or political instability. In Africa, much of which has seen long-term conflict and instability, per capita food production has dropped 12.4% on average during periods of violent conflict.

Natural disasters and environmental events also cause food crises by halting food production altogether. These occurrences have far more serious consequences in poor countries, where food production is already low, and they tend to happen more often in poor countries. Droughts, excess rainfall, earthquakes, and other environmental events have wreaked havoc in the agricultural sectors of underdeveloped and developing countries. Displacement is another consequence of natural disasters that increases the incidence of hunger in poor countries; when people are forced to flee after major disasters such as earthquakes or migrate due to severe weather conditions, pressure is placed on the areas in which they settle to produce enough food to support them.

The World Bank's 2006 report *Repositioning Nutrition as Central to Development: A Strategy for Large-Scale Action* states that a lack of food is just one of several factors contributing to malnutrition and undernutrition. Additional causes of severe malnutrition, especially in children, include a poor understanding of nutritional needs, insufficient knowledge about women's health in particular, and poor sanitation (the source of water-borne viruses and bacteria that cause diarrheal diseases). This suggests that investment in infrastructure would help reduce hunger and malnutrition.

LOW WAGES AND THE WORKING POOR

According to the International Labor Organization's (ILO) *World Employment Report 2004–05: Employment, Productivity, and Poverty Reduction*, there were 185.9 million unemployed people in the world in 2003. Perhaps more important for a discussion of poverty, of the total number of impoverished people in the world—approximately three billion living on less than two dollars per day—at least 1.39 billion of them were employed in 2003. About 550 million of those lived in extreme poverty—on less than one dollar per day. In all, 19.7% of working people around the world and 23.3% of workers in developing countries lived in extreme poverty.

These figures address one of the most common misperceptions about poverty: that poor people do not work. Regional rates of unemployment illustrate further the falsity of this assumption. The unemployment rate in sub-Saharan Africa, the overall poorest region in the world, with 751 million people, was 10.9% in 2003; in South Asia, which contains some of the poorest and most populous countries in the world, the unemployment rate was 4.8%; and in Latin America and the Caribbean the rate was 8%. Since most of the world's population is concentrated in poor countries, one would perhaps expect a greater percentage of the populations of these poor regions to be unemployed, but considering the large number of people living there, these percentages actually are rather low. By comparison, the unemployment rate in the United States, with 149.3 million people in the labor force, was 5.1% in 2005; out of Canada's labor force of 17.35 million people, 6.8% were unemployed in 2005; and in the European Union 9.4% of 218.5 million people in the labor force were unemployed.

The International Labor Organization defines "working poor" as those people whose earnings leave them unable to afford to lift themselves and their families above the poverty threshold (either the international line of one or two dollars a day or the poverty threshold of their individual country). The ILO also makes other distinctions regarding what it calls "working poverty":

It is important to note that, by definition, a person is counted as working poor only if that person is unable to lift himself or herself *and his or her family* above the poverty threshold. This means that somebody who earns only 50 cents a day would not be considered as working poor if somebody else in the family earns enough to make sure that each family member lives on more than US$1 a day. Conversely, somebody might earn as much as, for example, US$5 a day but with a family consisting of, say, 10 members (9 of them not working) each member would be living on less than US$1 a day. Such a person would still be counted as working poor. Finally, including the whole family in the concept of working poverty ensures that a rich young person in the developing world who has just started work life and works without remuneration in order to gain work experience is not considered to be working poor.

In the United States the working poor are defined as those people who work at least twenty-seven weeks per year in the labor force, either working or actively looking for work, but still live below the U.S. poverty threshold. According to the U.S. Bureau of Labor Statistics (BLS) publication *A Profile of the Working Poor, 2003* (March 2005), 7.4 million Americans could be classified as working poor in 2003. Furthermore, about three out of every five working poor Americans worked full time. As in the rest of the world, women (3.9 million) outnumbered men (3.5 million) in the working poor category. Unlike the working poor in developing countries, however, fewer working poor in the United States were employed in the informal economy, although informal work does exist in the United States. Most U.S. working poor are employed in service jobs; sales and office work; or production, transportation, and material moving. American working women who are heads of households are the most likely to be among the working poor, at a rate of 18.4%.

For most of the working poor around the world— including the United States—low wages, rather than unemployment, are a main cause of their situation. The BLS estimated that this was the case for about 62% of the working poor in the Unites States in 2003. In *Working Hard, Falling Short: America's Working Families and the Pursuit of Economic Security* (Working Poor Families Project, October 2004), Tom Waldron, Brandon Roberts, and Andrew Reamer reported that 9.2 million working families in the United States have low incomes, and 2.5 million of those families live below the poverty threshold. Although there is a link between low income and education level, the authors note that low wages leading to poverty do affect the well educated: 3.9 million working poor families had a parent with some post-secondary education.

The Working Poor in the Informal Economy

The International Labor Organization suggests that a large number of the world's working poor are employed in the informal labor sector, or informal economy. The term "informal economy" refers to the exchange of goods and services outside of national and international regulatory guidelines, meaning that the people who work in the informal economy receive no legal protection or employer-sponsored benefits, and have no official means by which to better their working situations. Unregistered self-employment and wage employment in informal work are the most common types of jobs in the informal economy, with self-employment accounting for about 33% of all nonagricultural employment in the world. Self-employment in the developing world typically refers to work that is home based (for example, garment workers, cigarette rollers, and embroiderers) or such enterprises as street vending and garbage collecting.

Work in the informal economy is more common in developing than developed countries, although informal labor does exist in wealthier countries, mostly in the form of self-employment and part-time and temporary work (the latter two are known as nonstandard wage employment). The ILO publication *Women and Men in the Informal Economy: A Statistical Picture* (2002) reports that 50% to 75% of nonagricultural workers in developing countries are employed in the informal economy. Estimates that include informal agricultural workers yield much higher percentages.

Although women have less of a presence in the overall labor force, they account for a greater percentage of informal workers. In developing countries 60% of women who work are employed in the informal economy, while in the largest developed countries women made up at least 60% of part-time workers, including 68% in the United States. Children also make up a large proportion of the informal economy, especially in developing countries. While the informal economy is not necessarily equated with the criminal economy, children (most notably girls) working in informal employment are particularly vulnerable to the abuses and exploitation of unregulated work; millions of child laborers end up being sold or tricked into the world of human trafficking, prostitution, pornography, slavery, and debt bondage. This kind of forced labor is not limited to so-called third world countries; it exists in the United States as well. (See Figure 2.4 and Table 2.3.)

FIGURE 2.4

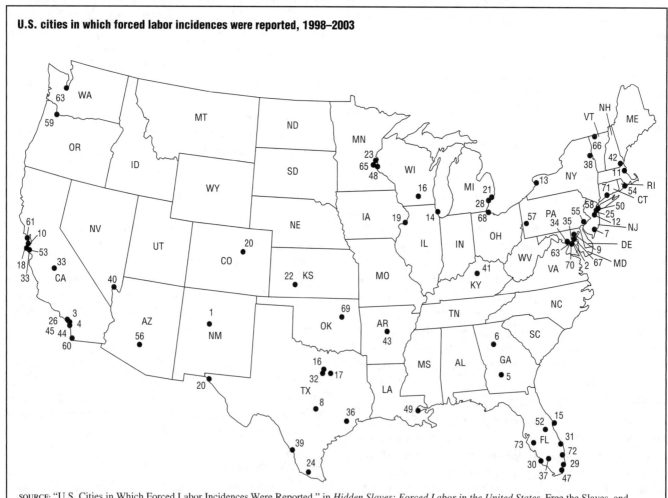

U.S. cities in which forced labor incidences were reported, 1998–2003

SOURCE: "U.S. Cities in Which Forced Labor Incidences Were Reported," in *Hidden Slaves: Forced Labor in the United States*, Free the Slaves, and Human Rights Center, September 2004, http://www.hrcberkeley.org/download/hiddenslaves_report.pdf (accessed April 10, 2006)

TABLE 2.3

Reported countries of origin of victims of forced labor, United States, 1998–2003

Reported country of origin of victims of forced labor	Number of cases	Estimated number of individuals
Mexico	25	ca 1,500
United States	20	ca 71
China	11	ca 10,000
Thailand	9	ca 150
India	9	ca 70
Bangladesh	8	ca 200
Russia	8	ca 100
Vietnam	6	ca 250
Honduras	5	ca 70
Philippines	5	ca 200
Korea	4	ca 6
Guatemala	3	ca 5
Indonesia	3	4
Cambodia	2	30
Cameroon	2	3
Estonia	2	15
Ghana	2	2
Kenya	2	2
Malaysia	2	5
Zambia	2	2
Albania	1	1
Brazil	1	1
Czech Republic	1	10
Ecuador	1	1
Ethiopia	1	3
Guyana	1	1
Haiti	1	1
Hungary	1	13
Jamaica	1	2
Kryghistan	1	1
Latvia	1	5
Micronesia	1	2
Nigeria	1	2
Peru	1	8
Romania	1	10
Tonga	1	4
Ukraine	1	29
Uzbekistan	1	1
Yugoslavia	1	1
Specific nationality not reported		
Asia	6	ca 10,000
Southeast Asia	4	ca 30
"Hispanic"	2	ca 70
Eastern European	1	1

Note: ca=circa (approximately).

SOURCE: "Reported Countries of Origin of Victims of Forced Labor," in *Hidden Slaves: Forced Labor in the United States*, Free the Slaves, and Human Rights Center, September 2004, http://www.hrcberkeley.org/download/hiddenslaves_report.pdf (accessed April 10, 2006)

Working conditions in the informal sector vary greatly. While some enterprises exist in the informal economy simply because they cannot afford to abide by the bureaucratic regulations of the formal economy, others deliberately avoid providing their workers with even the most reasonable legal protections. In *Decent Work and the Informal Economy* (2002) the ILO points out that working in the informal economy does not necessarily mean living in poverty or even earning low wages: "Many in the informal economy, especially the self-employed, in fact earn more than unskilled or low-skilled workers in the formal economy." However, the report

also notes that 75% of the poor living in developing countries lived in rural areas and worked in both agricultural and nonagricultural informal work. In addition, incomes among those working informally do average significantly less than the incomes of those working formally; this is particularly true of women and children, who are far more likely to experience abuses at the hands of employers.

EDUCATION AND LITERACY

In almost all societies a lack of education and literacy tends to result in a lower socioeconomic status. In its *Education for All Global Monitoring Report 2006: Literacy for Life* the United Nations Educational, Scientific, and Cultural Organization (UNESCO) names literacy as a basic human right and affirms its role in improving overall human development indicators at both the micro and macro levels. Nations with high levels of illiteracy tend to have high levels of poverty, and vice versa. Rates of literacy have risen more or less steadily since the 1950s, when 55.7% of the world's population was literate. Since 1970 the most dramatic increase in global literacy rates occurred in youths between the ages of fifteen and twenty-four. (See Table 2.4 and Table 2.5.) Despite these gains, illiteracy remains a significant problem around the world. As Table 2.6 shows, literacy has documented links to poverty, yet the global community has largely failed to ensure an educated populace. In 2002 ninety-nine million children did not attend primary school. (See Table 2.7.) Most of these not-in-school children were in developing countries, but developed countries and those in transition have problems as well. For example, according to UNESCO, in 2005 more than 40% of people aged sixteen to sixty-five in Chile, Italy, and Poland had a very low ability to comprehend information from written news sources or from fiction. (See Figure 2.5.)

In all countries with an adult literacy rate lower than 95%, literacy is less common among rural dwellers than among those who live in urban areas. (See Figure 2.6.) A large part of the education problem in developing and underdeveloped countries is the existence of school fees. (See Table 2.8.) With no reliable public education system, these countries charge families to send their children to school and sometimes to buy uniforms and supplies. In a 2005 World Bank report conducted for UNESCO, researchers found that 86% of the countries surveyed still charged fees for primary education—some of them legal and some of them not. Fees are considered illegal when they are not in accordance with a nation's laws or constitution. Education-related fees that adversely affect the poor contradict the spirit of the 1948 Universal Declaration of Human Rights, as well as the 1989 Convention on the Rights of the Child, which together guarantee free education as a basic human

TABLE 2.4

Global and regional trends in adult literacy rates, selected years 1950 to 2000–04

| | Adult literacy rates (percent) | | | | | | Increase in literacy rates (percent) | | |
	1950	1960	1970	1980	1990	2000–2004	1970 to 1980	1980 to 1990	1990 to 2000–2004
World	55.7	60.7	63.4	69.7	75.4	81.9	9.9	8.2	8.5
Developing countries	...	...	47.7	58.0	67.0	76.4	21.6	15.6	14.0
Developed and transition countries	...	...	94.5	96.4	98.6	99.0	2.0	1.8	0.5
Selected regions									
Sub-Saharan Africa	...	...	27.8	37.8	49.9	59.7	36.0	32.1	19.6
Arab states	...	18.9	28.8	39.2	50.0	62.7	36.1	27.7	25.3
East Asia and the Pacific	...	...	57.5	70.3	81.8	91.4	22.3	16.4	11.7
South and West Asia	...	...	31.6	39.3	47.5	58.6	24.4	20.8	23.5
Latin America and the Caribbean	...	...	73.7	80.0	85.0	89.7	8.5	6.3	5.5

SOURCE: "Table 7.3. Global and Regional Trends in Adult Literacy Rates, 1950 to 2000–2004," in *Education for All Global Monitoring Report 2006: Literacy for Life*, United Nations Educational, Scientific and Cultural Organization, 2005, http://www.unesco.org/education/GMR2006/full/chapt7_eng.pdf (accessed April 8, 2006). Data from the following sources: For 1950 and 1960: UNESCO (1978) Estimates and Projections of Illiteracy, CSR-E-29. Data refer to the 1972 assessment and are not necessarily comparable with data for subsequent years. For 1970 and 1980: UIS 2002 assessment based on the UN Population estimates and projections (2000 assessment). For 1990 and 2000–2004: data are from this report's statistical annex, Table 2A. Copyright © UNESCO, 2005

TABLE 2.5

Youth literacy rates by country development status and region, selected years 1970 to 2000–04

| | Youth literacy rates (percent) | | | | Increase in literacy rates (percent) | | |
	1970	1980	1990	2000–2004	1970 to 1980	1980 to 1990	1990 to 2000–2004
World	74.7	80.2	84.3	87.5	7.4	5.1	3.8
Developing countries	66.0	74.4	80.9	85.0	12.7	8.7	5.1
Developed and transition countries	99.0	99.3	99.5	99.7	0.3	0.2	0.2
Selected regions							
Sub-Saharan Africa	41.3	54.3	67.5	72.0	31.5	24.3	6.6
Arab states	42.7	54.7	66.6	78.3	28.1	21.8	17.6
East Asia and the Pacific	83.2	91.3	95.4	97.9	9.7	4.5	2.6
South and West Asia	43.3	52.6	61.5	73.1	21.6	16.8	18.9
Latin America and the Caribbean	84.2	89.5	92.7	95.9	6.2	3.6	3.4

SOURCE: "Table 7.4. Youth Literacy Rates by Country Development Status and Region, 1970 to 2000–2004, with Percent Increases in Each Decade," in *Education for All Global Monitoring Report 2006: Literacy for Life*, United Nations Educational, Scientific and Cultural Organization, 2005, http://www.unesco.org/education/GMR2006/full/chapt7_eng.pdf (accessed April 8,2006). Data from the following sources:For 1950 and 1960:UNESCO (1978) Estimates and Projections of Illiteracy, CSR-E-29. Data refer to the 1972 assessment and are not necessarily comparable with data for subsequent years. For 1970 and 1980: UIS 2002 assessment based on the UN Population estimates and projections (2000 assessment). For 1990 and 2000–2004: data are from this report's statistical annex, Table 2A. Copyright © UNESCO, 2005

right. In many regions, the average annual household income can actually be less than the cost of sending one child to school. For families who rely on subsistence farming for their livelihood, the cost simply is not worthwhile. Table 2.9 and Table 2.10 show the likelihood that countries will achieve the Millennium Development Goals of universal primary school education and universal literacy on time.

TABLE 2.6

Links between illiteracy and poverty, selected countries, 2003

	Gross national income per capita, 2003 (in PPP* US$)	Percent of population living below US$2 a day (most recent figures)	Belongs to heavily indebted poor countries
Number of illiterates is greater than 5 million and adult literacy rate is < 63%			
Bangladesh	1,870	83	
Egypt	3,940	44	
Ethiopia	710	78	X
Ghana	2,190	79	X
India	2,880	81	
Morocco	3,940	14	
Mozambique	1,060	78	X
Nepal	1,420	81	
Pakistan	2,040	66	
Sudan	1,760	—	X
Yemen	820	45	
Number of illiterates is greater than 5 million and adult literacy rate is > 63%			
Algeria	5,930	15	
Brazil	7,510	22	
China	4,980	—	
Democratic Republic of Congo	660	—	X
Indonesia	3,210	52	
Iran, Islamic Republic	7,000	7	
Mexico	8,980	26	
Nigeria	900	91	
Turkey	6,710	10	
Number of illiterates is between 1 and 5 million and adult literacy rate is < 63%			
Burkina Faso	1,170	81	X
Côte d'Ivoire	1,400	38	X
Mali	960	91	X
Niger	830	86	X

*Purchasing power parity.
Note: The figure of 63% to distinguish between high and low adult literacy rates is based on an examination of the distribution of all countries with rates below 95% and a calculation of the median.

SOURCE: "Table 7.7. The Literacy Challenge Compounded: Links to Poverty," in *Education for All Global Monitoring Report 2006: Literacy for Life*, United Nations Educational, Scientific and Cultural Organization, 2005, http://www.unesco.org/education/GMR2006/full/chapt7_eng.pdf (accessed April 8, 2006). Data from World Bank Development Indicators Database. Copyright © UNESCO, 2005

TABLE 2.7

Number of out-of-primary-school children, 1998 and 2002

	1998				2002			
	Total	Male	Female	Percent female	Total	Male	Female	Percent female
	Thousands				Thousands			
World	106,268	45,067	61,201	58	99,303	44,722	54,581	55
Developing countries	102,052	42,971	59,081	58	95,459	42,701	52,758	55
Developed countries	1,911	961	950	50	2,376	1,285	1,091	46
Countries in transition	2,304	1,135	1,170	51	1,468	736	732	50
Sub-Saharan Africa	44,581	20,648	23,933	54	40,370	18,367	22,003	55
Arab states	8,491	3,501	4,991	59	6,906	2,882	4,025	58
Central Asia	775	375	400	52	635	294	341	54
East Asia and the Pacific	8,309	4,158	4,151	50	14,782	7,410	7,372	50
South and West Asia	35,722	12,534	23,189	65	30,109	12,698	17,411	58
Latin America and the Caribbean	3,620	1,623	1,997	55	2,084	858	1,226	59
North America and Western Europe	1,429	718	711	50	1,848	1,012	836	45
Central and Eastern Europe	3,340	1,510	1,830	55	2,569	1,203	1,366	53

Note: Figures may not add to totals due to rounding.

SOURCE: "Table 2.4. Number of Out-of-Primary-School Children, 1998 and 2002," in *Education for All Global Monitoring Report 2006: Literacy for Life*, United Nations Educational, Scientific and Cultural Organization, 2005, http://www.unesco.org/education/GMR2006/full/chapt2_eng.pdf (accessed April 8, 2006). Copyright © UNESCO, 2005

FIGURE 2.5

Literacy challenges in selected countries and territories, percentage of adults aged 16–65 with very poor skills in prose literacy

Notes: The boundaries and names shown and the designations used on this map do not imply official endorsement or acceptance by United Nations Educational, Scientific, and Cultural Organization (UNESCO). Reported literacy data are derived from two surveys: the adult literacy and life skills survey and the international adult literacy survey. Each survey directly assessed literacy knowledge and skills in three domains—namely, prose, document, and quantitative literacy/numeracy—based on nationally representative samples of adults aged 16 to 65. The map presents information on adults with relatively poor literacy skills in the prose domain. Specifically, it refers to the percentage of adults in each country who had the weakest ability (level 1) to understand and use information from texts such as news articles or fiction.

SOURCE: "Literacy Challenges in Selected Countries and Territories," Percentage of Adults Aged 16 to 65 with Very Poor Skills in Prose Literacy," in *Education for All Global Monitoring Report 2006: Literacy for Life*, United Nations Educational, Scientific and Cultural Organization, 2005, http://www. unesco.org/education/GMR2006/full/chapt7_eng.pdf (accessed April 8, 2006). Copyright © UNESCO, 2005

FIGURE 2.6

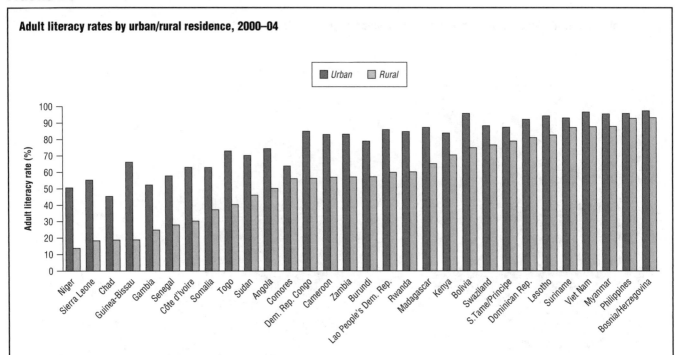

Adult literacy rates by urban/rural residence, 2000–04

Note: Only includes countries with an adult literacy rate lower than 95%.

SOURCE: "Figure 7.8. Adult Literacy Rates by Urban/Rural Residence, 2000–2004," in *Education for All Global Monitoring Report 2006: Literacy for Life*, United Nations Educational, Scientific and Cultural Organization, 2005, http://www.unesco.org/education/GMR2006/full/chapt7_eng.pdf (accessed April 8, 2006). Data from UNICEF MICS 2000, taken from Carr-Hill (2005). Copyright © UNESCO, 2005

TABLE 2.8

Education fees, selected countries, 2005

Legal fees	Albania; Argentina; Armenia; Azerbaijan; Benin; Bhutan; Bosnia/Herzegovina; Bulgaria; Burundi; Cameroon; Cape Verde; Chad; Comoros; Costa Rica; Côte d'Ivoire; Dominica; Dominican Republic; Egypt; El Salvador; Eritrea; Grenada; Guinea; Guinea-Bissau; Guyana; Haiti; India; Iran, Islamic Republic; Jordan; Lebanon; Madagascar; Maldives; Mauritania; Morocco; Niger; Papua New Guinea; Paraguay; Peru; Philippines; Romania; Russian Fed.; Rwanda; Solomon Islands; South Africa; Swaziland; Tajikistan; Thailand; The former Yugoslav Republic Macedonia; Timor-Leste; Togo; Trinidad/Tobago; Turkey; Uruguay
Illegal fees	Bolivia; Brazil; Colombia; Ethiopia; Ghana; Honduras; Lao People's Democratic Republic; Lesotho; Liberia; Mexico; Mozambique; Namibia; Nigeria; Panama; Tonga; Uganda; Ukraine; Vietnam
Both types of fees	Burkina Faso; China; Democratic Republic of Congo; Djibouti; Ecuador; Georgia; Indonesia; Kenya; Kyrgyzstan; Latvia; Mali; Mauritius; Mongolia; Nicaragua; Palestinian A. T.; Republic of Moldova; Vanuatu; Venezuela; Yemen

Note: Data was collected informally from World Bank task teams and may not reflect the most recent changes in policy and practice at the country level.

SOURCE: "Table 3.4. Fees Still Exist in a Large Number of Countries," in *Education for All Global Monitoring Report 2006: Literacy for Life*, United Nations Educational, Scientific and Cultural Organization, Paris, 2005, http://www.unesco.org/education/GMR2006/full/chapt3_eng.pdf (accessed April 8, 2006). Data from Bentaouet-Kattan (2005). Copyright © UNESCO, 2005

TABLE 2.9

Country prospects for the achievement of the adult literacy target by 2015

Level of adult literacy rate in 2000–2004			
High literacy (between 80% and 97%)	**Quadrant I** At risk of not achieving the goal 20 countries Brazil, Colombia, Dominican Republic, Ecuador, Honduras, Malaysia, Mauritius, Myanmar, Namibia, Panama, Peru, Philippines, Qatar, Saint Lucia, Sri Lanka, Suriname, Swaziland, Syrian Arab Republic, Turkey, Vietnam	**Quadrant II** High chance of achieving the goal 23 countries Bahrain, Bolivia, Bosnia and Herzegovina, Brunei Darussalam, Chile, China, Cyprus, Equatorial Guinea, Greece, Israel, Jordan, Macao (China), Maldives, Mexico, Palestinian Autonomous Territories, Paraguay, Republic of Moldova, Saudi Arabia, Serbia and Montenegro, Singapore, Thailand, TFYR[b] of Macedonia, Venezuela	
Low literacy (below 80%)	**Quadrant IV** Serious risk of not achieving the goal 30 countries Algeria, Angola, Belize, Benin, Burundi, Cambodia, Central African Republic, Chad, Côte d'Ivoire, Democratic Republic of the Congo, El Salvador, Guatemala, India, Kenya, Lao PDR[a], Madagascar, Mauritania, Nepal, Nicaragua, Niger, Pakistan, Papua New Guinea, Rwanda, Senegal, Sierra Leone, Sudan, Togo, Tunisia, U. R. Tanzania, Zambia	**Quadrant III** Low chance of achieving the goal 0 countries	
	Slow performers	Fast performers	
	Increase between 1990 and 2000–2004		

[a]People's Democratic Republic.
[b]The former Yugoslav Republic.

SOURCE: "Table 2.9. Country Prospects for the Achievement of the Adult Literacy Target by 2015," in *Education for All Global Monitoring Report 2006: Literacy for Life*, United Nations Educational, Scientific and Cultural Organization, 2005, http://www.unesco.org/education/GMR2006/full/chapt2_eng.pdf (accessed April 8, 2006). Copyright © UNESCO, 2005

TABLE 2.10

Country prospects for the achievement of universal primary education by 2015

Distance from 100% net enrollment rate (NER) in 2002			
Close or in an intermediate position	**Quadrant I** At risk of not achieving the goal 20 countries Albania, Bahrain, British Virgin Islands, CzechRepublic, Equatorial Guinea, Estonia, Georgia, Kuwait, Kyrgyzstan, Slovenia, Maldives, Malaysia, Netherlands Antilles, Palestinian A. T., Paraguay, Romania, South Africa, TFYR[a] of Macedonia, Uruguay, Vietnam	**Quadrant II** High chance of achieving the goal 20 countries Algeria, Belarus, Bolivia, Bulgaria, Cambodia, Colombia, Cuba, Guatemala, Indonesia, Ireland, Jamaica, Jordan, Lesotho, Lithuania, Malta, Mauritius, Morocco, Nicaragua, Vanuatu, Venezuela	
Intermediate position or far	**Quadrant IV** Serious risk of not achieving the goal 3 countries Azerbaijan, Papua New Guinea, Saudi Arabia	**Quadrant III** Low chance of achieving the goal 44 countries Bangladesh, Benin, Botswana, Burkina Faso, Burundi, Chad, Chile, Costa Rica, Côte d'Ivoire, Croatia, Djibouti, Egypt, El Salvador, Eritrea, Ethiopia, Gambia, Ghana, Guinea, Iran (Isl. Rep.), Kenya, Lao PDR[b], Latvia, Lebanon, Macao (China), Madagascar, Mali, Mauritania, Mongolia, Mozambique, Myanmar, Namibia, Niger, Oman, Republic of Moldova, Saint Vincent and the Grenadines, Senegal, Swaziland, Thailand, Trinidad and Tobago, United Arab Emirates, United Republic of Tanzania, Yemen, Zambia, Zimbabwe	
	Away from the goal	Towards the goal	
	Change over the period from 1990 to 2002		

[a]The former Yugoslav Republic.
[b]People's Democratic Republic.

SOURCE: "Table 2.8. Country Prospects for the Achievement of Universal Primary Education by 2015," in *Education for All Global Monitoring Report 2006: Literacy for Life*, United Nations Educational, Scientific and Cultural Organization, 2005, http://www.unesco.org/education/GMR2006/full/chapt2_eng.pdf (accessed April 8, 2006). Copyright © UNESCO, 2005

CHAPTER 3
POVERTY IN UNDERDEVELOPED COUNTRIES—THE POOREST OF THE POOR

Underdeveloped countries are at the very bottom of the global economy, with widespread extreme poverty and dire living conditions. They usually have little or no infrastructure or reliable health care and other social services. Many have experienced long-term political unrest in the form of civil war or armed conflict with other nations, or have been subject to unstable governments, dictatorships, and/or corruption. In addition, they may frequently suffer environmental events and natural disasters that cause famine, destruction, and displacement of large segments of their populations.

THE UNITED NATIONS' LIST OF LEAST DEVELOPED COUNTRIES

Many scholars and researchers refer to nations whose economies are almost completely lacking in industry and technology as "least developed countries" (LDCs). That term has a specific meaning according to the Economic and Social Council of the United Nations (UN), which maintains a list of countries it considers to be "least developed" according to whether they meet certain criteria:

- A low-income criterion, based on a three-year average per capita estimate of the gross national income (under $750 for inclusion on the list, above $900 to be removed from the list)

- A human resource weakness criterion, involving a composite Human Assets Index (HAI) based on indicators of nutrition, health, education, and adult literacy

- An economic vulnerability criterion, involving a composite Economic Vulnerability Index (EVI) based on indicators of the instability of agricultural production; the instability of exports of goods and services; the economic importance of nontraditional activities (the share of manufacturing and modern services in gross domestic product); merchandise export concentration

and the handicap of economic smallness (as measured through the population in logarithm); and the percentage of population displaced by natural disasters

Of the UN's list of least developed countries (LDCs) in 2006, thirty-four are in Africa, fourteen are in Asia and the Pacific, one is in the Caribbean/Latin America, and one is in the Arab states of the Middle East (http://www.un.org/special-rep/ohrlls/ldc/list.htm). Because the list automatically excludes very large economies—which necessarily have certain advantages over smaller economies—not all countries where large percentages of the population are extremely poor are represented on the list. (Africa is notable as a continent with many large economies that is nonetheless almost uniformly underdeveloped and impoverished.) The list is maintained and reviewed every three years by the Economic and Social Council. To be removed from the list a country must meet at least two of the criteria for two three-year reviews in a row. As of January 2006, Cape Verde, the Maldives, and Samoa were all under consideration for removal from the list.

AFRICA: THE POOREST CONTINENT

Africa is the second-largest continent on the planet (after Asia) in both land area and population—with more than 800 million people living in fifty-four countries. With a total land area of more than eleven million square miles, Africa accounts for 20% of the land on the planet; its population accounts for one-seventh of the population of earth.

Africa is typically discussed as two distinct regions: northern Africa—the area north of the Sahara Desert that is inhabited mostly by Arabic-speaking people whose ancestors come from the Middle East—and sub-Saharan Africa, the area south of the desert, in which many different tribes and nationalities live. These designations are not, however, absolutely definitive because political regional definitions differ from geographical regional definitions. For example, while the United Nations lists just seven territories as North African (Algeria, Egypt, Libya, Morocco, Sudan, Tunisia, and the Moroccan-occupied Western Sahara), geographically the Azores, Mauritania, Mali, Niger, Chad, Ethiopia, Eritrea, and Djibouti also are sometimes considered part of the North. Some commentators prefer the term "tropical Africa" to "sub-Saharan Africa," but others note that this excludes the country of South Africa, which falls outside the tropical zone. Regardless of political or geographic designation, however, Africa suffers from the overall highest rate of poverty in the world. Of the continent's fifty-four countries, thirty-four—all typically considered to be part of sub-Saharan Africa—are on the UN's list of least developed countries.

Colonialism and Slavery

Africa is unique in that, between the fifteenth and twentieth centuries, a great number of its native inhabitants were enslaved and shipped to other countries and almost the entire continent was colonized by outsiders. In simple terms, colonialism is when representatives of a wealthy country move to an underdeveloped country and set up a branch of their homeland government to rule over the indigenous people, usually profiting from the natural resources and local labor. Often the indigenous people are enslaved; almost always they are exploited and discriminated against. Even when a colonial government is successfully overthrown or voted out of power, poverty and injustice are often so deeply ingrained that liberated countries do not recover from their years as colonies. In the case of Africa—a continent with abundant natural resources such as gold, oil, and diamonds—the worldwide slave trade that relied on labor from the continent lasted for centuries, dispersing millions of native Africans all over the world, and even after the abolishment of slavery and the dismantling of the colonial system, the continent continued to be plagued by war and chronic poverty.

In the late fifteenth century, European slave traders, led by the Spanish and the Portuguese, began importing slaves from Africa. With the colonization of North and South America beginning in the 1500s and 1600s, the African slave trade increased dramatically, and within a century, many countries in Europe as well as North and South America were importing African slaves. The United States in particular relied on slave labor to fuel its southern farming economy. Native Africans were also forced into labor in Africa itself, to work in the burgeoning industries that exploited Africa's natural resources. Estimates vary, but it is believed that at least twenty-eight million Africans were kidnapped and enslaved.

At the same time, the European nations were colonizing African lands, and by the time World War I began in 1914, virtually all of Africa was occupied. The colonizers sought to make native Africans easier to rule by turning native groups against each other, deliberately inflaming old conflicts and creating inter-tribal strife, which later exploded into war and genocide.

By the turn of the twentieth century, public opinion abroad had begun to turn against colonialism, and a move toward independence gained strength in the 1920s and 1930s as descendants of slaves helped raise awareness of the injustices of foreign occupation in Africa. Anticolonialism increased within Africa as well, with frequent strikes and public protests that often ended in violence. In some countries the battle for independence was led by guerilla fighters, while protesters in other countries were inspired by the nonviolent resistance methods of Indian leader Mohandas Gandhi, who had led his country to independence from British rule in 1947. Most African nations had gained their independence by either peaceful or violent means by the late 1960s.

Cold War Politics

Sadly, the overthrow of the colonial governments did not guarantee a just society for native Africans. The rise of the United States and the Soviet Union as world powers resulted in a state of "neocolonialism," in which the two nations vied to secure allies during the cold war. Agents of both governments—including the Central Intelligence Agency (CIA) of the United States and the Komitet Gosudarstvennoy Bezopasnosti (KGB; "State Security Committee") of the Soviet Union—colluded with African political factions that had little interest in creating just and prosperous societies. The U.S. operatives were more successful than the Soviets in creating allies: helping to overthrow fledgling African governments that were based on Communist principles, the CIA supported the ascent of harsh dictators who would serve U.S. interests. Many of these leaders managed to amass great personal wealth while driving their own countries into economic ruin and further encouraging ethnic violence.

Ongoing Violence

Even after the end of the cold war, the continent was plagued by violence among ethnic groups. Especially noteworthy is the Rwandan genocide of 1994. During that conflict, ethnic tensions between the majority Hutus and minority Tutsis led to civil war and mass killings in which an estimated 800,000 people were slaughtered in just 100 days ("Rwanda: How the Genocide Happened," *BBC News Online*, April 1, 2004).

Violence in the vast Democratic Republic of Congo (DRC; formerly called Zaire) dates back to the country's independence in 1960. In the late 1990s Rwanda invaded the DRC in search of Hutu extremists in hiding; this ignited a rebellion that eventually involved Uganda, Angola, Namibia, and Zimbabwe, as well as Rwanda and the DRC. In 2003 the war ended in a tentative peace agreement, but not before three million Congolese had died either in the conflict or from the disease and malnutrition that followed its wake.

The East African country of Sudan has been in a near-constant state of civil war since about 1955. In 2003 tensions erupted in country's Darfur region between rebel fighters and the military government. Hostilities between black Arabs and non-Arabs, as well as between cattle herders and farmers fighting for scarce land and resources, turned into attacks on civilians that have been compared to the genocide in Rwanda. Hundreds of thousands of people have been murdered and about two million driven into exile. Hundreds of thousands more are expected to die of starvation because of the conflict.

Many other examples of conflict in Africa exist, such as the anarchy in Somalia, the tensions between Eritrea and Ethiopia, and rebel movements in scores of other countries. What all of these conflicts have in common is that they drain the nations involved of precious human, financial, and natural resources, weakening their societies and deepening their poverty.

THE POOR IN AFRICA

The United Nations tracks trends in poverty worldwide using its Human Development Index (HDI; see Chapter 1), which measures overall well-being in underdeveloped and developing countries. In its *Human Development Report 2005*, the UN indicated that the HDI has risen since the 1990s in almost all developing and underdeveloped areas of the world but two: the Russian Federation and sub-Saharan Africa. (See Figure 3.1 and Table 3.1.) As Table 3.1 shows, thirteen of the eighteen countries that have experienced significant reversals in their HDIs since 1990 are in sub-Saharan Africa. According to the UN, the African countries that experienced the sharpest declines in their HDI rankings between 1990 and 2003 are South Africa, with a drop of thirty-five places; Zimbabwe, with a drop of twenty-three places; and Botswana, with a drop of twenty-one places. The main indicators on the human development index include life expectancy and health, literacy and educational attainment, and income.

LIFE EXPECTANCY AND HEALTH. According to the UN's *Human Development Report 2005*, life expectancy has fallen dramatically in the countries of sub-Saharan Africa since 1990, when it saw a brief increase. This is due largely to the spread of the human immunodeficiency virus (HIV) and acquired immune deficiency syndrome (AIDS) on the continent. The UN's *Human Development Report 2005* estimates that, of the three million people

FIGURE 3.1

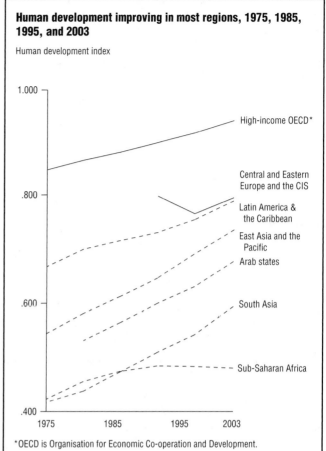

Human development improving in most regions, 1975, 1985, 1995, and 2003

Human development index

*OECD is Organisation for Economic Co-operation and Development.

SOURCE: "Figure 1.4. Human Development Improving in Most Regions," in *Human Development Report 2005*, United Nations Development Programme, 2005, http://hdr.undp.org/reports/global/2005/pdf/HDR05_complete.pdf (accessed April 10, 2006)

worldwide who died of AIDS in 2004, 70% were in Africa. Of the thirty-eight million total people infected with HIV, 25.8 million live in sub-Saharan Africa. In a press release at the XV International Conference on AIDS (July 14, 2004), the UN reported that in Zambia, a country in southern Africa with a total population of 10.4 million people, 16.5% of adults ages fifteen to forty-nine were infected with HIV or AIDS, and life expectancy had dropped from 47.4 years in 1990 to 32.7 years in 2004. In Zimbabwe 25% of adults among the country's 12.5 million people were HIV-positive, and life expectancy dropped from 56.6 years in 1990 to 33.9 years in 2002. Life expectancy in Swaziland, a small country bordering South Africa, dropped from 55.3 years in 1990 to 35.7 years in 2002; 38.8% of adults in Swaziland—with a total population of 1.1 million people—were HIV-positive in 2004. *Human Development Report 2005* noted that chances of survival for a person born in sub-Saharan Africa between 2000 and 2005 are not much better than those of individuals living in England and Wales during the 1840s.

TABLE 3.1

Countries experiencing HDI (human development index) reversal, 1980–90 and 1990–2003

1980–90	1990–2003
Congo, Dem. Rep. of the	Botswana
Guyana	Cameroon
Haiti	Central African Republic
Niger	Congo
Rwanda	Congo, Dem. Rep. of the
Zambia	Côte d'Ivoire
	Kazakhstan*
	Kenya
	Lesotho
	Moldova, Rep. of*
	Russian Federation*
	South Africa
	Swaziland
	Tajikistan*
	Tanzania, U. Rep. of*
	Ukraine*
	Zambia
	Zimbabwe

*Country does not have HDI data for 1980–90, so drop may have begun before 1990.

SOURCE: "Table 1.1. Countries Experiencing HDI Reversal," in *Human Development Report 2005*, United Nations Development Programme, 2005, http://hdr.undp.org/reports/global/2005/pdf/HDR05_complete.pdf (accessed April 10, 2006)

FIGURE 3.2

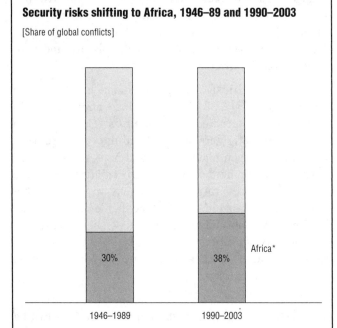

Security risks shifting to Africa, 1946–89 and 1990–2003

[Share of global conflicts]

*The entire continent, not just Sub-Saharan Africa.

SOURCE: "Figure 5.2. Security Risks Are Shifting to Africa," in *Human Development Report 2005*, United Nations Development Programme, 2005, http://hdr.undp.org/reports/global/2005/pdf/HDR05_complete.pdf (accessed April 10, 2006). Data calculated on the basis of data on armed conflict from Strand, Wilhelmsen and Gleditsch 2005.

According to the *AIDS Epidemic Update, December 2005*, published jointly by the Joint United Nations Programme on HIV/AIDS (UNAIDS) and the World Health Organization (WHO), AIDS in Africa cannot properly be called a single epidemic. Rather, each region and country has experienced its own trends in HIV/AIDS infection. Countries in southern Africa, for example, are considered the "epicenter" of the global epidemic. The report notes, however, that the epidemics in Zimbabwe, Kenya, and Uganda have, for the first time, shown signs of slowing down. Surveys have shown that the prevalence of HIV infection among pregnant women in Zimbabwe has fallen from 26% in 2002 to 21% in 2004. In the late 1990s HIV rates among adults in Kenya were as high as 10%; by 2003 the rate had dropped to 7%. In Uganda, which has experienced the most success among African countries in lowering rates of HIV/AIDS infection, 15% of the adult population was infected in the early 1990s; 2004 surveys found that the rate had dropped to 7%, although in some regions of the country surveys suggested that rates were rising among fifteen- to twenty-four-year-olds. In all three countries that have seen a decreasing rate of infection, there is strong evidence to suggest that changes in sexual behavior are the cause of the drops in rates—most notably, an increase in condom use.

While AIDS is certainly the most notable factor contributing to Africa's low life expectancy, it is not the only disease that takes millions of African lives a year and threatens the continent's economic stability.

Preventable disease is both a cause and a result of poverty. Unable to afford simple prevention, families often lose their primary breadwinner to these diseases, leaving them even deeper in poverty. Additionally, violent conflict has made Africa one of the most dangerous places on earth. Warfare that has become a routine part of life for Africans in many countries leads to malnutrition and outbreaks of disease, which sometimes kill more people than the violence itself. (See Figure 3.2.)

Malaria, a highly infectious but preventable disease that is spread through tropical regions by mosquitoes, is perhaps the most prominent example of this. According the World Health Organization (WHO), malaria costs Africa about $12 billion each year in lost gross domestic product and accounts for 40% of public health expenditures. Countries with high rates of malarial infection are known to have significantly lower GDP, slower rates of economic growth, and higher rates of poverty than those without. In the case of sub-Saharan Africa, the disease has had a significant impact on labor force participation and school attendance; children who suffer from repeat infections often develop permanent neurological damage that cuts short their education and hampers their ability to participate fully in the labor force as adults.

In the early twenty-first century poverty researchers began to recognize malaria's role in increasing impoverishment at the micro (family and community) level and diminishing economic advancement at the macro (national and global) level in countries prone to epidemics of the disease. Aside from the obvious difficulties facing poor families who cannot afford treatment or prevention, the wider effects of frequent epidemics include impeded market activity and tourism industries as traders and potential tourists avoid areas with heavy infection rates. Even agricultural trends can shift with malaria rates; farmers dependent on the availability of workers during harvest seasons will be less likely to plant labor-intensive cash crops, instead relying on subsistence crops.

According to the *World Malaria Report 2005*, published by the Roll Back Malaria (RBM) campaign—a global partnership of the World Health Organization, UNICEF (United Nations Children's Fund), the World Bank, and the United Nations Development Program—66% of the total population of Africa is at risk of developing malaria. There are as many as twelve million cases of malaria reported every year in Africa, more than a million of them fatal in 2002; about 90% of all deaths from malaria worldwide occur in Africa. Children are particularly vulnerable to the disease. In those under age five, nearly 20% of all deaths in sub-Saharan Africa are directly attributable to malaria. Considerably more are believed to be indirectly related to the disease because repeated malarial infections can lead to severe anemia, which in turn makes children more susceptible to other illnesses. Additionally, infection of pregnant women raises the rate of infant mortality because it can cause low birth weight and other complications.

The WHO reports that malaria is particularly common in sub-Saharan Africa because of the prevalence of *plasmodium falciparum* (http://www.rbm.who.int/cmc_upload/0/000/015/370/RBMInfosheet_3.htm)—the most deadly strain of the disease—and of the species of mosquito most likely to spread the disease. In addition, the infection's resistance to the most effective and affordable antimalarial drug, chloroquine, is high in African countries, and resistance to the second most commonly used drug, sulfadoxine-pyrimethamine, is growing. More effective drugs are available, but they are prohibitively expensive.

Prevention of malaria is relatively simple. The most effective way to prevent its spread is the use of insecticide-treated mosquito nets (ITNs) draped over beds at night, when most disease-carrying mosquitoes bite. Early trials of the nets in the 1980s and 1990s showed that they could help reduce malaria-related deaths in children by 20%. Unfortunately, the RBM campaign has found that there are two ongoing problems with the use of ITNs. First, the nets and the materials used to make them have been subject to high taxes and import tariffs that make them too expensive for most African families to afford. As of 2005, negotiations were underway throughout Africa to reduce or

eliminate taxes and tariffs on the nets and the materials used to make them; twenty countries had already done so. Second, WHO studies have shown that, even when ITNs are used routinely, fewer than 5% are regularly retreated with insecticide to continue their effectiveness. The WHO has been working with ITN manufacturers to develop nets that would require less frequent or no re-treating and is encouraging families to participate in community "dipping" events to re-treat their nets at least once a year. Additionally, African governments are instituting public health education campaigns to promote the use of ITNs.

In June 2005 U.S. President George W. Bush announced plans for a $1.7 billion aid package for Africa, $1.2 billion of which was to go to combating malaria infection (Peter Baker, "Bush Pledges $1.2 Billion for Africa to Fight Malaria," *Washington Post*, July 1, 2005). Scheduled to be distributed over five years, the money would be used for insecticide spraying, stronger combination drug therapies, and longer-lasting ITNs. In June 2006 R. Timothy Ziemer was named U.S. Malaria Coordinator for the President's Malaria Initiative to oversee all malaria programs and policy at USAID, the U.S. government foreign aid agency.

In October 2005 the Bill and Melinda Gates Foundation announced it would donate $258.3 million to fund research on malaria—$107.6 million toward developing a vaccine, $100 million for new treatment drugs, and $50.7 million for ITNs and other forms of mosquito control (http://www.gatesfoundation.org/globalhealth/pri_diseases/malaria/announcements/announce-051030.htm). In November 2005 the Gates Foundation, which was founded by Microsoft pioneer Bill Gates and his wife, Melinda, helped organize a project to combat the disease in Zambia, donating another $35 million. Zambia, where 30,000 people die annually of the disease, had already begun waging a somewhat successful campaign to cut malaria-related deaths. Money from the Gates Foundation will be used to step up the campaign, in the hopes of providing effective protection for 80% of Zambia's population ("A Model Fight against Malaria," *New York Times*, November 22, 2005).

Literacy and Education

According to the *Millennium Development Goals Report 2005* (United Nations, http://unstats.un.org/unsd/mi/pdf/MDG%20Book.pdf), 42% of children in sub-Saharan Africa did not attend school in 2001. The United Nations Educational, Scientific, and Cultural Organization (UNESCO) reported in *EFA Global Monitoring Report 2006: Literacy for Life. Regional Overview: Sub-Saharan Africa* that in more than half of the countries in the region only about 6% of children were enrolled in preprimary education during 2002; on average, 63% of children were enrolled in primary

TABLE 3.2

Estimates of adult illiterates and literacy rates, population aged 15 and over, by region, 1990 and 2000–04

	Number of illiterates (thousands)		Literacy rates (percent)		Change from 1990 to 2000–2004 in:		
					Number of illiterates		Literacy rates
	1990	2000–2004	1990	2000–2004	Thousand	Percent	Percentage points
World	871,750	771,129	75.4	81.9	−100,621	−12	6.4
Developing countries	855,127	759,199	67.0	76.4	−95,928	−11	9.4
Developed countries	14,864	10,498	98.0	98.7	−4,365	−29	0.7
Countries in transition	1,759	1,431	99.2	99.4	−328	−19	0.2
Sub-Saharan Africa	128,980	140,544	49.9	59.7	11,564	9	9.8
Arab states	63,023	65,128	50.0	62.7	2,105	3	12.6
Central Asia	572	404	98.7	99.2	−168	−29	0.5
East Asia and the Pacific	232,255	129,922	81.8	91.4	−102,333	−44	9.6
South and West Asia	382,353	381,116	47.5	58.6	−1,237	−0.3	11.2
Latin America and the Caribbean	41,742	37,901	85.0	89.7	−3,841	−9	4.7
Central and Eastern Europe	11,500	8,374	96.2	97.4	−3,126	−27	1.2
North America and Western Europe	11,326	7,740	97.9	98.7	−3,585	−32	0.8

Note: Figures may not add to totals because of rounding.

SOURCE: "Table 2.6. Estimates of Adult Illiterates and Literacy Rates (Population Aged 15+) by Region, 1990 and 2000–2004," in *Education for All Global Monitoring Report 2006: Literacy for Life*, United Nations Educational, Scientific and Cultural Organization, 2005, http://www.unesco.org/education/GMR2006/full/chapt2_eng.pdf (accessed April 8, 2006). Copyright © UNESCO, 2005

school; an average of 28% of children were enrolled in secondary school. Children in sub-Saharan Africa spend an average of 7.8 years in school (versus an average of twelve years in developed countries); of those who enroll in school, fewer than 60% complete their education.

The prevalence of disease—particularly HIV/AIDS—takes an especially heavy toll on school-age children in sub-Saharan Africa. Along with the many children who must leave school because they suffer from such diseases as HIV and malaria, many others are indirectly affected; the UN reports that in 1999 almost one million children in the sub-Saharan region lost teachers to AIDS. The likelihood of qualified teachers becoming available quickly to take the place of the millions who have died of AIDS is small. Carole Palma, acting director of USAID, projected in October 2004 that 15% to 20% of teachers in the sub-Saharan region would have died of AIDS by 2005. Moreover, children whose parents or other family members become ill with or die from diseases such as AIDS usually must leave school, either to care for the sick relative or to go to work to support the family. At the broader level, the African educational system overall suffers from a lack of funding because of the drain of AIDS on public monies and human resources.

The persistent military conflicts in many African countries also make it nearly impossible for many children, particularly those living in rural areas, to attend school, even if schools still exist. Decades of political, economic, and social turmoil have decimated the educational sector on the continent. Schools have been destroyed; students and teachers have been killed; teaching materials and supplies are virtually nonexistent. For

many children merely walking to school can be deadly; as of 2001 there were an estimated nine to fifteen million land mines in Angola and more than two million in Mozambique, as well as an unknown number newly laid along the border of Eritrea and Ethiopia ("Reconstruction from War in Africa: Communities, Entrepreneurs, and States," *CSAE Conference 2001: Development Policy in Africa—Public and Private Perspectives*, Center for the Study of African Economies, University of Oxford, March 29–31, 2001).

The *EFA Global Monitoring Report 2006: Literacy for Life. Regional Overview: Sub-Saharan Africa* reports that rates of adult literacy in Africa range from below 40% in Benin, Burkina Faso, Chad, Mali, Niger, Senegal, and Sierra Leone to more than 90% in Seychelles and Zimbabwe. Only South and West Asia have a lower literacy rate than sub-Saharan Africa. (See Table 3.2.) According to UNESCO, 140.5 million adults in sub-Saharan Africa are illiterate. Countries with the highest rates of poverty have correspondingly high rates of illiteracy; similarly, the larger a country's rural population is, the higher its rate of illiteracy will be.

Not all of the news about Africa's educational sector is bad, however. In the early twenty-first century some countries have seen marked improvements in access to education and literacy among children. In Zambia, for example, a Primary Reading Program was instituted in 1998 to increase literacy at all grade levels by focusing on reading and writing activities in grades one through seven. Within a year, the literacy rate of children in primary schools—87% of which are located in rural areas—rose 64% (Francis K. Sampa, "Zambia's Primary Reading Program [PRP]: Improving Access and Quality

Education in Basic Schools," Association for the Development of Education in Africa, 2005). One of the main goals of the program, and of Zambia's Ministry of Education overall, has been to provide free education for all, including girls, rural and poor children, special needs children, and orphans. The Primary Reading Program also includes texts about HIV/AIDS and other social issues in its materials for school children.

In Nigeria there are an estimated 9.3 million nomads, 3.1 million of them children. Only about 0.2% to 2% of Nigerian nomads—most of whom earn their living herding sheep and fishing—are literate (Gidado Tahir et al., "Improving the Quality of Nomadic Education in Nigeria: Going beyond Access and Equity," Association for the Development of Education in Africa, 2005). Nomadic people have a difficult time sending their children to school consistently for several reasons: they relocate frequently to find grazing and water for their livestock and to find more available fish; children are an essential source of labor, which makes adults reluctant to send them to school; the rigid time schedules of traditional schools do not account for the nomadic lifestyle; nomads often live in inaccessible areas where terrain is difficult to navigate; and, in Nigeria, a land tenure system often prohibits nomadic people from acquiring permanent settlement land. In response to these problems, the Federal Ministry of Education of Nigeria developed the Nomadic Education Program (NEP), under the direction of the National Commission for Nomadic Education (NCNE), established in 1989. Key components of the NEP include developing a curriculum that is relevant to the experience of nomadic children, who are generally regarded as living outside the mainstream in almost every way; educating nomadic parents and adults about the importance of schooling for their children; and creating flexible, "moveable" schools that take into account the nomads' seasonal relocations. The case study "Access to Basic Education: A Focus on Nomadic Populations of Nigeria" presented at the 1999 biennial meeting of the Association for the Development of Education in Africa found that, in the ten years since the creation of the NCNE, total school enrollment among nomadic children rose from 18,831 in 1990 to 155,786 in 1998. The number of nomadic schools rose from 329 in 1990 to 1,098 in 1997. Gender parity in schools (the ratio of girls to boys attending school) rose from 54% in 1990 to 85% in 1998. In addition, the number of nomadic children completing school rose from 2,077 in 1994 to 7,632 in 1998. According to the NCNE, by 2002, 229,944 nomadic children were enrolled in school.

Economic Well-being in Africa

In its *World Development Report 2006: Equity and Development*, the World Bank notes:

An individual's consumption, his or her income, or his or her wealth have all been used as indicators of the command of an individual over goods and services that can be purchased in the market and that contribute directly to well-being. It is clear too, that individuals' economic status can determine and shape in many ways the opportunities they face to improve their situations. Economic well-being can also contribute to improved education outcomes and better health care. In turn, good health and good education are typically important determinants of economic status.

The interconnectedness of health, education, and economic status is true in countries around the world. As was discussed above, however, certain circumstances in Africa—the colonial presence, government corruption, the AIDS epidemic—have led to a long and well-documented history of extreme poverty. In the large West African country Mali, for example, the average monthly income in 1994 was $54 a month (less than two dollars a day), whereas the average monthly income for Americans in 1994 was $1,185 a month (World Bank, *World Development Report 2006*). Poverty researchers agree that it is not merely a coincidence that the people of Mali spend an average of less than two years in school.

According to the World Bank, poverty rates worldwide have declined since the 1980s in almost every region of the world but sub-Saharan Africa, where, in 1981, there were about 160 million people living on less than one dollar a day; by 2001 the number had doubled, to 313 million. In 2003 the region's total unemployment rate for people ages fifteen to twenty-four was 21.1%—18.6% among women and 23% among men. Unemployment in this age group represented 62.8% of sub-Saharan Africa's total jobless rate.

According to the United Nations Development Program's Human Development Index, average annual income for women in sub-Saharan African countries in 2003 ranged from a low of $325 in Sierra Leone to a high of $10,771 in Equatorial Guinea. For men, average annual income in 2003 ranged from $717 in Malawi to $27,053 in Equatorial Guinea. By comparison, men in the United States earned an average of $46,456 in 2003, while U.S. women averaged annual incomes of $29,017 (http://hdr.undp.org/statistics/data/pdf/hdr05_table_25.pdf).

ASIA: THE LARGEST AND MOST POPULOUS CONTINENT

In terms of both land mass and number of people, Asia is the largest continent on earth, with four billion people in approximately fifty countries covering about 17.2 million square miles, including parts of Siberia (North Asia); China, Japan, Taiwan, and the Korean Peninsula (East Asia, or the Far East); the Middle East, including the Arabian Peninsula, the Persian Gulf countries, Armenia, Georgia, Azerbaijan, the Near East countries of Israel,

Jordan, Syria, Lebanon, and Iraq, and parts of North Africa (West Asia); India, Pakistan, Nepal, Bhutan, Bangladesh, Sri Lanka, and the Maldives (South Asia, or the Indian Subcontinent); Indonesia, Malaysia, the Philippines, Vietnam, Thailand, Laos, and Cambodia (Southeast Asia); Afghanistan and the Central Asian republics of Kazakhstan, Kyrgyz Republic, Tajikistan, Turkmenistan, and Uzbekistan (Central Asia). Because the borders around Asia have never been permanently defined, experts disagree on the total number of countries on the continent, and even the distinctions outlined here are in dispute. Sometimes, for example, East and Southeast Asia are discussed together as "East Asia and the Pacific."

The continent of Asia is home to two-thirds of the world's people—and almost two-thirds of the world's poor. There are approximately 2,269 distinct living (currently used) languages spoken in Asia—415 of them in India alone—and no fewer than nine major religions were founded and continue to be practiced on the continent. With such geographic, ethnic, and cultural diversity, Asia is a region of immense economic differences, housing at the same time some of the wealthiest people in the world and some of the most startlingly poor, many of whom reside in the fourteen least developed Asian countries.

LEAST DEVELOPED COUNTRIES OF ASIA AND THE PACIFIC

In *Voices of the Least Developed Countries of Asia and the Pacific: Achieving the Millennium Development Goals through a Global Partnership* (Elsevier, 2005), the United Nations Development Program (UNDP) reported that the least developed Asia/Pacific countries—Afghanistan, Bangladesh, Bhutan, Cambodia, Kiribati, Lao People's Democratic Republic, Maldives, Myanmar, Nepal, Samoa, Solomon Islands, Timor-Leste, Tuvalu, and Vanuatu—together account for 37% of the total population of all LDCs. These countries range in size from Bangladesh, which has 130 million people, to Tuvalu with 11,000. Between 1990 and 2000 Asia/Pacific LDCs saw overall improvement in some areas: average per capita gross domestic product increased, the total adult literacy rate increased from 60% to 71%, life expectancy went from fifty-eight years to sixty-two years, and the infant mortality rate dropped from seventy-seven to fifty-five deaths per 1,000 live births.

While Asia as a whole has experienced much growth and the very large Asian economies of China and India have expanded in the early twenty-first century and reduced their rates of overall poverty, the least developed countries of the Asia/Pacific region are in general not on track to meet the Millennium Development Goals—in particular the first goal of halving extreme poverty by 2015. (See Table 3.3.) According to the UNDP, 22% of the population of developing countries in Asia live on less then one dollar a day, but 38% of the population of Asia/Pacific LDCs live on less than a dollar a day. So although Asia/Pacific least developed countries account for 7% of the total population of the region, they account for 12% of the region's extremely poor. Furthermore, 46.8% of the Asia/Pacific LDC population live below the region's individual country poverty lines. In individual least developed countries in the region, according to UNDP estimates, the national poverty rates range from 34% in Cambodia to 56% in Afghanistan.

As in Asia/Pacific countries such as China and India that are experiencing unprecedented economic growth but a wider poverty gap, least developed countries in the region have seen increasing disparities in income, wealth, and consumption: Cambodia's consumption rose by 18% among the country's wealthiest segment but only 1% among the poorest. However, even among a single economic category of countries in a region, such as the LDCs of Asia/Pacific, great differences exist in levels of poverty and human development indicators.

Afghanistan

About a year after signing the 1978 Treaty of Friendship, Cooperation, and Good Neighborliness with Afghanistan, the Soviet Union invaded the country and deposed the Afghan president, sparking a bloody civil war between Soviet supporters and anticommunist rebels. By the time the Soviets withdrew in 1989, more than five million Afghans had fled to refugee camps in Pakistan and Iran. The civil war, however, continued after the Soviet withdrawal, creating a state of chaos between competing warlords and eventually giving rise in 1996 to the Taliban, an extreme Islamic nationalist movement that stabilized the country to a degree but also controlled nearly every aspect of Afghan citizens' lives. The Taliban were responsible for massive human rights abuses, including torturing and killing thousands of Afghan civilians. Devastating earthquakes hit the country in 1998 and 1999, further displacing tens of thousands of Afghans. When terrorists associated with the Islamic fundamentalist group al-Qaeda struck the United States on September 11, 2001, the U.S. retaliated militarily against the Taliban—and therefore against Afghanistan—for sheltering al-Qaeda leader Osama bin Laden. Afghanistan was again torn by war.

Afghanistan is considered the least developed country in the world. According to the United Nations Development Program's *Afghanistan National Human Development Report 2004*, more than two decades of near-constant war and natural disasters have left Afghanistan with one of the worst human development indexes (HDI) in the world, at 0.346, ranking 171 out of 177 countries. As a comparison, Norway had the world's highest human development ranking in 2003 at 0.963; the United States ranked tenth at 0.944. Niger, with the lowest HDI in the world, had a score

TABLE 3.3

Progress toward attainment of the MDGs (Millennium Development Goals) in Asia-Pacific least developed countries, 2005

Country	Goal 1, target 1: proportion of population below poverty line	Goal 1, target 2, indicator 4: prevalence of underweight children under 5 years of age (UNICEF[a]-WHO[b])	Goal 1, target 2, indicator 5: proportion of population below minimum level of dietary energy consumption (FAO[c])	Goal 2, target 3, indicator 6: net enrollment ratio in primary education (UNESCO[c])	Goal 2, target 3, indicator 8: literacy rate of 16- to 24-year-olds (UNESCO[c])	Goal 4, target 5, indicator 13: under-5 mortality rate (UNICEF[a]-WHO[b])	Goal 4, target 5, indicator 14: infant mortality rate (UNICEF[a]-WHO[b])	Goal 7, target 10, indicator 30: proportion of population with sustainable access to an improved water source, rural (UNICEF[a]-WHO[b])	Goal 7, target 10, indicator 30: proportion of population with sustainable access to an improved water source, rural (UNICEF[a]-WHO[b])	Goal 7, target 10, indicator 31: proportion of population with access to improved sanitation, rural (UNICEF[a]-WHO[b])	Goal 7, target 10, indicator 31: proportion of population with access to improved sanitation, urban (UNICEF[a]-WHO[b])
Afghanistan	n/a	n/a	Underachiever, deteriorating trend	Underachiever, slow pace of achievement	n/a	Underachiever, slow pace of achievement	Underachiever, slow pace of achievement	n/a	n/a	n/a	n/a
Bangladesh	Underachiever, slow pace of achievement	On track	Underachiever, slow pace of achievement	On track	Underachiever, slow pace of achievement	On track	On track	Underachiever, slow pace of achievement	Underachiever, deteriorating trend	On track	Underachiever, slow pace of achievement
Bhutan	n/a	On track	n/a	Underachiever, slow pace of achievement	n/a	On track	Underachiever, slow pace of achievement	n/a	n/a	n/a	n/a
Cambodia	On track	Underachiever, slow pace of achievement	Underachiever, slow pace of achievement	On track	Underachiever, slow pace of achievement	Underachiever, deteriorating trend	Underachiever, deteriorating trend	n/a	n/a	n/a	n/a
Lao People's Democratic Republic	On track	Underachiever, slow pace of achievement	On track	On track	Underachiever, slow pace of achievement	On track	Underachiever, slow pace of achievement	n/a	n/a	n/a	n/a
Maldives	n/a	On track	n/a	On track	On track	On track	Underachiever, slow pace of achievement	Underachiever, deteriorating trend	Underachiever, deteriorating trend	n/a	On track
Myanmar	n/a	Underachiever, deteriorating trend	On track	Underachiever, deteriorating trend	Underachiever, slow pace of achievement	Underachiever, slow pace of achievement	Underachiever, slow pace of achievement	On track	On track	On track	On track
Timor-Leste	n/a	n/a	n/a	n/a	n/a	Underachiever, slow pace of achievement	Underachiever, slow pace of achievement	n/a	On track	n/a	n/a
Nepal	Underachiever, slow pace of achievement	n/a	Underachiever, slow pace of achievement	Underachiever, slow pace of achievement	Underachiever, slow pace of achievement	On track	On track	On track	Underachiever, deteriorating trend	Underachiever, slow pace of achievement	Underachiever, slow pace of achievement
Kiribati	n/a	n/a	n/a	On track	n/a	Underachiever, slow pace of achievement	Underachiever, slow pace of achievement	On track	Underachiever, slow pace of achievement	Underachiever, slow pace of achievement	On track
Samoa	n/a	n/a	n/a	Underachiever, deteriorating trend	On track	On track	On track	Underachiever, deteriorating trend	Underachiever, deteriorating trend	On track	On track
Solomon Islands	n/a	n/a	n/a	n/a	n/a	On track	On track	n/a	n/a	Underachiever, slow pace of achievement	No improvement

TABLE 3.3

Progress toward attainment of the MDGs (Millennium Development Goals) in Asia-Pacific least developed countries, 2005 [CONTINUED]

Country	Goal 1, target 1: proportion of population below poverty line	Goal 1, target 2, indicator 4: prevalence of underweight children under 5 years of age (UNICEF[a]-WHO[b])	Goal 1, target 2, indicator 5: proportion of population below minimum level of dietary energy consumption (FAO[c])	Goal 2, target 3, indicator 6: net enrollment ratio in primary education (UNESCO[d])	Goal 2, target 3, indicator 8: literacy rate of 16- to 24-year-olds (UNESCO[d])	Goal 4, target 5, indicator 13: under-5 mortality rate (UNICEF[a]-WHO[b])	Goal 4, target 5, indicator 14: infant mortality rate (UNICEF[a]-WHO[b])	Goal 7, target 10, indicator 30: proportion of population with sustainable access to an improved water source, rural (UNICEF[a]-WHO[b])	Goal 7, target 10, indicator 30: proportion of population with sustainable access to an improved water source, rural (UNICEF[a]-WHO[b])	Goal 7, target 10, indicator 31: proportion of population with access to improved sanitation, rural (UNICEF[a]-WHO[b])	Goal 7, target 10, indicator 31: proportion of population with access to improved sanitation, urban (UNICEF[a]-WHO[b])
Tuvalu	n/a	n/a	n/a	n/a	n/a	Underachiever, slow pace of achievement	Underachiever, slow pace of achievement	On track	On track	On track	On track
Vanuatu	n/a	n/a	n/a	On track	n/a	On track	On track	Underachiever, deteriorating trend	Underachiever, deteriorating trend	n/a	n/a
APLDCs[e] (weighted averages)	Underachiever, slow pace of achievement	On track	Underachiever, slow pace of achievement	Underachiever, slow pace of achievement	Underachiever, slow pace of achievement	On track	Underachiever, slow pace of achievement	On track	On track	On track	On track

[a]United Nations Children's Fund.
[b]World Health Organization.
[c]Food and Agriculture Organization.
[d]United Nations Educational, Scientific and Cultural Organization.
[e]Asia-Pacific least developed country. These estimates refer to various points of time and are based on population-weighted averages of countries for which data were available.
Note: "n/a" indicates data not available.

SOURCE: "Box 2. Progress toward Attainment of the MDGs in Asia-Pacific Least Developed Countries," in *Voices of the Least Developed Countries of Asia and the Pacific: Achieving the Millennium Development Goals through a Global Partnership*, United Nations Development Programme, Elsevier, 2005, http://www.undp.org.in/events/LDC/LDC-MDGAsiaP.pdf (accessed April 10, 2006). Information compiled and estimated on the basis of latest available data from the United Nations Millennium Database and national Millennium Development Goal (MDG) Progress Reports for Afghanistan, Bangladesh, Bhutan, Cambodia, Lao People's Democratic Republic, Nepal and Timor-Leste.

TABLE 3.4

Selected indicators for poverty, vulnerability, and risk in Afghanistan, 2003

	GDPª per capita (US$) (2002)	Life expectancy at birth (years) (2002)	Infant mortality rate per 1,000 live births (2002)	Population without sustainable access to an improved water source (percent) (2000)
Afghanistan	190	44.5	115ᵇ	60ᵇ
Iran	1,652	70.1	35	8
Pakistan	408	60.8	83	10
Tajikistan	193	68.6	53	40
Turkmenistan	1,601	66.9	76	—
Uzbekistán	314	69.5	52	15
Least developed countries	298	50.6	99	38
South Asia	516	63.2	69	15
Low human development countries	322	49.1	104	38
Low-income countries	451	59.1	80	24
World	5,174	66.9	56	18

ªGross domestic product.
ᵇFigures for 2003.

SOURCE: "Table 2.2. Selected Indicators for Poverty, Vulnerability, and Risk in Afghanistan," in *Afghanistan National Human Development Report 2004: Security with a Human Face*, United Nations Development Programme, 2004, http://www.undp.org/dpa/nhdr/af-files/afnhdr2004-ch2.pdf (accessed April 10, 2006). Data from UNDP global *Human Development Report 2004*, UNICEF/CSO MICS 2003 and CSO *Statistical Yearbook 2003*.

of 0.281. Afghanistan's gender-related development index (GDI) was 0.300. The gender development index examines basic quality of life but is adjusted for inequalities between men and women. Norway again ranked first in the world, with a GDI rating of 0.960; the United States was eighth at 0.942. Of the 140 countries ranked using the GDI, Niger was again last at 0.271.

Individual poverty indicators are equally low, especially compared with those of Afghanistan's neighboring countries. Per capita gross domestic product in 2002 was $190—the lowest in the region—and only 23% of Afghans have access to safe drinking water. All of the country's poverty indicator numbers were the worst in the region: As indicated in Table 3.4, Afghanistan's per capita GDP was lower, its life expectancy at birth was lower, its infant mortality rate was higher, and its population without access to an improved water source was higher than other countries in the region, than the average of countries with low human development, and than the average of low-income countries.

Because of the constant wartime conditions in Afghanistan, the idea of poverty encompasses more than income and human deprivation as they are discussed in Chapter 1. Overall "human security" includes not only security in the physical sense of safety from armed violence but also security that allows for economic development and even access to safe water, sanitation services,

and farmable land. In *Human Security and Livelihoods of Rural Afghans, 2002–2003* (June 2004), the Feinstein International Famine Center at Tufts University used data collected by the United Nations Food Program and the Ministry of Rural Rehabilitation and Development's Nationwide Risk and Vulnerability Assessment (NRVA) of 2003, which found that Afghans living in rural provinces who were asked about their physical and economic conditions overwhelmingly reported a lack of access to safe water sources, health care, education, and economic opportunities and said that this lack of essential services posed as much of a threat to their security as the ongoing armed conflict. As in most developing and underdeveloped countries, women and children are the most vulnerable members of Afghan society.

The Tufts study revealed that Afghan people by and large have a very different idea of their country's biggest challenges than do those in the international community:

> Rural people throughout Badghis, Herat, Kabul, Kandahar, and Nangarhar provinces defined security as having access to health care, education, employment, clean drinking water, reproductive choices, political participation, good governance, and housing. This conception of security illustrates a marked difference from the understanding of security on the part of the international community (i.e., a lack of armed attacks and fighting). It also more accurately reflects the reality of "security issues" in the lives of rural Afghans.

Regarding the differing perceptions of men and women, the report notes: "In contrast to men's overwhelming concerns regarding physical security, women consistently ranked poverty as their top concern."

Eighty-five percent of Afghans live in rural areas. The UNDP identifies seven critical factors that influence the country's high poverty level in addition to chronic violent conflict:

- Lack of income

- Lack of access to basic necessities

- Social, political, and economic exclusion and isolation

- Lack of marketable skills and exposure to technologies; lack of assets such as tools, livestock, and machinery

- Lack of property ownership rights and access to credit

- Vulnerability to environmental risks, natural disasters, and other poverty risk factors

- Erosion of indigenous cultures, values, and social support networks

HEALTH AND MORTALITY IN AFGHANISTAN. According to the UNDP report, life expectancy in Afghanistan is 44.5 years; healthy life expectancy (the number of years a newborn can expect to live in full health) is just 33.4 years. Afghans live about twenty fewer years than those in their neighboring countries and about 18.7 fewer than the average of South Asia overall. Mortality rates of infants, children, and mothers are some of the highest in the world: UNICEF's *State of the World's Children 2006* reports that 257 out every 1,000 children—one out of every five and the fourth worst rate in the world—die before reaching the age of five (85,000 children annually die from diarrhea); and a woman dies of pregnancy-related causes every thirty minutes. An estimated 50% of the population suffers from chronic malnutrition, as do 50% of children under five. Fewer than 15% of pregnant women receive medical attention during labor and delivery; only eleven of the country's thirty-one provinces have obstetric care available, and Afghan women report that the care they do receive is inadequate.

The Afghan population suffers from high rates of malaria infection—an estimated two to three million per year. Afghanistan also has a high number of tuberculosis cases, with 72,000 new cases annually and about 15,000 deaths (at least 12,000 to 13,000 of which are women). Because fewer than 40% of Afghan children receive preventative vaccinations, diseases such as measles and polio—which have been largely eradicated in developed countries—continue to afflict Afghans; there are approximately 35,000 cases of measles every year, and in 2001 the country had eleven cases of polio. (Afghanistan is one of only six countries where polio still exists.) *State of the World's Children 2006* reports that 54% of Afghan children under age five suffer from stunted growth, and 39% are moderately or severely underweight. The main causes of death for children under five are diarrhea disease (accounting for 25% of under-five deaths), respiratory tract infections (19%), and measles (16%).

Additionally, the UNDP reports that most Afghans suffer from some degree of mental illness or stress disorder due to the country's almost chronic state of war since 1978. The World Health Organization estimates that as many as one in five Afghans have some form of mental disorder related to stress, including severe anxiety, depression, insomnia, and post-traumatic stress disorder. A large percentage of Afghans is also believed to have serious health problems related to drug use, although exact figures are unavailable. Health officials fear that, as heroin injection increases among drug users, rates of HIV/AIDS and hepatitis infection will also increase, although, again, numbers are not available.

EDUCATION AND LITERACY. As a result of the country's longstanding military engagements, about 80% of its schools have been seriously damaged or destroyed, according to the UNDP. So although Afghanistan's constitution of 1964 guaranteed free and compulsory (required) education for all citizens, by 1999 almost 70% of Afghans (85% of women) were illiterate and its education system was considered one of the worst in the world. In the Tufts study fewer than 10% of women in rural areas reported having attended any school at all. After the American invasion in late 2001 and the subsequent fall of the Taliban, which had outlawed education for girls, pressure from the international community led to the enrollment of nearly four million children in grades one through twelve in 2002—a higher enrollment than the country had ever experienced.

Nonetheless, access to education is limited and schools remain substandard. Most classes are held in tents or the open air, with few materials available. Disparities exist between urban and rural areas as well, with only about one-third of schools located in rural provinces (2,233 out of 6,870 total). In more remote areas schools often are located inside mosques, where girls and women are not allowed. In areas where gender segregation is enforced, schools must either hold separate sessions for girls and boys, or there must be separate schools altogether. With teachers earning only about $30 a month, there is little incentive to work double the hours to educate both boys and girls equally. Many parents continue to resist sending their daughters to school as well because of cultural beliefs. In a country where most girls have no options for higher education or careers, educating them seems like a waste of time and money that could be better spent elsewhere. Additionally, traditional beliefs hold that girls have lesser capabilities and will never have to support their families financially. In 2002 more than twice as many Afghan boys attended school as girls (2,533,272 boys versus 1,171,963 girls).

ACCESS TO NATURAL RESOURCES. The ongoing military conflict in Afghanistan is another example of a cyclical situation that is both a cause and a consequence of poverty. On the one hand, it has caused environmental destruction that prevents many Afghans from earning a good living. On the other hand, because they cannot earn a living wage, Afghans continue to join militias and fight, thus causing more damage to natural resources and preventing other Afghans from getting out of poverty. In addition to the environmental affects of war, Afghanistan has suffered from natural soil erosion and drought, which make agricultural work extremely difficult. A rapidly diminishing water table due to drought and infrastructure mismanagement has made safe water and sanitation rare in Afghanistan.

In fact, water scarcity is considered one of the greatest threats to human development in Afghanistan, according to the UNDP. Wetlands in the country have disappeared, along with the wildlife they housed and the agriculture they supported. Overall, a lack of reliable water supplies has caused widespread loss of income. The UNDP reports that many families reduce their food intake, take out loans, and sell possessions to cope with the inadequate water supply. The quality of water in Afghanistan is also a danger to the poor, causing water-borne illnesses such as cholera outbreaks. Only 8.5% of Afghans had access to indoor piped water in 2003—23.8% of urban residents and 2% of those living in rural areas. The rest of population relied on surface water and wells for drinking, bathing, and cleaning. Sanitation causes equally serious problems for the poor. In six provinces less than 20% of households had access to a flush or pit toilet. Only one province had near 100% toilet access. Open sewers spread communicable diseases that can cause severe illness or death, especially in children.

Access to farmable land also threatens the health and livelihoods of impoverished Afghans. Just 12% of Afghanistan's land can be used as farmland, but about 80% of Afghans rely on farming for food; 85% of the population lives in rural areas. Competition among rural farmers over land and water often leads to outbreaks of violence, and families can become displaced—forced to move to urban areas to survive—when they lose valuable land on which to farm or let their livestock graze, leaving them even more vulnerable to malnutrition and disease. One survey cited by the UNDP found that 37% of Afghan households have become displaced due to the shrinking supply of arable land. Such competition increases both the rate and the depth of poverty by pitting the relatively well off against those who are already poor.

Timor-Leste

While Afghanistan is the world's least developed country in terms of social and human development indicators, Timor-Leste (formerly known as East Timor) is commonly cited as the world's poorest in terms of income poverty. As with many extremely poor countries, Timor-Leste has experienced violent conflict that has in many respects truncated its potential for economic development and kept much of the population in poverty.

A TURBULENT HISTORY. Timor-Leste makes up half of the island of Timor in Oceania, surrounded by the Banda Sea to the north and the Timor Sea to the south. Portugal colonized the island in the mid-sixteenth century, but a treaty in 1859 ceded the western half of the island to the Dutch. During World War II Imperial Japan occupied Timor-Leste, but Japan's defeat in the war in 1945 returned colonial rule to Portugal. A military coup in Portugal in 1974 led to a decolonization process in all of Portugal's territories, including Timor-Leste. In August 1975 the Timorese Democratic Union Party launched a coup, which was followed by a short civil war with the Revolutionary Front for an Independent Timor-Leste. The Democratic Union Party was forced into West Timor (the other half of the island), which was under Indonesian rule. Indonesian forces began entering Timor-Leste in September 1975. In November 1975 the Revolutionary Front declared Timor-Leste an independent state; in December Indonesia launched a full-scale military attack.

Although Indonesia's takeover of Timor-Leste was never recognized by the United Nations, its insistence that the Revolutionary Front was a communist organization incited fear—many Western countries, including the United States, supported Indonesia's brutal regime in Timor-Leste to prevent the spread of communism, even though an estimated 100,000 to 250,000 Timorese died because of the violence and starvation caused by the Indonesian occupation. Finally, in January 1999 the Indonesian government allowed the Timorese to vote to choose between remaining under the rule of Indonesia and establishing an independent state. In August 1999, 75% percent of Timorese voters chose independence, but in September an anti-independence front of militias rampaged through the country, burning three-quarters of the houses and destroying most of the infrastructure, schools, and utility systems. More than a thousand Timorese were killed, a thousand Timorese women raped, and another 250,000 to 300,000 people were forced into West Timor to live as refugees. Late in September peacekeeping forces from Australia entered Timor-Leste to end the violence. In August 2001 the United Nations supervised elections, and in May 2002 Timor-Leste officially became an independent republic recognized by the global community. In April 2005 Indonesia and Timor-Leste signed an agreement to demarcate their borders.

Timor-Leste has continued to experience phases of violence and unrest. According to the Office of the United Nations High Commissioner for Refugees (UNHCR) 2006 "Country Operations Plan" for Timor-Leste (September 1, 2005), further violence is expected during the scheduled 2006 elections.

ECONOMIC CONDITIONS SINCE INDEPENDENCE. Timor-Leste has valuable natural resources, particularly petroleum reserves. However, the political unrest over the second half of the twentieth century caused such disruption in essential services, food production, and livelihoods in general that extreme poverty became the norm. The joint publication by the World Bank, Asian Development Bank, Japanese International Cooperation Agency, United Nations Development Program, UNICEF, United Nations Mission of Support in Timor-Leste, and the Government of Timor-Leste, titled *Timor-Leste. Poverty in a New Nation: Analysis for Action* (May 2003), reports that in 1999—the year Timorese citizens voted in favor of independence, followed by the violent militia crackdown—Timor-Leste's gross domestic product fell 38.5% and its agricultural output fell 48.4%. In 2000 and 2001 recovery began in earnest, with GDP increasing 15% in 2000 and 18% in 2001, and food production increased 15% in 2000. Reconstruction of roads and residential and commercial buildings also began shortly after the UN-supervised elections—almost 70% of damaged or destroyed houses have been or are being rebuilt. Utilities, however, have not been fully restored: electricity in particular remains unavailable in much of the country, especially rural areas.

As of the publication of the World Bank's joint report in 2003, the poverty line in Timor-Leste was US$15.44 per capita a month, or about fifty cents per day. Just less than 40% of the population lives below this poverty line. About 75% of Timorese live in rural areas; six out of seven poor people in the country are rural dwellers.

HEALTH. According to the International Monetary Fund's July 2005 Country Report on Timor-Leste, Timor-Leste's rate of maternal mortality is one of the highest in the region, at about 800 per 100,000 live births. The rate of infant mortality is also high, at seventy to ninety-five per 1,000 live births. The mortality rate of children under age five is 126 per 1,000 live births. The World Health Organization (WHO) reports that life expectancy was fifty-five years for males and sixty-one years for females in 2003; healthy life expectancy was 47.9 years for males and 51.8 years for females. In 2002, 23.6% of births were attended by skilled practitioners.

The WHO reports in *Health Profile: Democratic Republic of Timor-Leste* (October 2002) that 80% of Timorese had access to health care as of 2002, but distance is a problem: on average, people must walk about seventy minutes to reach one of the country's four hospitals, sixty-five community health centers, or eighty-two health posts. Timor-Leste has had a serious shortage of doctors since the violence of 1999, when many health care professionals fled to Indonesia. The lack of technical services, clean water, reliable electricity, and communications systems adds to the inadequacy of the medical system.

Common childhood diseases include acute respiratory and diarrheal diseases, malaria, and dengue fever. Additionally, as many as 80% of Timorese children suffer from intestinal parasites, which can lead to severe malnutrition. In fact, hunger and its consequences are major health problems in Timor-Leste. In March 2000 the WHO estimated that 45% of children ages six months to five years were underweight, and 41% had stunted growth. About 35% of mothers were also found to be underweight. According to the WHO, several deadly and/or communicable diseases are prevalent in Timor-Leste, including malaria, leprosy, lymphatic filariasis (an infection of the lymph system by parasitic worms), Japanese encephalitis, yaws (a bacterial infection of the skin), and tuberculosis. In 2002 communicable diseases were responsible for about 60% of deaths in Timor-Leste. Although the immunization program was revived in 2000, in 2002 fewer than 50% of children five years and younger had received basic immunizations.

ACCESS TO ESSENTIAL SERVICES. As in Afghanistan, access to essential services such as water and sanitation is a strong indicator of poverty in Timor-Leste, especially among those living in rural areas. Only 4% of the rural population has access to safe water, sanitation, and electricity, versus almost 50% of urban dwellers. According to the *Health Profile* of Timor Leste prepared by the World Health Organization, of the country's 850,000 citizens, 620,000 have no electricity and 560,000 have no radios, making daily conveniences and communication across even short distances almost nonexistent.

EDUCATION. Before the 1999 vote for independence, 80% of sixteen- to eighteen-year-olds in Timor-Leste had completed grades one, two, and three of primary school, compared with nearly 100% of Indonesians in the same age group. During the violence that followed the independence referendum, 95% of schools were destroyed, and 20% of primary school teachers and 80% of secondary school teachers fled the country. By 2001, however, about 86% of schools had been rebuilt at least to the point of being usable, with overall enrollment in primary school increased from 65% in 1998–99 to 75% in 2000–01—girls made up 45% of those enrolled. Among adults, however, literacy and educational attainment are very low, with 57% reporting little or no formal schooling. Less than 40% of Timor-Leste's wealthiest adults age thirty and older are literate; in the poorest group only about 15% are literate. This poses a problem for the development of the country's education system because it means the pool of potential teachers is extremely small.

CHAPTER 4
EMERGING AND TRANSITION ECONOMIES: WIDENING THE POVERTY GAP

An emerging economy is one that is moving from developing to developed (or industrial), while a transition economy is one evolving from a planned economy (meaning one controlled by the government, as in the former Soviet bloc countries) to a free market economy like those in North America and Europe. A country may be both emerging and transitional. Countries undergoing these economic shifts experience varying degrees of progress regarding their impoverished citizens. Generally, a great number of people are able to enter the middle class during such a transition because of increased business opportunities. At the same time, the incidence of poverty and extreme poverty can increase as the very poor have little or no access to such opportunities.

Researchers of poverty use a measurement called the Gini coefficient to discuss income equality—that is, the poverty gap. Developed by the Italian statistician Corrado Gini in 1912, the Gini coefficient is a number between zero and one, with zero representing perfect equality and one representing perfect inequality. Scholars often use the Gini coefficient to express how wide the gap is between the very poor and those with higher incomes.

ASIA

In the early years of the twenty-first century several countries—most notably China and India—that had suffered long-term extreme poverty began to experience unprecedented economic growth. Reasons include rapidly expanding economies and increasing acceptance into the global marketplace; the burgeoning fields of technology and science in both East Asia and the Indian subcontinent that have allowed for greater educational and employment opportunities; the outsourcing of jobs from developed countries to the developing world; and the relative loss in value of the U.S. dollar, which has in general increased the values of foreign currencies.

Despite near record high oil prices around the world, a disappointing agricultural harvest in Southeast Asia,

and a softening electronics market, all in 2006, economic growth in the developing countries of Asia is expected to continue. In 2005 the Asian Development Bank's *Asian Development Outlook 2005 Update* (http://adb.org/documents/books/ado/2005/ado2005.pdf) projected the region's gross domestic product (GDP) would continue to grow at an average of 6.6% in 2006, down from 2004's 7.4%, but still a high rate. (By comparison, the U.S. GDP grew at an annual rate of 3.8% in the third quarter of 2005, according to the Bureau of Economic Analysis, October 28, 2005). High oil prices have been a mixed blessing for Asia. The countries of Central Asia (as defined by the Asian Development Bank: Azerbaijan, Kazakhstan, Kyrgyzstan, Tajikistan, Turkmenistan, and Uzbekistan) have abundant oil supplies that make them a major region of net oil exports. In 2004 the regional GDP for the Central Asian republics grew at a remarkable 10.4%, according to the *Asian Development Outlook*, with a rate of 8.8% growth projected for 2006 and 9.2% projected for 2007. Turkmenistan, Kazakhstan, and Azerbaijan in particular have rapidly expanding economies and are experiencing growth in such industries as tourism, communications, and oil and natural gas. Furthermore, government investment in modern infrastructure has increased employment and exports in other industries.

In East Asia—which includes Hong Kong, Mongolia, the People's Republic of China, the Republic of Korea, and Taiwan—GDP growth has been strong since 2000 and was projected at 7% for 2006. The acceptance in 2001 of the People's Republic of China into the World Trade Organization (WTO) added to the economic expansion of East Asia, which was led largely by exports from China. In China relaxed government policies have allowed entrepreneurs to compete—many for the first time—in the global marketplace. In addition to the success of such exported products as steel, real estate in China has boomed.

The countries in South Asia (Afghanistan, Bangladesh, Bhutan, India, Maldives, Nepal, Pakistan, and Sri Lanka) have also experienced some of the strongest rates of growth, allowing many people in the region to attain relative prosperity in the early years of the twenty-first century. The resulting consumer spending in such countries as India and Pakistan has fueled the economies even further. Even war-torn Afghanistan—the least developed country in the world as of 2005—was estimated to achieve GDP growth of 7.5% in 2005, despite the massive social and political upheavals since September 11, 2001. In 2005 the Indian government announced its creation of the Building India program, which will invest $40 billion over four years in improving rural infrastructure, with the goal of moving more of India's rural population into the middle class.

However, despite Asia's unprecedented economic growth in the first few years of the twentieth-first century, extreme poverty persists in the region, and the Gini coefficient is actually rising. According to the report *Enhancing the Fight against Poverty in Asia and the Pacific: The Poverty Reduction Strategy of the Asian Development Bank* (December 2004, http://www.adb.org/Documents/Policies/Poverty_Reduction/2004/prs-2004.pdf), 720 million Asians lived on less than one dollar a day in 2000.

A majority of Asia's poor are concentrated in South Asia, mostly in the large economies of India, Bangladesh, and Pakistan, but the rest of the continent has many poor people as well. According to the Asian Development Bank in *Poverty in Asia: Measurements, Estimates, and Prospects* (2004), 1.9 billion Asians lived on less than two dollars a day in 2002, 690 million of them on less than one dollar a day.

Even with its strong economic growth, Kazakhstan maintains a high rate of poverty, at about 24% in 2002 ("Kazakhstan: Poverty Persists Despite Impressive Economic Growth," IRINnews.org, May 13, 2004). In Tajikistan, the poorest of the Central Asian republics, more than 83% of the population lives below the country's poverty line; in Kyrgyzstan 44% and in Turkmenistan 58% live in poverty. According to the United Nations, 70% of the population of Afghanistan lives below the poverty line; only 23% of Afghans have access to safe drinking water, and just 12% have access to adequate sanitation (http://www.undp.org.af/about_us/overview_undp_afg/default.htm).

In all regions of Asia the rapidly growing economies have actually increased the numbers of the working poor—that is, those who are steadily employed but still live below their country's official poverty line. Perhaps more troubling, the gap between the rich and poor has expanded dramatically, particularly in two of the most populous countries on earth: China and India.

THE PEOPLE'S REPUBLIC OF CHINA

According to the Central Intelligence Agency's *World Factbook* (June 2006, http://www.cia.gov/cia/publications/factbook/geos/ch.html), China is the most populous country in the world, with 1.3 billion people—20% of the earth's population—and about fifty-six different ethnic groups. The country has the second-largest economy in the world, after the United States, with a GDP of $8 trillion in 2005. In the *China Human Development Report 2005* (2005, http://hdr.undp.org/docs/reports/national/CPR_China/China_2005_en.pdf), the United Nations Development Program (UNDP) reported that China ranked eighty-fifth on the United Nations human development index (HDI) in 2003—a ranking that fell about in the middle of the list of 177 countries. China's widespread poverty—as well as its contemporary status as an emerging and transitional economic power—has many causes, forged in large part by its complex political history.

From Dynasties to Communism to a Free(er) Market Economy

China is one of the oldest ongoing civilizations in the world, with organized city-states having been developed about 5,000 years ago. Early human beings are believed to have inhabited the region 65,000 years ago, and agriculture is known to have developed around 6000 BCE. Two thousand years ago the region was unified for the first time under a single system of government, although over the centuries China experienced periods of political upheaval followed by reunification.

Until the early twentieth century China was governed by a series of dynasties—that is, unified governments controlled by a single leader, with leadership passed down to successive generations. This system of political elitism depended heavily on a massive rural peasant class, who provided all of China with crops for food and other purposes. This social and political organization is known as feudalism and still exists in China.

Over the centuries conflict between the ruling elite class and the poverty-stricken peasants often erupted into rebellions. The Republican Revolution of 1911 brought an end to the dynastic system. For the next several decades, China was nominally unified at best. Warlords and factions controlled various regions, sometimes supporting a national government and other times not.

Among the groups vying for power were the Communists. The Chinese Communist Party (CCP) officially formed in 1920, and quickly grew in strength. It benefited from the anger many Chinese felt towards Western nations, which were supporting Japanese control over the Chinese region of Shantung. Mao Tse-tung was one of the early members of the CCP, by the 1931 he rose to become its leader. By this time the CCP was one of the two most powerful factions in China, the other being the Nationalists, also called the Kuomintang.

When Japan invaded China in 1937, both the Communists and the Nationalists fought back, while remaining at odds with each other. Fighting with Japan continued throughout World War II (1939–45) and was marked by brutal atrocities by the Japanese. Under Mao's direction, the Communist Red Army succeeded in waging guerrilla warfare against the Japanese, gaining further support for the CCP. Mao also further developed his political theory during this time, refining his beliefs that the answers to the poverty among China's peasants lay in land reform and full participation in the social and political arenas. With the surrender of Japan at the end of World War II in 1945, China was free from occupation, but the country was soon plunged into civil war between the Communists and Nationalists. The Red Army conquered most of China by 1949, due largely to Mao's successful recruiting of peasants, and the formation of the People's Republic of China (PRC) was declared. The Nationalists remained in control of the island of Taiwan.

Mao created what was called a "democratic dictatorship," meaning that all the classes of Chinese society were represented by the centralized government; however, detractors from Mao's system were dealt with in prison camps or were simply executed. No one knows exactly how many people were killed under Mao's democratic dictatorship; he admitted to having approximately 800,000 people executed, but the number is believed to be in the millions.

Despite Mao's stated commitment to empowering the peasantry, many of contemporary China's problems with rural poverty can be traced to his economic policies. As a communist country, the government strictly controlled most aspects of the economy, and Mao directed much of its resources towards collectivization, industrialization, and modernization, regardless of the cost to average Chinese. The purges of the Cultural Revolution (1966–76) nearly bankrupted the country intellectually and economically by ridding China of anyone accused of holding "counterrevolutionary" ideas.

China was drawn back into the international community after years of isolation due to communism and the split with Taiwan when U.S. President Richard Nixon visited the country in 1972 and reestablished relations, officially recognizing the PRC as the only legitimate China. Mao died in 1976, and reforms began soon after that loosened state controls somewhat and boosted productivity. Calls for democratic reform were suppressed, however, including the massacre that ended the Tiananmen Square protests of 1989.

In 1998 the Chinese government began a program to privatize some of the economy. Diplomatic relations with the United States improved after a summit with U.S. President Bill Clinton in 1998. By November 1999 the United States and China had reached a trade agreement that loosened trade barriers and made way for China's acceptance into the WTO; China officially earned WTO membership in December 2001. Since then, China has experienced unprecedented economic growth—nearly 10% annually, according to most estimates. It has become one of the world's largest and most important manufacturing centers, much of it for export but also for its expanding domestic market.

China's Growing Middle Class

A large part of the success of China's economy since the late 1990s has been the expansive building and business boom in its cities, which has fueled the urban economy by increasing employment opportunities. With so many more people finding work in China's large cities, and massive government investment in fueling this urbanization, the urban middle class has expanded. Although China's per capita annual income was just $1,000 in 2004 ("China's Middle Class Revolution," October 11, 2004, http://news.bbc.co.uk/1/hi/world/asia-pacific/3732914.stm), People's Daily Online (English version; "Chinese Middle-Class Families Defined," June 2, 2004, http://www.sinoptic.ch/embassy/presseschau/2004/20040601-0604.htm) reports that by 2010, 100 million Chinese families are expected to be included in the middle-class category of people with assets totaling approximately $75,000. Most of those included in this group are the highly educated professionals, managers, and other white-collar employees. In September 2005 People's Daily Online reported that 11.9% of Chinese citizens could be defined as middle class, meaning they earned 5,000 Yuan per month, or about $617, had earned at least a bachelor's degree, and were employed in professional or technical occupations (http://english.people.com.cn/200509/03/eng20050903_206346.html).

This new middle class is both the result and a cause of China's evolution from an agrarian economy to an industrial one. The more people move to urban settings, the more they need items such as automobiles, which changes the way they shop and do business, which in turn increases the likelihood that they will pay for goods and services they would not have needed before, thus increasing overall consumerism. In "China through the Middle Class—Some Distortion but Real Nonetheless" (February 6, 2004, http://www.asiapacificbusiness.ca/apbn/pdfs/bulletin144.pdf), the *Asia Pacific Bulletin* reports that private ownership of vehicles and property—which had been anathema to Communist Party leaders throughout much of the twentieth century—was on the rise: in 2003 there were 12.4 million privately owned automobiles in China (up 24.8% from 2002), and private ownership accounted for 82% of real estate in urban areas. In addition, *Asia Pacific Bulletin* notes an increasing demand for improved health care and education services, as well as more personal spending on travel and eating out—formerly looked down on in the country as indulgent luxuries.

A History of Inequitable Income Distribution

Inevitably, as a large segment of a country's population moves up in social and economic status, the divide between the rich and poor becomes wider and deeper. In countries that have had a planned economy, in which the centralized government controls prices and wages, income is distributed to ensure a certain level of equality, and market competition is discouraged. In China, however, the rural communal farm system was never really equitable. While urban factories were owned and wages administered by the central government, with workers receiving a low but dependable level of health care and compulsory education, the farm communes in the countryside were operated, and wages were controlled, by provincial landlords. To guarantee the health of the urban economy so that China could compete on the world market, investment was concentrated in manufacturing centers along the coast, while the prices of crops produced in the interior were suppressed. This guaranteed that more money would be available for the country to pursue industry, but it also created inequalities between urban and rural dwellers' incomes and standards of living. According to the *China Human Development Report 2005*, the urban per capita income in 1978 was already 2.6 times that of the rural provinces. The World Bank reports that the disparity in the incomes between rural and urban dwellers continued to increase from 1990 through 2002. (See Table 4.1.)

Government economic reforms in the 1980s and 1990s sought to gradually privatize certain businesses; at this point even some rural farmers who took advantage of the expanding free market benefited. However, as privatization spread in China's cities, competition forced many businesses to cut wages and lay off workers, leading to a class of unemployed urban workers. Regardless, fluctuating grain prices kept most rural Chinese poor from the late 1990s to the present, and most of those living in rural provinces never attained the same kinds of opportunities that became available to urban dwellers during the economic reform period.

Poverty Decreases, Especially among Rural Peasants

Nonetheless, great advancements have been made in the country's human development indicators since government reforms began in the late 1970s. The *China Human Development Report 2005* states that the number of rural citizens living in absolute poverty dropped from 250 million in 1978 to 26.1 million in 2005. A direct result of this is that between 1980 and 2001 the average life expectancy rose from sixty-seven to seventy years, while the infant mortality rate dropped from forty-two deaths per 1,000 live births to thirty-one deaths per 1,000 live births. (See Table 4.2.) Furthermore, the *China Human Development Report 2005* reports that in 2002 the adult literacy rate was 85.8% and the youth literacy rate 95.4%, better than the average levels in developing countries, which were 75% and 85%, respectively. Overall, China's incidence of poverty has been steadily decreasing. In 1990 the national rate of poverty at one dollar per day of income was 23.1, and by 2000 it had dropped to 8.8. There was a similar decrease in the national rate of poverty at one dollar per day of consumption, from 32.9 in 1990 to 16.1 in 2000. (See Table 4.3.)

While the poverty rate has declined and the human development ranking has improved, the gap between the rich and poor has grown. CHINAdaily.com reports that, as of June 2004, there were 236,000 Chinese whose

TABLE 4.1

Poverty reduction and rural–urban inequality in China, selected years 1990–2002

	1990	1993	1996	1999	2000	2001	2002	Change (avg. annual, %)		
								1991–93	1994–96	1997–02
Household real income										
Rural	686	765	922	1,044	1,066	1,111	1,164	3.7	7.1	3.6
Urban	1,510	1,945	2,299	2,749	2,925	3,174	3,599	8.8	4.4	7.2
Urban/rural	*2.2*	*2.5*	*2.5*	*2.6*	*2.7*	*2.9*	*3.1*	*4.4*	*−1.9*	*4.4*
Household consumption spending										
Rural	585	632	826	829	878	908	961	7.3	4.0	3.0
Urban	1,279	1,593	1,862	2,167	2,328	2,456	2,818	4.8	2.7	7.9
Urban/rural	*2.2*	*2.5*	*2.3*	*2.6*	*2.7*	*2.7*	*2.9*	*4.3*	*−2.7*	*4.7*

SOURCE: "Table 1.5. Poverty Reduction and Rural–Urban Inequality, 1990–2002," in *China: Promoting Growth with Equity: Country Economic Memorandum*, Report No. 24169-CHA, World Bank, Poverty Reduction and Economic Management Unit, East Asia and Pacific Region, October 15, 2003, http://www.worldbank.or g.cn/English/content/cem03.pdf (accessed April 10, 2006). Data from China Statistical Yearbook.

TABLE 4.2

Progress in health, by selected regions and selected characteristics, China and East Asia, 1980 and 2001

	China		East Asia and Pacific		Lower middle-income countries		High income countries	
	1980	**2001**	**1980**	**2001**	**1980**	**2001**	**1980**	**2001**
Life expectancy at birth (years)	67	70	64	69	65	69	74	78
Mortality infant (per 1,000 live births)	42	31	53	34	55	33	12	5
Mortality under 5 (per 1,000 live births)	64	39	79	44	83	41	15	7

SOURCE: "Table 1.3. Progress in Health," in *China: Promoting Growth with Equity: Country Economic Memorandum*, Report No. 24169-CHA, World Bank, Poverty Reduction and Economic Management Unit, East Asia and Pacific Region, October 15, 2003, http://www.worldbank.org.cn/English/content/cem03.pdf (accessed April 10, 2006). Data from World Health Report and World Bank World Development Indicators.

TABLE 4.3

Recent trends in poverty reduction in China, selected years 1990–2000

	1990	1992	1996	1998	1999	2000
Poverty headcount rate at $1/day income						
National	23.1	21.6	10.6	7.9	7.8	8.8
Rural	31.0	30.0	14.9	11.4	11.2	13.7
Urban	0.9	0.0	0.2	0.0	0.25	0.3
Poverty headcount rate at $ 1/day consumption						
National	32.9	30.2	17.4	17.8	17.8	16.1
Rural	44.4	41.4	24.8	26.2	27.0	25.0
Urban	1.0	0.8	0.4	1.0	0.5	0.5

Note: Estimates based on official household survey data available only until 2000.

SOURCE: "Table 1.4. Recent Trends in Poverty Reduction," in *China: Promoting Growth with Equity: Country Economic Memorandum*, Report No. 24169-CHA, World Bank, Poverty Reduction and Economic Management Unit, East Asia and Pacific Region, October 15, 2003, http://www.worldbank.org.cn/English/content/cem03.pdf (accessed April 10, 2006)

FIGURE 4.1

Trends in per capita income of urban and rural residents in China, 1990–2003

[At variable prices]

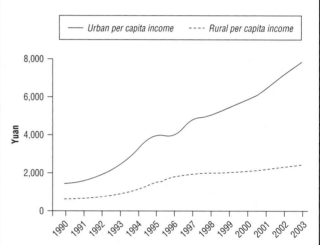

SOURCE: "Figure 2.1. Trends in Per Capita Income of Urban and Rural Residents, 1990–2003 (at Variable Prices)," in *China Human Development Report 2005*, United Nations Development Program, China Development Research Foundation, 2005, http://www.undp.org.cn/downloads/nhdr2005/NHDR2005_complete.pdf (accessed April 10, 2006). Data from National Bureau of Statistics, 2004.

---

assets totaled at least $1 million (http://www.chinadaily.com.cn/english/doc/2004-06/18/content_340483.htm). At the same time, China is home to hundreds of millions of peasants, most of whom live in poverty. Although the per capita income for both urban and rural citizens has risen from 1990 to 2003, the urban per capita income saw a considerable increase. (See Figure 4.1.) A 2002 study by the Chinese Academy of Social Sciences found a remarkable income discrepancy between those who reside in urban and rural centers: 93% of those in China's highest income category were urban dwellers, while 7% were rural dwellers (UNDP, *China Human Development Report 2005*). Income inequality between urban and rural residents fluctuated during the 1990s and then rose dramatically between 1997 and 2003. (See Figure 4.2.) Table 4.4 shows the level of dependence of poor and nonpoor Chinese households on agriculture; peasants living in rural regions are obviously most dependent.

Besides the inequality of incomes, there is also a significant difference in health. The infant mortality rate has been decreasing for both rural and urban infants since 1991. Regardless, in 2000 the rural rate was thirty-seven infant deaths per 1,000 live births, as opposed to the urban rate of twelve infant deaths per 1,000 live births. While the maternal mortality rate has likewise seen a decrease during this same period, the rural rate was still seventy deaths per 10,000 live births in 2000, compared to the urban rate of twenty-nine deaths per 10,000 live births. (See Table 4.5.)

SURVEY OF CHINESE PEASANTS. In October 2004 the German magazine *Lettre International* (http://www.lettre-ulysses-award.org/authors04/chen_wu.html) awarded its top prize—the Lettre Ulysses Award for the Art of Reportage—to a married couple from China's peasant class whose book, *Survey of Chinese Peasants*, became the country's most notorious publication in decades by exposing the true conditions of life for China's 900 million poverty-stricken peasants. The *Survey*'s authors, Chen Guidi and Wu Chuntao, spent their life savings to travel for three years to fifty towns in the agricultural province of Anhui, living among the peasants and interviewing thousands of them as well as local and central government officials.

The study was initially published in the Chinese literary magazine *Dangdai* in late 2003. The issue sold 100,000 copies and went through ten printings. In January 2004 the unabridged version appeared in book form, selling an estimated seven to eight million copies despite being officially banned by China's Communist Party Propaganda Department in March 2004; it has since continued to circulate in pirated editions. Because much of the book focuses on corruption among the party officials who govern peasant villages, and exposes conditions that do not match the government's official version of poverty in China, Chen and Wu were the targets of a libel suit filed against them by one of the officials they discuss in their book. The trial, which was called China's "trial of the century" (Pepe Escobar, "Part 4: The Peasant Tiananmen Time Bomb," January 21, 2005, http://www.atimes.com/atimes/China/GA22Ad01.html), had massive implications for the future freedom of Chinese journalism. Chen and Wu were permitted to travel to Berlin, Germany, to accept the Lettre Ulysses Award, and they were allowed to grant some interviews, but they were also forced to send their young son to live elsewhere for fear of government retaliation. In March 2005 Chen and Wu were found guilty of libel and given heavy fines.

What the *Survey of Chinese Peasants* reports is a situation far worse than anything nonpeasants and Westerners have imagined: rural farmers and laborers sometimes earning less than $30 a year, living in mud huts, and paying exceptionally high taxes (taxes on peasants are four times higher than those on city dwellers) to support the government's urban industrialization program, without any of the health, pension, or education benefits of the cities. Furthermore, Chen and Wu assert that systematic bribery and extortion, as well as beatings, mass arrests, and murders, are commonplace in rural villages, where local officials rule without repercussions.

FIGURE 4.2

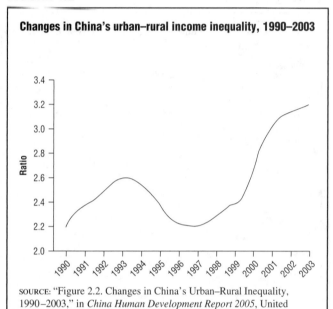

Changes in China's urban–rural income inequality, 1990–2003

SOURCE: "Figure 2.2. Changes in China's Urban–Rural Inequality, 1990–2003," in *China Human Development Report 2005*, United Nations Development Program, China Development Research Foundation, 2005, http://www.undp.org.cn/downloads/nhdr2005/NHDR2005_complete.pdf (accessed April 10, 2006). Data from National Bureau of Statistics, 2004.

TABLE 4.4

Poor and nonpoor households' dependence on agriculture by region in China, 1998

	Non-poor average	Poor average	Region I	Region II	Region III	Region IV
Agricultural income (including forestry) (%)	49.6	68.3	49.5	70.1	69.8	84.8
of which from crop production (%)	45.0	58.4	47.0	57.5	60.0	78.3
Income from other household business (%)	26.7	18.1	24.0	16.2	17.7	8.4
Other income (%)	23.7	13.6	26.5	13.7	12.5	6.8
Land per capita (mu)	2.1	1.6	0.7	1.3	1.6	5.9
Grain yield per mu (kg/mu)	347	165	400	268	181	147
Grain production per capita (kg)	714	406	266	353	295	865
Production inputs per capita (RMB)	668	289	259	316	274	572
Production inputs per mu (RMB)	318	181	370	243	171	97

Notes: Region I: Economically developed with limited poverty, less than 5% of Chinese poor. Provinces: Shanghai, Beijing, Tianjin, Zhejiang, Jiangsu, Fujian, and Guangdong. Region II: Large areas of shallow poverty, home to 55% all poor. Provinces: Hebei, Shanxi, Liaoning, Anhui, Jiangxi, Shangdong, Henan, Hubei, Hunan, Guangxi, Hainan, Chongqing, and Sichuan. Region III: Areas of concentrated and extreme poverty, home to 35% of the total poor. Provinces: Guizhou, Yunnan, Shaanxi, Gansu, Qinghai, Ningxia, and Xinjiang. Region IV: Cold area with limited poverty, home to 68% of the total poor population. Provinces: Inner Mongolia, Jilin and Heilongjiang. 1 mu=666.67 square meters. RMB is Ren Min Bi (currency of People's Republic of China).

SOURCE: "Table 4.3. Poor and Non-Poor Households' Dependence on Agriculture by Region, 1998," in *China: Promoting Growth with Equity: Country Economic Memorandum*, Report No. 24169-CHA, World Bank, Poverty Reduction and Economic Management Unit, East Asia and Pacific Region, October 15, 2003, http://www.worldbank.org.cn/English/content/cem03.pdf (accessed April 10, 2006). Data from China Rural Poverty Monitoring Report, 2000, National Bureau of Statistics, Rural Social Economic Survey Team.

TABLE 4.5

Recent trend in health indicators for maternal and child mortality in China, 1991–2000

	Infant mortality		Under 5-year mortality		Maternal mortality	
	Rural	Urban	Rural	Urban	Rural	Urban
1991	58	17	71	21	100	46
1992	53	18	66	21	98	43
1993	50	16	61	18	85	39
1994	46	16	57	18	78	44
1995	42	14	51	16	76	39
1997	38	13	49	16	80	38
1998	38	14	48	16	74	29
1999	38	12	48	14	80	26
2000	37	12	46	14	70	29

Note: Infant mortality and under 5 year of age mortality rates are per 1,000 of live births. Maternal mortality rate is per 10,000 of live births.

SOURCE: "Table 1.9. Recent Trend in Health Indicators," in *China: Promoting Growth with Equity: Country Economic Memorandum*, Report No. 24169-CHA, World Bank, Poverty Reduction and Economic Management Unit, East Asia and Pacific Region, October 15, 2003, http://www.worldbank.org.cn/English/content/cem03.pdf (accessed April 10, 2006). Data from China Health Statistical Digest, 2001.

One phenomenon peculiar to China and its feudal socioeconomic system of peasants and elites is the *mingong*: the migrant peasant worker. According to Escobar, more than 200 million *mingong* throughout China have migrated to cities to take on jobs in construction, manufacturing, food service, and other manual labor. Ten-plus-hour workdays are common, and 97% of *mingong* have no medical coverage. Robert Marquand, writing in the *Christian Science Monitor*, reports that most of the peasants work at least twenty-eight days per month, and their pay is frequently withheld from them by managers ("China's Peasants Opt for Urban Grindstone," January 23, 2004). They live in city shelters and are required to register with the government every two months. According to David Wank of Sophia University in Tokyo, the growing Chinese economy depends heavily on the *mingong*. He told Marquand: "Without migrants, the whole structure would collapse. They staff the shops, restaurants, factories, construction. It all depends on migrants."

INDIA

India has one of the oldest civilizations in the world, with evidence of permanent human settlements dating back 9,000 years. It is also the world's largest democracy and is home to the greatest concentration of poor people—out of one billion people living on approximately 1.1 million square miles of land, 25% live below the country's poverty line (*World Factbook*, June 2006, http://www.cia.gov/cia/publications/factbook/geos/in.html). According to the World Bank's Issue Brief *Poverty in India* (September 2004, http://siteresources.worldbank.org/INTINDIA/Data%20and%20Reference/20283013/Poverty_India_Brief.pdf), per capita average annual income was $460 as of 2001.

Like Africa, India was colonized by outsiders from the sixteenth century until it achieved independence in 1947. Like China, India has had a class system designed to keep many people (known as "untouchables") in extreme poverty, performing the kinds of labor that wealthier citizens refuse to do. These two factors together have caused much of India's poverty. Since 1991 India has experienced economic expansion akin to China's, which has left its population even more divided between the so-called haves and have-nots.

Colonialism and the Caste System in India

India is the site of origin for four major world religions: Hinduism, Buddhism, Jainism, and Sikhism. This has made the country rich with cultural and philosophical traditions, but it has also led to violent disputes that made India vulnerable to colonial takeover, wars with neighboring countries, and the creation of Hinduism's caste (class or birth ranking) system that continues to keep many Indians in poverty, in part due to the legal entrenchment of castes during the period of British colonialism from 1757 to 1947.

According to the *World Factbook*, Hinduism is India's dominant religion, with 80.5% of Indians counted as followers. One tenet of Hinduism that has strongly influenced secular Indian society is that of castes—the categories into which different kinds of occupations are placed based on the labor or social class into which a person was born. Castes are believed by some to have been instituted by the conquering Indo-European (Aryan) people who invaded northwest India around 1500 BCE and imposed the castes as a way to organize the conquered peoples, although other scholars dispute this theory. As in early China, early Indian government was based on a series of dynasties, which further aggravated tensions between the rich and poor.

In "The Caste System and the Stages of Life in Hinduism" (2005, http://www.friesian.com/caste.htm), Kelley L. Ross reports that there are thousands of "subcastes" throughout India—many of them regionally based—but the five traditional rankings are Brahmins (priests and teachers), Ksytrias (warriors and rulers), Vaisyas (farmers, merchants, and artisans), Sudras (laborers), and Untouchables (polluted laborers, also known as "outcastes"). Typical occupations of untouchables include anything dealing with dead bodies, such as disposing of dead animals and unclaimed human bodies, and tanning leather. Castes are not, however, based on economic factors in the same way that class is. According to the Bhagavad Gita (the main religious text of Hinduism), Brahmins, Ksytrias, and Vaisyas are "different, in harmony with the three powers of their born nature." In other words, the three top castes are inborn states of being, not based on economic status. Ross also notes that when the British created their official census for India in the mid-nineteenth century, they included their own interpretations of the castes: "Existing tribal people as well as Untouchables are also called the 'scheduled castes,' since the British drew up a 'schedule' listing the castes that they regarded as backwards, underprivileged, or oppressed."

While in Hinduism one's caste is not necessarily a fixed position (a person can advance to another caste through reincarnation by his or her actions, although movement is not possible in one lifetime), when the British instituted their census in 1872 they included questions on religion and ethnic identity, in keeping with the European preoccupation at the time with establishing a link between social status and racial purity (the British associated Indian castes with race, an association that some Indians came to share). This led to a deepening of the chasm between the classes as well as the castes, as British social policy was imposed on the Indians.

THE INDIAN APARTHEID. The result of centuries of adherence to the caste system is a social structure that still closely resembles that of South Africa's apartheid. The caste formerly called untouchables are now called Dalits, but they are nonetheless at the bottom of India's social hierarchy, especially in the rural states and villages. According to the Human Rights Watch (2006, http://www.hrw.org/campaigns/sasia/india.htm), there are at least 160 million Dalits in India, even though the concept and practice of "untouchability" was outlawed by India's constitution in 1950. The Dalits are routinely discriminated against: they typically cannot own or access land; they must work in the most undesirable occupations (as always, dealing with corpses and waste); they are abused by local police and denied rights; their living quarters and public spaces are strictly segregated; and their children do not receive equal education. Dalit children are also the ones most commonly sold into debt bondage and forced labor. Dalit workers commonly earn just $0.38 to $0.88 per day. Women of the Dalit caste suffer perhaps the most: they are routinely raped as punishment for any offenses their family members commit, and their numbers are increasing in the commercial sex trade because of poverty and lack of other financial opportunities.

Economics of Contemporary India

India is an example of a country that is both emerging and transitional: although it has been a democracy since its independence, certain elements of its economy have been planned because of efforts to encourage social equality. To make up for centuries of discrimination against the lower-caste Indians by the British rulers, the post-independence Indian government developed a mixed economy, with a certain amount of market freedom in the private sector (independent, privately owned businesses) and socialist-style control of the public sector (services such as the railroad and postal systems). With India

failing to keep up with the huge growth of other Asian economies in the 1980s, the Indian government began in 1991 to open up the country's markets—including parts of the public sector—to private ownership, foreign investment, and increased trade in an effort to stimulate the economy.

According to Bloomberg.com ("India Economy Likely Grew 7.7% in Dec. Qtr on Consumer Spending," February 22, 2006), the Indian economy grew at a rate of 8.1% in 2005. By comparison, the growth rate of the United States in the same period was 3.1%, and that of the European Union countries was 1.7%. The main reason for this high rate of growth—outside of the loosening of the country's markets—is India's abundance of well-educated, English-speaking workers who are willing to accept relatively low wages for steady jobs. Western countries, therefore, began to outsource jobs and set up operations in India to save money and take advantage of the labor force's talents. At the 2005 India Economic Summit, the Indian prime minister Manmohan Singh announced that India could achieve a 10% annual growth rate within two to three years if infrastructure and agriculture were improved and the savings rates increased ("10% Growth for India Could Soon Be a Reality, Says PM Singh," November 29, 2005, http://www.weforum.org/site/homepublic.nsf/Content/10%25+growth+for+India+could+soon+be+a+reality,+says+PM+Singh).

INDIA'S NEW AFFLUENCE. Yet, as in China, the divide between those who are benefiting from India's wealth and those who are not is larger than ever. Amy Waldman reported in "Mile by Mile, India Paves a Smoother Road to Its Future," (*New York Times*, December 4, 2005) that in 1999 the Indian government committed more than $12 billion to update and expand India's crumbling highway system. (Indian infrastructure has been notoriously bad for decades.) The National Highways Development Project (NHDP) is a fifteen-year plan to significantly improve 40,000 miles of roadways running through thirteen of India's thirty-five official states and territories, including the major cities of Mumbai, New Delhi, Calcutta, and Zhenhai. The highway's name, the Golden Quadrilateral, points to the symbolic significance of the project, which the Indian government has promised will increase the country's competitiveness and improve the lives of India's citizens.

The Golden Quadrilateral, however, was quickly coming to highlight the growing gulf between the rich and poor. Discussing the highway's promise to unite and uplift India, Waldman stated:

> But coherence may bring collision. Since 1991, India's population of poor has dropped to 26% from 36%, yet the poor seem poorer than ever. India now juxtaposes pre- and postindustrial societies: citizens who live on dirt floors

without electricity and others who live like twenty-first-century Americans, only with more servants. The highway throws these two Indias into jarring proximity.

Waldman further reported ("In Today's India, Status Comes with Four Wheels," *New York Times*, December 5, 2005), that 250 million people have entered India's middle class since the mid-1990s and that many others have become "super-rich." For these middle- and upper-class Indians, their new wealth has opened them up to an abundance of consumer choices. In fact, one of India's most popular consumer items in the early twenty-first century has been luxury automobiles—an apparent paradox in a country where so many citizens still rely on walking and ox carts for transportation.

With a massive public roadway winding through the country, it is possible that opportunities will be brought to India's many poor rural villages. However, India is also experiencing a migration—similar to China's—to its cities, which many Indians believe hold the most promise for lifting them out of poverty. The rural poor in India are some of the most impoverished people in the world. According to statistics from the Indian government cited by Jayati Ghosh in "Income Inequality in India" (February 17, 2004, http://www.countercurrents.org/eco-ghosh170204.htm), while per capita consumption has increased 40% since 1989–90 for the richest 20% of the country's urban population, India's poorest group, the bottom 80% of rural dwellers (approximately 600 million people), has actually experienced a drop in consumption since 1989–90, signaling a significantly growing gap in income. (India measures poverty by household consumption rather than by income.) Because India's agricultural sector has seen slow and even negative growth in the first part of the twenty-first century, farming is now seen as a dead-end life for poor families, who often send a young adult member to a large city or industrial center to work and who in turn sends money back home.

. . . AND PERSISTENT POVERTY. There is no question that overall poverty in India has dropped since the 1980s, when 44.5% of the country lived below the poverty threshold. In fact, several human development indicators have improved. Life expectancy, just fifty-six years in the 1980s, rose to sixty years in the 1990s, and then increased to sixty-one years in 2000. (See Table 4.6.) According to the World Bank in "Poverty in India," primary school enrollment rose from 68% in 1992–93 to 82% in 2000, with 108 million children ages six to ten attending school. The fertility rate has dropped since the 1960s, from an average of six children per Indian woman to an average of three. Infant mortality has also improved, from 146 deaths per 1,000 live births in 1950 to sixty-eight in 2004.

Other indicators have worsened, however. The maternal mortality rate has increased from 424 deaths per 100,000 live births to 540 per 100,000, and, as of 2000, there were four million known cases of HIV—a

TABLE 4.6

Progress on social indicators in India, selected years 1980–2000

	1980s	1990s	2000
Poverty			
Poverty incidence (%)	44.5	36.0	26.1
Adjusted poverty incidence (%)			28.6
Education			
Overall literacy rate: 7+ years (%)	44	52	65
Female literacy rate as a percent of male literacy rate (%)	53	61	71
Net enrollment rate (NER): grades 1–5 (%)	47	51	77
Female NER as a percent of male NER: grades 1–5 (%)	70	80	81
Health			
Life expectancy at birth (years)	56	60	61
Infant mortality rate 0–4 years (per 1,000 live births)	115	79	68
Maternal mortality rate (per 100,000)	n.a.	424	540
Prevalence of HIV (million people)	n.a.	3.5	4.0
Sanitation			
Access to improved water resources (%)	n.a.	68	78
Number of households with toilet facility (%)	n.a.	30	36

Note: n.a. is not applicable.

SOURCE: "Table 1. Progress on Social Indicators, 1980–2000," in *India: Sustaining Reform, Reducing Poverty*, Report No. 25797-IN, The World Bank, Poverty Reduction and Economic Management Sector Unit, South Asia Region, July 14, 2003, http://www.wds.worldbank.org/servlet/WDS ContentServer/WDSP/IB/2003/07/18/000012009_20030718114757/ Rendered/PDF/257970IN.pdf (accessed April 10, 2006)

situation that is expected to worsen as India's commercial sex industry grows along with its big cities. While the Indian government has stepped up investment in infrastructure, only 36% of Indian households had a toilet in 2000. (See Table 4.6.) In "Hazeltine Scholar Documents Problem of Illiteracy in India" (Fall–Winter 2003–04, http://www.journalism.indiana.edu/alumni/newswire/stories/ hazeltine.html), Sheila B. Lalwani reported that India is believed to be the most illiterate country in the world, with an estimated 350 million citizens who cannot read or write. According to the Human Rights Watch 1996 report *The Small Hands of Slavery: Bonded Child Labor in India* (http://hrw.org/reports/1996/India3.htm), India also has the highest number of working children in the world—an estimated sixty to 115 million (more current statistics on child labor in India are difficult to come by because of the country's many levels of bureaucracy and inaccurate statistical measurements).

CASTE-BASED VIOLENCE. As poverty deepens in India's poor, rural states, tensions between the castes is on the rise. Alexander Zaitchik reported in "Bihar's Blues" (January 20, 2006, http://www.freezerbox.com/ archive/article.php?id=406) that Maoist guerilla fighters claiming to represent Dalit interests were seeking revenge on the higher castes in India's poorest states, such as Bihar in the northeast, where the Dalits are routinely subjected to such horrifying violence as mass immolation (being burned alive). However, the situation is not as simple as rebels protecting the country's poorest and most vulnerable citizens. The Maoists have been known to kill anyone they believe to be sympathetic to the higher castes, with or without evidence.

According to Zaitchik, until the 1960s Bihar—where Buddha is said to have achieved enlightenment—was considered one of the most successful states in post-independence India, with many universities, abundant natural resources, and a well-educated citizenry. Bihar leaders in the 1960s, however, failed to implement needed land reforms that would have distributed land equitably among the castes. Instead, the Dalits remained landless and increasingly impoverished. As of 2006 more than half of Bihar's citizens were illiterate. The culture of corruption that arose led to a ruling body and police officials that fail to prosecute or even investigate crimes against Dalits. As the poverty gap widens in India, caste-based violence is spreading throughout the country.

In October 2005 representatives of the human rights organization Amnesty International testified before the U.S. House of Representatives' Committee on International Relations, Subcommittee on Africa, Human Rights, and International Operations, that the following abuses against Dalits are common in India:

- Socioeconomic discrimination
- Beatings, slashings, and other forms of torture
- Arson—the burning of Dalit communities
- Violence against women
- Rape, gang rape, and the parading of women through the streets naked as a form of punishment, as the right of the upper-caste male, or to punish or embarrass the woman's family
- Beating and torture of women
- Summary execution, many times by burning alive
- Bonded labor
- Denial of rights, especially land rights
- Police abuses against Dalits and custodial abuse

CHAPTER 5

POVERTY IN THE DEVELOPING WORLD

Developing countries are those with incomes (in terms of gross domestic product, or GDP) that fall between the least developed countries and the industrialized nations. Most countries in the world can be described as "developing": neither hopelessly poor nor hopefully rich. These countries have segments of deep, absolute poverty and instances of great wealth in their populations, but their overall economies fall below even that of a middle-income country such as Russia. At the same time, however, in terms of government and general standards of living, progress can be seen over time. Industry and technology in developing nations shows progress, too—often aided by an abundance of natural resources—but they may be hampered by militarism, violent unrest between classes and ethnic groups, political instability, and persistent poverty. Nevertheless, many developing countries have experienced impressive economic growth because of their increasingly important role in the global market as they open their economies to international trade and learn to leverage their natural resources for greater returns.

LATIN AMERICA AND THE CARIBBEAN

The 2006 World Bank report on Latin America, *Poverty Reduction and Growth: Virtuous and Vicious Cycles*, cites the region's under-$2-a-day poverty rate of 25% as one of the major causes and consequences of its overall low growth rate of 4.2% in 2005. As Figure 5.1 shows, the poverty rate in Latin America was halved from 60% in 1950 to less than 30% in 2000. However, during the same time period income inequality remained more or less the same, making both poverty reduction and economic growth more difficult; as in other countries with a wide income gap—even developed ones—the challenge is to increase the incomes of the lower economic groups at a faster rate than those of the wealthier groups. In reality, economic growth rarely works this way. Latin American income inequality is drastic: the

average annual per capita income is $4,000, but the region is home to many millionaires and billionaires. The fourth richest person in the world, Carlos Slim, whose worth was estimated at $23.8 billion in 2005, is Mexican.

In the article "Not Everyone Celebrates Improved Poverty Statistics" (August 23, 2005, http://www.global policy.org/socecon/develop/quality/2005/0823mexico.htm), Diego Cevallos states that Latin America's poverty numbers can be deceptive. He uses the example of an impoverished woman in Mexico City who makes a living picking through garbage and has seen her monthly income increase from $70 to $85 because she has begun collecting discarded tin cans besides paper. While she theoretically has increased her income enough to lift her out of extreme poverty, in reality she is no better off. This, Cevallos argues, is the case with many Latin Americans who are considered above the official poverty line but in reality are still impoverished. Cevallos explains that any poverty line is necessarily subjective, quoting José del Val, the coordinator of the Mexico Multicultural Nation program at the National Autonomous University of Mexico: "Poverty is a condition, a global social state that is not modified just because someone earns a few more dollars."

Colonization and Inequality in Latin America

Latin American social, political, and economic inequality dates back to the late fifteenth century, when the region was first colonized by explorers from Spain and Portugal (including Christopher Columbus). Besides the region's climate and soil fertility, South America in particular is rich in mineral, precious metal, and oil reserves. European explorers recognized this and began moving to expand their territories by taking control. The indigenous peoples of what are now the Caribbean, Mexico, Central, and South America had lived there in complex civilizations for thousands of years. When the

FIGURE 5.1

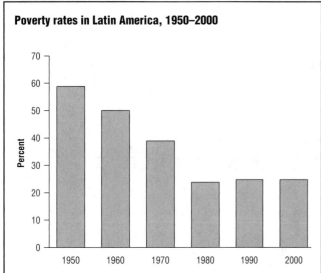

Poverty rates in Latin America, 1950–2000

Note: We used a poverty line of US$2 a day; poverty rates for 1950–1980 are estimated using a lognormal approximation.

SOURCE: Guillermo E. Perry, Omar S. Arias, J. Humberto Lopez, William F. Maloney, and Luis Serven, "Figure 1.3. Poverty Rates in Latin America, 1950–2000," in *Poverty Reduction and Growth: Virtuous and Vicious Cycles*, World Bank, 2006, http://siteresources. worldbank.org/EXTLACOFFICEOFCE/Resources/870892 1139877599088/virtuous_circles1_complete.pdf (accessed March 28, 2006). Data from authors' calculations for 1950–1980; Gasparini, Guitierrez, and Tornarolli (2005) for 1990 and 2000.

Europeans arrived, however, they brought with them infectious diseases against which the native inhabitants had no natural immunity. By the time the conquest was over, around the 1530s, up to 90% of the indigenous population had died—some in battle against the Europeans and others as a result of the brutal working conditions imposed on them by the conquerors, but most because of diseases such as smallpox, typhoid fever, influenza, and measles. To make up for the loss in potential workers, the colonizers began importing slaves from Africa. The Europeans, Africans, and natives occasionally intermarried. Instead of creating a society of equals, however, intermarriage actually resulted in a group of permanent underclasses; children of mixed unions, as well as descendants of natives, continue to be socially and economically oppressed even into the twenty-first century.

A History of Unequal Land Distribution

As in all countries and regions with a history of colonization and slavery, the distribution of property and income in Latin America is inequitable: overall, descendants of native, African, and mixed-race conquered people and slaves earn less money and have less access to workable land than the descendants of Europeans. Samuel Morley writes in *The Income Distribution Problem in Latin America and the Caribbean* (UN Economic Commission for Latin America and the Caribbean, 2001)

that the Latin American region has averaged the most unequal distribution of income in the world since at least the middle of the twentieth century. According to Morley, in the 1990s the top 5% of Latin Americans earned 25% of total income, while the bottom 30% earned 7.5%. Morley contrasts this with the countries of Southeast Asia, where the wealthiest 5% earned 16% of total income and the poorest 30% earned 12.2%. The main difference, Morley says, between Latin America and other developing and even underdeveloped areas such as Africa (the second most unequal region after Latin America) is that inequality did not decrease even after the economic recovery began in the 1990s following the severe recession of the 1980s (sometimes called the "lost decade" for the entire region).

A major cause of the dramatic inequities in income in Latin America is the region's history of land distribution. The World Bank's Office of Land Policy and Administration reports that Latin America's forty million indigenous peoples have not historically been given land rights because government priority has always leaned toward allowing for the greatest—usually corporate or business-oriented—use of natural resources. In *Models for Recognizing Indigenous Land Rights in Latin America* (World Bank, October 2004), Roque Roldán Ortiga reports that historically, Latin America's indigenous land rights system was essential for the livelihoods, culture, inheritance patterns, and basic survival of the native people.

In his foreword to Ortiga's report, the World Bank's Alfredo Sfeir-Younis writes that once the conquering Europeans realized that the region was not as rich in gold as they had initially thought, they began dividing up huge pieces of land, sometimes much of entire countries, and distributing it to individuals without regard to traditional land tenure customs. Over the centuries, the two land distribution techniques overlapped, producing a confusing system. As Sfeir-Younis explains, "The lack of coherence in the land tenure and land titling policies in the mid-eighties constituted one of the main sources of poverty—particularly for women—and of unsustainable agricultural practices." The reason is that in much of Latin America a title to a piece of land, even for a small plot in the city, can be used as collateral to gain access to credit. Without land, people have no way to acquire credit, which leaves them with very few financial options. Additionally, land has a symbolic, religious, and social significance for traditional cultures that often is not understood by nontraditional societies. "Thus," writes Sfeir-Younis, "whenever governments or the private sector move people away, or alienate them, from those sacred sites, this process is almost always accompanied by social disruption, instability and conflict."

Ortiga explains that the conquering Europeans used force, in the form of imposing Christianity and European languages and social norms, on the native people of the region to assimilate them into the dominant culture. "State authorities were particularly keen to abolish the institutions of collective territorial property and communal government of the native peoples of the Americas." Until the twentieth century, the goal was to create a single, overarching culture, eliminating any ethnic or social distinctions. Around the 1930s and 1940s, however, indigenous people began to agitate for recognition of their distinct backgrounds. Native land claims were first officially addressed when the countries of Latin America and the Caribbean all adopted the International Labor Organization's (ILO) Convention 107 in 1957, which recommends methods for protecting and assimilating native peoples while recognizing their individual rights and cultures. Since the 1970s native land rights have become a central issue in Latin American legal and social reform. In 1989 the ILO updated and expanded Convention 107 with Convention 196—the Indigenous and Tribal Peoples Convention—which was adopted by twelve out of twenty Latin American and Caribbean (LAC) countries.

Income Poverty Statistics

As with other countries, researchers use the $2-a-day standard to measure poverty in LAC countries. However, the countries within the region each have their own standard for measuring poverty, most of which differ significantly from each other. The World Bank explains that LAC countries tend to define poverty using a line higher than $2 a day, but in several countries the line is lower than $2 a day. According to the World Bank, in some LAC countries people are officially classified as poor who would not be considered poor in other countries. Likewise, in LAC countries with lower poverty lines fewer people are considered poor than would be in nations with a higher official poverty line. Furthermore, there is no consistency throughout the region on measuring poverty using income and measuring it using expenditures. This lack of consistency makes it difficult to compare rates of poverty in different LAC countries.

The LAC poverty rate (measured according to the standard of under $2 a day) averaged about 25% in 2005, with individual country rates ranging from 4% in Uruguay to 47% in Nicaragua. (See Figure 5.2.) Falling in the middle is the "Southern Cone" region of Argentina, Bolivia, Brazil, Chile, Paraguay, and Uruguay, which averaged 18.8%; Central America and Mexico averaged 29.2%; and the region of the Andean Mountains averaged 31.4%. (See Table 5.1.) The rates measuring against the poverty lines of individual countries yield a somewhat different picture. In Honduras, for example, 72% of the population in 2005 lived below the country's poverty line, while 36% lived on less than $2 a day. In Chile 5% of the population lived on less than $2 a day, but 19% lived

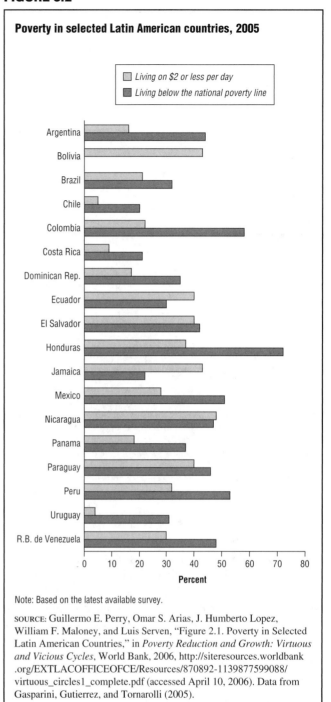

FIGURE 5.2

Poverty in selected Latin American countries, 2005

Note: Based on the latest available survey.

SOURCE: Guillermo E. Perry, Omar S. Arias, J. Humberto Lopez, William F. Maloney, and Luis Serven, "Figure 2.1. Poverty in Selected Latin American Countries," in *Poverty Reduction and Growth: Virtuous and Vicious Cycles*, World Bank, 2006, http://siteresources.worldbank.org/EXTLACOFFICEOFCE/Resources/870892-1139877599088/virtuous_circles1_complete.pdf (accessed April 10, 2006). Data from Gasparini, Gutierrez, and Tornarolli (2005).

below the country's poverty line. By contrast, in Jamaica about 22% of people lived below the country's poverty line, but 43% made less than $2 a day. In El Salvador the numbers were nearly the same, 39% and 41%, respectively. (See Figure 5.2.) Figure 5.3 shows a different aspect of poverty, in that of the fourteen countries cited, only Jamaica had a higher percentage of poverty in its urban areas, as opposed to its rural areas in 2005.

In 2005 and 2006 several Latin American countries began ushering in what was viewed as an era of change.

TABLE 5.1

Poverty in Latin America, by region, early 1990s to early 2000s

[US$2 a day headcount poverty]

Region	Early 1990s (i)	Early 2000s (ii)	Last survey (iii)	Change (iii)–(i)
A. Southern Cone				
Poverty (weighted) (%)	23.6	19.0	18.8	−4.9
Poverty (unweighted) (%)	18.1	16.2	17.1	−1.1
Population (million)	204.4	244.4	246.4	42.1
Number of poor (million)	48.3	46.5	46.2	−2.1
B. Andean community				
Poverty (weighted) (%)	24.8	34.9	31.4	6.6
Poverty (unweighted) (%)	30.6	37.2	34.0	3.4
Population (million)	94.4	118.3	118.0	23.6
Number of poor (million)	23.4	41.3	37.1	13.7
C. Central America and Mexico				
Poverty (weighted) (%)	30.5	29.2	29.2	−1.3
Poverty (unweighted) (%)	36.5	30.0	30.1	−6.4
Population (million)	112.7	140.4	139.6	26.8
Number of poor (million)	34.4	41.0	40.8	6.4
Latin America (A+B+C)				
Poverty (weighted) (%)	25.8	25.6	24.6	−1.2
Poverty (unweighted) (%)	29.3	28.1	27.4	−1.9
Population (million)	411.5	503.1	504.0	92.6
Number of poor (million)	106.1	128.8	124.1	18.0

Note: Weighted refers to population-weighted averages.

SOURCE: Guillermo E. Perry, Omar S. Arias, J. Humberto Lopez, William F. Maloney, and Luis Serven, "Table 2.1. Poverty in Latin America (US$2 a Day Headcount Poverty)," in *Poverty Reduction and Growth: Virtuous and Vicious Cycles*, World Bank, 2006, http://siteresources.worldbank.org/EXTLACOFFICEOFCE/Resources/870892-1139877599088/virtuous_circles1_complete.pdf (accessed April 10, 2006). Data from Gasparini, Gutierrez, and Tornarolli (2005).

FIGURE 5.3

Rural and urban headcount poverty rates, 2005

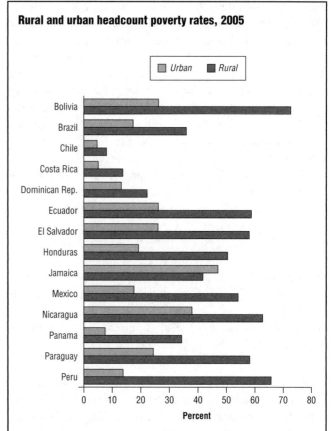

Note: Poverty is defined here as living on $2 or less per day.

SOURCE: Guillermo E. Perry, Omar S. Arias, J. Humberto Lopez, William F. Maloney, and Luis Serven, "Figure 5.5. Rural and Urban Headcount Poverty Rates," in *Poverty Reduction and Growth: Virtuous and Vicious Cycles*, World Bank, 2006, http://siteresources.worldbank.org/EXTLACOFFICEOFCE/Resources/870892-1139877599088/virtuous_circles1_complete.pdf (accessed April 10, 2006). Data from Gasparini, Guitierrez, and Tornarolli (2005).

In Bolivia, Latin America's poorest country, the first indigenous Bolivian was sworn in as president in January 2006. In Chile the region's first woman president was elected the same month. Costa Ricans reelected their president, a Nobel Peace Prize–winner, for a second term. Nine more LAC countries were scheduled to hold elections before the end of 2006. Others, such as Argentina and Venezuela, were undergoing political and social transitions that affected their economies and rates of poverty.

ARGENTINA'S ECONOMIC CRISIS. As the most "European" country in South America, Argentina has fewer people living in extreme poverty than other Latin American countries because it has an unusually large middle class. In fact, Argentina does as well as most developed countries in terms of human development indexes. According to "Country Sheet: Argentina" (2006, http://hdr.undp.org/statistics/data/countries.cfm?c=ARG), the United Nations Human Development Program reports that Argentines had a life expectancy of 74.5 years and a total school enrollment of 95% in 2003, with a 97.2% literacy rate. The infant mortality rate in 2003 was seventeen per 1,000 live births; the under-five mortality rate was twenty per 1,000. The average per capita GDP in 2003 was $12,106.

Historically, Argentina has been through phases of wealth and stability punctuated by periods of political and economic chaos. The events in the early years of the twenty-first century, however, were extreme in the number and kinds of people who were thrown into poverty, known in the country as the "new poor." Incidences of social problems such as suicide, substance abuse, and domestic violence increased as a result.

In 2001 the economy of Argentina fell into a recession. By November of that year the government, unable to repay its international debts, moved toward freezing citizens' bank accounts throughout the country so that it would have access to enough money to keep it stable through the crisis. The threat of having the accounts frozen threw Argentines into a panic, and they began withdrawing as much of their funds as possible. Because of these fears, bank deposits declined by 35% throughout 2001, according to Jennifer L. Rich in "Argentines, Fearing a Freeze, Withdraw Savings from Banks" (*New York Times*, December 1, 2001). Two days later, on December 3, the government froze most assets and limited withdrawals to $250 per week. This temporarily prevented a run on the banks, but not for long.

On December 19 four days of sporadic unrest in a few cities—with Argentines surrounding and in some cases storming grocery stores demanding food—erupted into nationwide rioting. Argentina's economy had been in decline for four years, resulting in an unemployment rate of 20% and a 14% drop in per capita income. The threat of a total economic collapse quickly caused widespread anxiety and chaos. In response, the government declared a "state of siege," a thirty-day period during which most of Argentina's constitutional guarantees were suspended. After President Fernando de la Rúa announced the state of siege, poor Argentines marched through the streets to the presidential palace, banging pots and pans in protest.

Within days de la Rúa was forced out of office. Poor, middle- and working-class Argentines who were unemployed resorted to looting and picking through garbage heaps for food. By January 2, 2002, the country was on its fifth president in two weeks, three more having resigned after de la Rúa. The new government immediately devalued the peso by 30% and froze all bank accounts over $3,000 for a full year. With banks still closed, Argentines were not only unable to access their accounts but were also prevented from cashing checks or using debit services and credit cards. They were effectively rendered penniless indefinitely. By the time the crisis began to ease in April 2002, at least twenty-seven people had been killed in food riots and millions of Argentines had been reduced, at least temporarily, to poverty.

According to the World Bank report *Argentina—Crisis and Poverty 2003: A Poverty Assessment* (Report No. 26127AR, July 24, 2003), poverty rose from 37% in 2001 to 58% at the end of 2002 because of the economic events of that year. Extreme poverty rose from 6% to 28%—a remarkable increase in a country with such a large and highly educated middle class. In fact, of the 825,000 jobs lost between May 2001 and May 2002, 90% were in the private sector, and two-thirds were salaried employees, meaning that most job losses affected the nonpoor. By contrast, the informal sector—which typically employs more poor people—actually grew by 170,000 jobs between 1998 to 2002, which implies that more people were forced into less secure, lower-wage jobs. Besides rising prices and unemployment rates, Argentines experienced an overall decrease in income between the late 1990s and the early 2000s, mostly during the crisis period. For the bottom 10% of Argentines, income fell 49%; for the top 10%, income declined 37%. Because of the large size of already-poor families in Argentina before the economic crisis, the poverty rate for children up to age fourteen rose from 45% in 1998 to 70% in 2002.

BOLIVIA'S POLITICAL UPHEAVAL. Bolivia, in central South America, is a country that has experienced nearly 200 political coups since it won independence from Spain in 1825. Although the country is rich in natural resources—including silver, tin, rubber, and natural gas—a history of human rights abuses (especially against indigenous Indians), involvement in the drug trade with its coca crops (used to produce cocaine), and a series of military dictatorships that mismanaged the economy left Bolivia the poorest country in the Latin American region, with two-thirds of its estimated nine million citizens living in poverty in 2005. According to the U.S. State Department in *Background Note: Bolivia* (April 14, 2005, http://www.state.gov/r/pa/ei/bgn/35751.htm), hyperinflation (inflation that increases quickly at extreme rates) in Bolivia had reached an annual rate of 24,000% by 1985.

The economy was temporarily stabilized during the mid-1980s under the presidency of Paz Estenssoro. Estenssoro implemented an intensive restructuring program that turned the economy around between 1985 and 1989, but not without serious social unrest because the "shock therapy" left tens of thousands of government workers unemployed. Two more presidents were democratically elected. In 1993 Gonzalo Sánchez de Lozada became president and began a program of "capitalization"—privatizing government services such as communications, utilities, and railroads, which proved very unpopular with the public. Violent protests were common under the Lozada administration. The next president, Hugo Banzer, continued with privatization, but less successfully. Economic growth and job creation slowed. Banzer also began a campaign to destroy Bolivia's illegal coca crops, on which most rural indigenous farmers depended for their livelihoods. In 2002 Sánchez de Lozada returned to office, but his administration was unpopular. In February 2003 a protest turned violent and thirty people were killed. More deadly violence erupted in September during protests against privatization of the natural gas industry. Sánchez de Lozada resigned in October, partly because of pressure from an Indian union leader named Evo Morales, who had led the movement to nationalize the gas industry and return most of the profits to the Bolivian people.

Two more presidents entered and exited office before the election of December 2005, when Morales became Bolivia's first indigenous Indian president, elected with 54% of the vote—an unusually high percentage in a country that rarely sees a majority vote. A former coca leaf farmer, Morales ran on a platform of antiprivatization as well as social and government reform. Morales's pro-socialist leanings are perceived as a threat by many, including the United States, which has aggressively campaigned against Bolivia's coca growing by physically eradicating crops and objects to Morales's close ties with the socialist regimes of Cuba and Venezuela.

The unsettled political situation has been detrimental to human development in the country. As of 2003 the UNDP Human Poverty Index ranked Bolivia 113th out of 177 countries. Annual gross domestic product per capita was $892 in 2003, an amount with purchasing power equal to $2,587 in the United States. The World Health Organization (2006, http://www.who.int/countries/bol/en/) reports that life expectancy in 2004 was sixty-five years, and healthy life expectancy (the years a newborn could expect to live in full health) was 54.4 years in 2002. UNICEF estimated that 18,000 deaths occurred among children under five years old in 2004, which equaled a rate of sixty-nine per 1,000 (http://www.unicef.org/infobycountry/bolivia.html). According to the non-profit organization Food for the Hungry, Bolivia, chronic malnutrition is a contributing factor in 28% of child deaths; overall, 40% of children aged three to thirty-five months suffered from chronic malnutrition in 2004. UNICEF also noted that approximately 2,500 unaccompanied children were living on the streets of Bolivian cities in 2004.

Poverty in Bolivia is more prevalent among indigenous people than among the population overall. According to the World Bank's *Indigenous Peoples, Poverty, and Human Development in Latin America, 1994–2004* (March 2006), in 2002 (the most recent data available) the poverty rate for indigenous people in Bolivia was 74%; for nonindigenous people it was 53%. The rates of extreme poverty were 52% for indigenous people and 27% for nonindigenous. For the indigenous rural population the extreme poverty rate was 72%; for nonindigenous rural dwellers it was 52%. Indigenous Indians in Bolivia averaged between 5.9 years of formal schooling (3.5 for those living in rural areas); nonindigenous Bolivians averaged 9.6.

THE CENTRAL ASIAN REPUBLICS

The Central Asian republics—Kazakhstan, Kyrgyzstan, Tajikistan, Turkmenistan, and Uzbekistan—were all republics of the Soviet Union until they achieved independence in 1991. (See Figure 5.4.) Officially, they are now a part of the

FIGURE 5.4

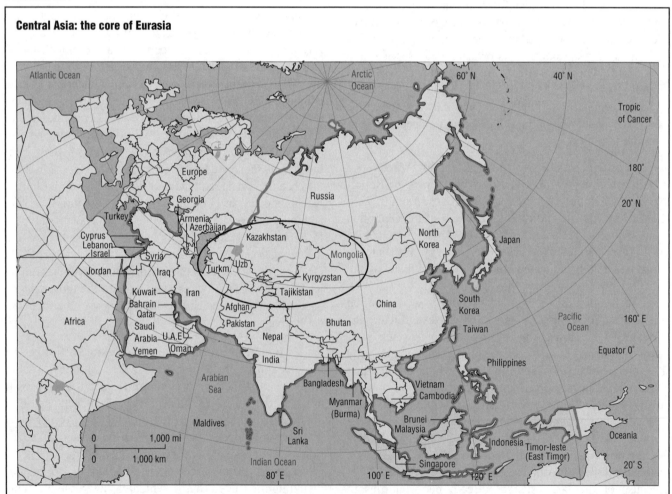

Central Asia: the core of Eurasia

SOURCE: Johannes Linn, "Figure 1.1. Central Asia: The Core of Eurasia," in *Central Asia Human Development Report—Bringing Down Barriers: Regional Cooperation for Human Development and Human Security*, United Nations Development Programme, 2005, http://europeandcis.undp.org/?wspc=CAHDR 2005%20 (accessed April 10, 2006). Copyright 2003 National Geographic Society.

FIGURE 5.5

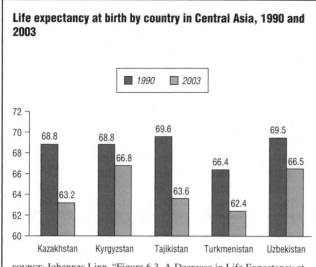

Life expectancy at birth by country in Central Asia, 1990 and 2003

SOURCE: Johannes Linn, "Figure 6.3. A Decrease in Life Expectancy at Birth (Total Years between 1990 and 2003)," in *Central Asia Human Development Report—Bringing Down Barriers: Regional Cooperation for Human Development and Human Security*, United Nations Development Programme, 2005, http://europeandcis.undp.org/?wspc= CAHDR2005%20 (accessed April 10, 2006)

Commonwealth of Independent States, which is dominated by Russia and includes all the former Soviet states of the Eurasia region. However, the Central Asian republics, while having a twentieth-century history rooted in the Soviet bloc and still politically tied to Russia, are fundamentally different ethnically, religiously, and economically. In one sense, the Central Asian republics are transition economies: they all had planned economies during the Soviet era and have since the 1990s gradually opened to the international market. However, their general adherence to authoritarianism and their high rates of extreme poverty make them far less developed than other former Soviet countries. The Central Asian republics have abundant natural resources and growing economies, but their human development indicators are in general seriously lacking because overall poverty has increased and human security has decreased since independence. As Figure 5.5 shows, these countries have experienced a decline in life expectancy at birth in the years since the dissolution of the Soviet Union. According to some international observers, nearly all the Central Asian republics are in danger of igniting an explosive political situation, putting the human needs even more at risk of not being met.

Kazakhstan

The United Nations Development Program (UNDP) reports in *Human Development Report: Kazakhstan 2004* (2004, http://hdr.undp.org/docs/reports/national/KAZ_Kazakhstan/Kazakhstan_2004_en.pdf) that Kazakhstan saw a dramatic decline in its human development indicators immediately after independence from the Soviet Union in 1991, dropping in rank from fifty-fourth to ninety-third on the UN's Human Development Index

(HDI) of 177 countries. Between 1996 and 2002, though, Kazakhstan rose on the HDI to seventy-eighth place, due largely to its steady economic growth that averaged 10.4% annually from 2000 to 2004, and as of 2005 it ranked eightieth. However, as with other developing regions, a growing economy has not necessarily translated to a decrease in poverty or an increase in the standard of living for ordinary people, especially for those living in rural areas.

The World Bank's *Dimensions of Poverty in Kazakhstan, vol. 2: Profile of Living Standards in Kazakhstan in 2002* (November 9, 2004) reports that the total poverty rate in 2002 was 15% (about one in six people), down from 18% in 2001. Sixty-four percent of the poor lived in rural regions and 15% in large cities. As in Russia, poverty in Kazakhstan tends to be shallow, meaning that the greatest number of the poor are concentrated near the poverty line. The UNDP's *Millennium Development Goals in Kazakhstan, 2005* reports a large gap between urban and rural households in the availability of in-house utilities. While 81% of urban households had piped water in 2004, only 8.3% of rural households did, with just 0.8% of rural houses having a hot water supply, versus 56.1% of urban houses. Although nearly 100% of both rural and urban households had electricity, just 1.9% of rural homes had central heating, contrasted with 68.6% of urban homes. Sanitation was also lacking in rural households: only 4.3% had improved sewage systems, while 73.7% of urban households did. This situation in particular seems to be worsening over time. In 1999, 73.9% of urban and 10.4% of rural houses had access to a sewage system. Given that the public expenditure on health has been decreasing since 1995, this is a partial explanation for these worsening conditions. (See Figure 5.6.)

According to the UN's report *MDG1: Eliminate Extreme Poverty and Hunger* (2005, http://www.undp.kz/library_of_publications/files/1568-75446.pdf), Kazakhstan has already achieved the first MDG of halving extreme poverty by 2015, reducing its total poverty incidence from 39% of the population in 1998 to 16.1% in 2004. In rural regions, however, the poverty rate averaged 24.8%, almost three times the rate of 9.2% in urban regions. This huge gap indicates uneven development and growth throughout the country. The average annual per capita GDP was $7,363 as of 2005.

EDUCATION AND LITERACY. Kazakhstan has already exceeded the MDG of universal primary school education: 84% of children are enrolled in primary school, and the adult literacy rate is 99.5%, according to the UNDP report *The Great Generation of Kazakhstan: Insight into the Future* (2005, http://www.undp.kz/library_of_publications/files/5811-13639.pdf). However, the country has a high inequality ratio because of the great differences between rural and urban areas, especially in secondary education.

FIGURE 5.6

Public expenditure on health, by country in Central Asia, 1995 and 2002

[Percent of gross domestic product]

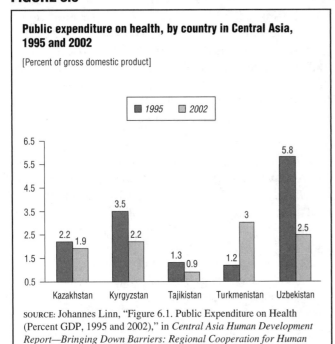

SOURCE: Johannes Linn, "Figure 6.1. Public Expenditure on Health (Percent GDP, 1995 and 2002)," in *Central Asia Human Development Report—Bringing Down Barriers: Regional Cooperation for Human Development and Human Security*, United Nations Development Programme, 2005, http://europeandcis.undp.org/?wspc=CAHDR2005%20 (accessed April 10, 2006)

According to the UNDP report *MGD2: Achieve Universal Primary Education* (2005, http://www.undp.kz/library_of_publications/files/1569-52013.pdf), 47% of school-age children live in rural areas. Hundreds of Kazakhstan's rural communities have no schools, and even in the areas where schools are present children may have to travel long distances to attend them. As a result, rural children find it increasingly difficult to attain the skills they will need to succeed. Furthermore, the smaller of Kazakhstan's one hundred or more ethnic groups have problems in school because Kazakh and Russian are the dominant languages used in schools. The quality of teacher training is also an issue in Kazakhstan, with 18% of urban teachers and 42% of rural teachers rating as unqualified. Overall government spending on education has increased, from 3.1% of GDP in 2001 to 3.8% in 2004. The increase has not been uniform across oblasts, or provinces, however. In some regions, spending has decreased, including in the heavily impoverished Mangystau oblast, where education spending dropped from 2.6% to 2.2% from 2001 to 2004.

HEALTH AND MORTALITY. Life expectancy in Kazakhstan is fairly low: fifty-six years for men and sixty-seven years for women in 2004, according to the World Health Organization (2006, http://www.who.int/countries/kaz/en/). Healthy life expectancy at birth in 2002 was 52.6 years for men and 59.3 years for women. Under-five child mortality in 2002 was eighty-three per 1,000 live births for males and sixty-two for females. Different agencies within the country report different numbers for maternal mortality, and there are to date no official statistics. The Kazakhstan Ministry of Health reports that there were 75.8 deaths per 100,000 live births in 1990, while the Agency for Statistics reports fifty-five. Both groups report a decrease between 1990 and 2004, to 36.9 deaths per 100,000, although the number is still considered unreasonably high, particularly in light of the fact that nearly 100% of births in Kazakhstan are attended by health professionals. This indicates an issue with the quality of obstetric care.

One of the biggest health challenges confronting Kazakhstan since the dissolution of the Soviet Union is drug use. Because of its location on the drug trafficking route between the major drug producers of Southwest Asia to major drug-consuming regions such as Russia and Eastern Europe, Kazakhstan has become a major link on the route. According to the Silk Road Studies Program and the Central Asia–Caucasus Institute's "Country Factsheet, Eurasian Narcotics: Kazakhstan 2004" (2004), Kazakhstan's customs union with Russia, Belarus, and the Ukraine permits the passage of closed containers without inspection across borders, making it especially attractive to smugglers. Kazakhstan, however, does not just provide a passage through which illicit drugs can easily pass. The country is also becoming a bigger producer of heroin and cannabis for use within its own borders. As in all countries with a high rate of intravenous drug use, HIV infection is on the rise in Kazakhstan. The Silk Road Studies fact sheet reports that as many as 3% of the country's citizens are believed to be intravenous drug users, and about 23,000 people are believed to be HIV-positive, with 84% of those infected being intravenous drug users. Suicide is a major cause of death among the HIV-positive population of Kazakhstan.

Kyrgyzstan

Kyrgyzstan is a small, almost entirely mountainous, landlocked country of about five million people. Historically, the people of the region were nomadic, but when it was incorporated into the Soviet Union in 1924, Kyrgyzstan was converted to an agricultural-manufacturing lifestyle and economy. By the time the Central Asian republics were granted independence in 1991, Kyrgyzstan's manufacturing sector relied almost entirely on the Soviet Union's military-industrial complex. With its collapse, Kyrgyzstan's manufacturing sector also fell apart, which left its economy in ruins.

POVERTY AND HEALTH INDICATORS. By 1999 the rural poverty rate was 60%, according to Kyrgyzstan's *National Poverty Reduction Strategy, 2003–2005* (April 2004, http://poverty2.forumone.com/files/Kyrgyz_PRSP.pdf), and the urban rate was 42.4%. In 2001 the numbers had declined to 51% for rural dwellers but had risen to 47.6% for those in urban areas. As in much of the rest of the world, poverty in Kyrgyzstan is heavily concentrated in rural regions. While 65.3% of the total Kyrgyzstani population lives in rural areas, 70% of the poor are rural dwellers. The overall rate of extreme poverty in 2001 was 13.5%. For those in rural regions the extreme poverty rate dropped between 2000 and 2001, from 20.5% to 15.6%, as did the urban regions rate, from 12.7 to 9.6%.

According to the UN Human Development Program's "Country Sheet: Kyrgyzstan" (2006, http://hdr.undp.org/statistics/data/countries.cfm?c=KGZ), Kyrgyzstan's literacy rate and primary school enrollment are high: 98.7% of adults were literate in 2002, and 82% of children were enrolled in primary, secondary, and tertiary schools. According to the World Health Organization (2006, http://www.who.int/countries/kgz/en/), in 2004 life expectancy was fifty-nine years for men and sixty-seven for women. The healthy life expectancy at birth was 52.2 years for men and 58.4 years for women in 2002. In 2004 the under-five child mortality was seventy-two per 1,000 live births for boys and sixty-three per 1,000 for girls. The average per capita GDP in 2005 was $1,751. In 2003 Kyrgyzstan ranked 109 out of 177 countries on the UN's Human Development Index.

Like Kazakhstan, Kyrgyzstan has a growing presence in the international drug trade and, consequently, an increasing number of intravenous drug users and HIV cases. In fact, according to the British nongovernmental organization One World UK (2006, http://uk.oneworld.net/guides/kyrgyzstan/development), unofficial sources estimate that there may be as many as 6,000 cases of HIV, most unreported, in the country. Additionally, Kyrgyzstan has high rates of deaths from circulatory and respiratory diseases, and incidences of tuberculosis, syphilis, and malaria have increased since the 1990s.

Tajikistan

After independence in 1991, Tajikistan fell into a civil war that lasted from 1992 to 1994. The conflict seriously deteriorated conditions throughout the country, which has not entirely recovered as of 2006. The World Bank reports in *Republic of Tajikistan Poverty Assessment Update* (January 6, 2005, http://www.untj.org/files/reports/Tajikistan%20Poverty%20Assessment%20Update.pdf) that Tajikistan is the poorest of the former Soviet republics, indeed, one of the poorest countries in the world, with 64% of its population living on less than $2.15 a day in 2003. This is down substantially from 81% in 1999. The rate of extreme poverty (less than $1.08 a day) in 2003 was 18%, down from 36% in 1999. In 2002 the average gross national income per capita was less than $200, despite economic growth averaging 8% since 2000. Tajikistan does not have a national poverty line, so all calculations are based on the international lines (adjusted to $1.08 and $2.15 per day based on 2000 purchasing power parity).

The UNDP's *Investing in Sustainable Development: Millennium Development Goals Needs Assessment* (May 2005, http://www.undp.tj/home/MDG_NA_Full_Eng.pdf) for Tajikistan reports that steady economic growth and increased income and consumption have not really improved living standards for most Tajiks, even though extreme poverty has decreased by as much as fifty-five percentage points in some provincial regions since 1999.

HUNGER AND FOOD INSECURITY. Food insecurity and malnutrition are key poverty-related problems for Tajiks: the UNDP Millennium Development Goals report states that 83% of the population suffered from nutrition-related poverty in 2003. Families reported cutting down on food consumption and relying on food given as gifts to get by. Unbalanced diets that cause a number of nutritional deficiencies are the norm in Tajikistan, especially an over-dependence on bread as a primary source of nutrition. Children are the demographic group most affected by nutritional deficiencies. Of children aged six-months to fifty-nine months old, 36% are chronically malnourished, and 5% have acute malnutrition. Poor maternal nutrition results in 15% of Tajik babies being born malnourished.

The most common nutritional problems, other than simply a lack of food, in Tajikistan are deficiencies of iodine, folic acid, vitamin A, and iron. Iodine and folic acid deficiencies cause mental retardation and enlarged thyroids; in 2003, 89% of Tajik children had low levels of iodine, and 58% were deficient in folic acid. About 10% to 15% of Tajiks of all ages were believed to have enlarged thyroids. Vitamin A deficiency can cause blindness and increases susceptibility to infectious diseases. In Tajikistan approximately 52% of children aged six-months to fifty-nine months were Vitamin A deficient in 2003. Iron deficiency—the most common nutritional deficiency in the world, affecting 66% to 80% of the world's population—is experienced most often by children and pregnant women. In fact, anemia (very low levels of iron in the blood) is a factor in up to 20% of all maternal deaths. In Tajikistan 37% of preschool children, 40% of women, and 48% of pregnant women were believed to be anemic in 2003.

Overall malnutrition and food insecurity increased in Tajikistan between 2003 and 2004, according to a March 2005 press release from the UNDP's donors agency. Twenty-seven percent of rural Tajik households were either chronically food insecure or at risk of food insecurity. Hunger, food insecurity, and malnutrition were not limited to Tajikistan's poorest households. Even steadily employed householders reported a lack of adequate food. Low income was not, however, the only reason for such widespread food insecurity. The UNDP press release cites a Tajik survey that found a 17% drop in the country's cereal production from 2003 to 2004.

EDUCATION AND LITERACY. All the former Soviet republics have generally high rates of primary school enrollment and literacy because of the former Soviet Union's compulsory education system. In Tajikistan the pre-Soviet literacy rate was 4% for men and 0.1% for women. Even after the Soviets introduced their program of state-run schools into the country, the subject of education was not always welcomed by the native population; Islamic leaders vocally opposed public education, and antieducation violence resulted in school burnings and the murders of teachers. By the 1980s Tajik education was well below that of other Soviet republics, with only 55% of adults having completed secondary schooling. Nevertheless, in "Country Sheet: Tajikistan" (2006, http://hdr.undp.org/statistics/data/countries.cfm?c=TJK) the UNDP reports that the literacy rate in Tajikistan was 99.5% in 2003, and the primary school enrollment was 94% in 2002–03. Even though factors such as poverty and hunger make it increasingly difficult for children to attend school, an estimated 88% of enrolled children attend school.

HEALTH AND MORTALITY. According to the World Health Organization (2006, http://www.who.int/countries/tjk/en/), life expectancy in Tajikistan was sixty-three years in 2004, sixty-two years for males and sixty-four years for females. Healthy life expectancy at birth was 53.1 years for males and 56.4 years for females in 2002. Under-five child mortality was 120 deaths per 1,000 live births for males and 115 per 1,000 live births for females in 2004. Data on infant mortality vary by source. Existing birth and death records are not considered reliable in Tajikistan. However, in January 2005 IRINnews.org reported that infant mortality rates appear to be going up in the northern provinces of the country. The article cites estimates for 2003 from both the United Nations Children's Fund (UNICEF) and the U.S. Agency for International Development (USAID). According to UNICEF, the infant mortality rate was ninety-two deaths per 1,000 live births, but USAID's rate was 112.1 deaths per 1,000. Tajikistan's health ministry chief believed the numbers could actually be three or four times higher.

As in the other Central Asian republics, HIV/AIDS cases are on the rise in Tajikistan because of the country's geographical location on the trafficking route and because of an increase in intravenous drug use and prostitution. In fact, if the number of HIV cases continues to increase at its 2005 rate, experts say the number could double every thirteen months ("Tajikistan: Donors Call on Country to Strengthen Battle against HIV/AIDS," February 23, 2006, http://www.aegis.com/news/IRIN/2006/IR060259.html). Besides its role in the drug trade, Tajikistan has many citizens who temporarily migrate abroad—mostly to Russia—for work. Increasingly, these migrant workers become infected abroad and bring the disease back to Tajikistan, where they spread HIV.

Turkmenistan

Turkmenistan is considered the most closed society in the former Soviet bloc. In July 2004 the last international radio outlet to broadcast in the country—Russia's Mayak radio station—was cut off by Turkmenistan's authoritarian government, leaving the Turkmen people with no access to outside information. According to an article from the Power and Interest News Report (PINR; "The Erosion of Political Institutions in Turkmenistan," December 30, 2004, http://www.pinr.com/report.php?ac=view_report&report_id=250&language_id=1), as of 2006 Turkmenistan and North Korea were the only countries in the world to retain their Stalinist regimes, meaning that they were ruled by dictators who control every aspect of their societies. The PINR lists many problems with the Turkmen government:

> documented human rights violations, forced resettlement of ethnic minorities, rigid press censorship, high unemployment, a drug epidemic among the youth, widespread corruption, a declining educational system . . . , vast symbolic building projects (including an ice palace in the desert), isolation of the country from the rest of the world, collapsing public health (including reported cases of plague), and a political system in which no opposition to the government is tolerated.

Although exact figures are difficult to obtain because Turkmenistan does not have an established poverty line and what calculations the government does keep are not widely available, poverty is believed to be high and human development indicators low despite the potential for national wealth because of the country's huge oil and natural gas reserves. Turkmen president Saparmurat Niyazov has ruled Turkmenistan since independence in 1991, but in 1999 he declared himself "president for life" and adopted the title "Turkmenbashi," which means "father of all Turkmen."

According to Bernd Rechel and Martin McKee's report *Human Rights and Health in Turkmenistan* (April 2005, http://www.lshtm.ac.uk/ecohost/projects/turkmenistan%20files/Turkmen%20report.pdf), Turkmenistan has evolved to become the most oppressive of all the former Soviet republics. The Turkmen government controls all media and communications and refuses to report health data to the World Health Organization or development information to the United Nations. In March 2003 the Turkmen government imposed a ban on the issuance of exit visas to its citizens, preventing them from leaving the country. Threats of trade sanctions from the United States caused the Turkmen regime to abandon the exit visa ban in January 2004, although the government maintains a blacklist of people not allowed to travel.

Because of this atmosphere, the United Nations has been unable to research and publish a human development report on Turkmenistan since the 1990s. As of early 2006 the country was on uneasy terms with the World Bank because it refused to report its international debt, so all statistics related to poverty are speculative and based on data that are in most cases ten years old. Rechel and McKee, however, deduce from the information available in the World Bank's 1998 Living Standards Measurement Survey that urban unemployment in Turkmenistan was approximately 50% in 2003, and rural unemployment about 70%. In 1998 an estimated 44% of Turkmen lived below the international poverty line of $2 per day. Rechel and McKee note that "there is anecdotal evidence that the economic situation has deteriorated considerably since then."

Like all other statistics about the country, information on the health and education status of the Turkmen people is of dubious accuracy; the last time the country reported health data to the World Health Organization was in 1998. In February 2006 EURASIANET.org reported in "Turkmenistan Vulnerable to Public Health Catastrophe" (http://www.eurasianet.org/departments/recaps/articles/eav020606.shtml) that health care in Turkmenistan since independence has been deliberately targeted by President Niyazov, who has officially denied the existence of contagious diseases such as AIDS in the country, leaving citizens with no real options for medical aid. When they are able to see a doctor, extortion is not uncommon because the medical system is essentially a black market: for example, a parent taking her child in for a doctor visit might be forced to undergo testing herself so that the doctor makes more money. In 2004 Niyazov dismissed 15,000 health care professionals and replaced them with untrained military conscripts (people who have been drafted into the military involuntarily) to cut down on government spending. In 2005 he announced that all hospitals outside the capital city of Ashgabat would be closed indefinitely. In 2002 the World Health Organization (2006, http://www.who.int/countries/tkm/en/) estimated that the mortality rate was 51.6 years for men and 57.2 years for women. The child mortality rate for those under five years old had risen from ninety-seven per 1,000 live births in 1990 to 103 per 1,000 in 2004, as reported by UNICEF; an estimated 11,000 Turkmen children under five years old died in 2004 (http://www.unicef.org/infobycountry/Turkmenistan_statistics.html).

In late 2005 the Turkmen government began cutting benefits to about 100,000 of the country's 400,000 people, mostly the elderly, who receive government pensions. Other government benefits have been cut by 20%, according to IRINnews.org ("Turkmenistan: Pension Cuts Begin to Bite," February 6, 2006, http://www.irinnews.org/report.asp?ReportID=51553&SelectRegion=Asia&SelectCountry=TURKMENISTAN). This move was expected to push thousands of older people into almost instant poverty. IRINnews.org notes that unemployment in Turkmenistan is believed to be as high as 80%.

Uzbekistan

Uzbekistan is the most populous of the Central Asian republics, with 25.8 million people—36.7% in urban areas and 63.3% in rural, according to the UNDP's "Country Sheet: Uzbekistan" (2006, http://hdr.undp.org/statistics/data/countries.cfm?c=UZB). Poverty in Uzbekistan is not generally as dire as in some of the other Central Asian republics. The country is the fourth-largest producer of cotton in the world and the seventh-largest producer of gold; in addition, it has large reserves of gas and oil. However, rising unemployment, a government crackdown on civil liberties, and economic policies that many observers consider disastrous have put Uzbekistan on the brink of total disarray.

According to "Country Sheet: Uzbekistan," in 2003 Uzbekistan ranked 111 out of 177 countries on the Human Development Index, ahead of Kyrgyzstan's 109 and Tajikistan's 122, but behind Kazakhstan's 80 and Turkmenistan's 97. As in all the other Central Asian republics, life expectancy decreased in Uzbekistan between 1990 and 2003, from 69.17 to 66.68 years. The UNDP's *Central Asia Human Development Report: Bringing Down Barriers—Regional Cooperation for Human Development and Human Security* (2005, http://hdr.undp.org/docs/reports/regional/CIS_Europe_CIS/Central_Asia_2005_en.pdf) states that in 2003, 47% of Uzbekistan's population lived below the international poverty line of $2.15 per day, compared to a high of 74% in Tajikistan and a low of 21% in Kazakhstan. Yet, Uzbekistan's annual economic growth lagged behind that of all the other Central Asian republics, at around 7.5%.

As in all the Central Asian republics, HIV and AIDS pose a risk not just to the physical health but also to the economy of Uzbekistan. In "A Silent Killer Threatens Central Asia" (December 28, 2004, http://www.eurasianet.org/departments/civilsociety/articles/pp122804.shtml), Antoine Blua states that the projected long-term loss in economic growth in Uzbekistan because of HIV and AIDS infection could total 21% by 2015. However, unlike the rest of Central Asia, the cause of the burgeoning epidemic in Uzbekistan is not so much intravenous drug use as a huge increase in prostitution since independence in 1991. According to Gulnoza Saidazimova in the article "HIV Infections Build in Uzbekistan as Prostitution Rises" (December 29, 2004, http://www.eurasianet.org/departments/civilsociety/articles/pp122904.shtml), Uzbekistan's large population, high unemployment—especially among women—and role as a major transit stop for truck drivers throughout the republics has caused an increasing number of women to turn to prostitution to earn a living. With an average monthly income in the country at just $15, condoms to prevent HIV and antiretroviral drugs to treat it are too expensive for prostitutes to afford.

Of further concern to the international community is the potential for widespread unrest in the region if Uzbekistan should become even more unstable. A government crackdown on civil liberties began after armed protesters stormed a prison in the city of Andijon in May 2005 to free twenty-three men accused of membership in an extreme Islamic group. Government troops were sent to stop the insurgency, but eyewitness accounts say they fired indiscriminately into crowds of people, killing as many as 1,000 Uzbek citizens; since then, the International Crisis Group has called leadership in Uzbekistan one of the most repressive regimes in the world. With political refugees from Uzbekistan fleeing to other Central Asian republics, especially the already-fragile Kyrgyzstan, the entire region could, according to some observers, fall into total disarray. The United States and the European Union both condemned the May 2005 government massacre and have since cut off nearly all ties to Uzbekistan. After the events of May 2005, Uzbek leaders halted the activities of at least 60% of nongovernmental organizations in the country. With aid groups forced to close facilities and leave the country, the Uzbek people have become even more vulnerable to the effects of poverty.

According to the International Crisis Group's Policy Briefing "Uzbekistan: In for the Long Haul" (February 16, 2006, http://www.crisisgroup.org/home/index.cfm?id=3952&l=1), the ruling party's economic policies have been disastrous for the Uzbek people. Although the country is the world's second biggest exporter of cotton (which is used mostly to produce blue jeans for the U.S. and European markets), the rural farmers—mostly women and children—who grow and cultivate it are essentially slave labor, with all the revenues going to the small but powerful upper class. Unrest has continued since the Andijon uprising despite the government's increase in the minimum wage to $9 a month. A growing number of Uzbeks are leaving the country for Russia and Kazakhstan to work as illegal, and therefore unprotected, temporary laborers.

NORTH KOREA

The peninsula on which both North and South Korea are located was under Japanese rule until the end of World War II in 1945. At that point the United States began occupying the southern half and the Soviet Union took over the northern half. The two countries' inability to agree on unification led to the formation of two separate governments in the north and south. War broke out between them in 1950 and ended in 1953, with a permanent demilitarized zone separating the two countries; this area has been called the most dangerous place on earth. From the end of the war until his death in 1994, Kim Il-Sung, who called himself (and demanded that all North Koreans call him) "Great Leader," ruled North Korea. Following his death, leadership went to his son Kim Jong-Il, who is known as "Dear Leader." Between their two periods of leadership, the father and son created a cult of personality and amassed military strength that enriched them and the country's upper class and left North Korea's ordinary citizens in such severe poverty that in the late 1990s as many as three million died of starvation (estimates vary; the North Korean government claims 600,000 died, while some nongovernmental organizations and human rights watchdog groups say one million). Human rights abuses abound in the country as well. In fact, North Korea is known for having one of the worst records in the world for the treatment of its own citizens.

It is also one of the most secretive societies in the world. Even photographs from inside the country are rare. Because everything is so tightly controlled by the authorities, valid statistics are generally nonexistent, although some nongovernmental organizations do manage to obtain data, and the government of South Korea keeps statistics as well. According to the South Korean Ministry of Unification (2006, http://www.unikorea.go.kr/en/index.jsp), the average annual income in North Korea was $818 in 2003. Because poverty numbers and other human development information provided by the government of North Korea are known to be inaccurate, the country is not ranked by the UNDP Human Development Index. In the early 1990s authorities were believed to be inflating the numbers to receive more foreign aid. By the late 1990s they were downplaying the severity of the problem. As of December 2005 the government was denying the presence of starvation in the country and planning to expel all nongovernmental aid organizations (Jehangir Pocha, "Cult of Ideology: North Korea Struggles to Save Face by Resisting Crucial Foreign Aid," December 5, 2005, http://www.inthesetimes.com/site/main/article/2420/).

Death Camps, Famine, and the Pursuit of Nuclear Weapons

For his article "A Gulag with Nukes: Inside North Korea" (July 17, 2005, http://www.opendemocracy.net/globalization-institutions_government/north_korea_2686.jsp), Jasper Becker interviewed refugees from North Korea who had firsthand knowledge of the inner workings of the country, from slave labor camps to the palaces of Kim Jong-Il. Becker refers to these refugees as "escapees from the last slave society left in the world." David Hawk of the U.S. Committee for Human Rights in North Korea concurs. In *The Hidden Gulag: Exposing North Korea's Prison Camps—Prisoners' Testimonies and*

Satellite Photographs (2003, http://hrnk.org/HiddenGulag. pdf), Hawk estimates that 150,000 to 200,000 North Koreans are held in penal colonies throughout the country. The prisoners are people who may or may not have committed crimes but are perceived as criminals by authorities. Relatives of the prisoners are abducted and imprisoned as well. Detainment for alleged criminals is frequently lifelong, and there is no legal recourse. In fact, the accused are never actually arrested or charged with anything. They are simply snatched off the street and taken to interrogation facilities, where they may be tortured into confessing. Family members—usually parents, children, and grandparents—are kept in separate camps for "reeducation"; eventually, they may be released. This notion of "guilt by association" dates back to 1972, when Kim Il-Sung proclaimed that the blood lines of prisoners should be wiped out for three generations.

Prisoners detained in the camps are fed a starvation diet, meaning they are given the least possible amount of food to keep them alive and allow them to perform brutally difficult labor at least twelve hours a day, seven days a week. According to Sung Hun Han's article "Poverty Line in North Korea" (2005, http://www. bepress.com/peps/vol11/iss1/3/), adult prisoners are given the same amount of food that is allotted in the government's grain rationing program to two- to four-year-old children. The below-subsistence diet causes long-term physical deformities, and the dangerous working environment results in high numbers of amputations and disabilities. Additionally, feeding prisoners the absolute bare minimum creates an atmosphere of distrust and suspicion among them, making them fight each other for extra scraps of food and the clothing of those who have died. They are also known to turn each other in to the guards for indiscretions. Punishment is either confinement in a boxlike structure whose size makes both standing and lying down impossible, causing circulation to be cut off and slow death, or prisoners are killed by hanging or by a firing squad in front of other prisoners.

According to the Korea Institute for National Unification's annual White Paper on Human Rights in North Korea, 2004, North Korea operates a rations system, under which all citizens receive food, clothing, medical care, housing, education, and pensions directly from the government. The thinking behind the system is that it will instill gratitude in the people, yet, because of the small amount of goods they receive, they are being kept from becoming lazy and frivolous. The grain distribution system had collapsed by the 1990s, with citizens receiving less than one-third the amount they needed to survive. In late 1996 grain rations were stopped altogether, leaving people to acquire their own food, mostly from the black market. Those who lacked the resources to buy food off the black market faced starvation. In fact, from 1996 to 1999 millions did starve to death in one of the largest famines in modern history. Exact figures are unknown because of the North Korean government's strict control of all information entering and leaving the country, but as many as three million people are believed to have starved to death, mostly children.

In 2004 the government loosened its control of food supplies slightly by allowing some markets to operate privately and expand their selection of goods. Some farms were also privatized. However, in October 2005 authorities reversed these policies and again prevented the sale of grain in markets. The decision to expel all aid organizations from the country by the end of 2005 because they were creating an atmosphere of "dependency" and because the harvest was allegedly expected to improve alarmed international agencies, who warned that another famine could be imminent without emergency food aid. With tensions escalating over North Korea's pursuit of nuclear weapons, the United States announced in May 2005 that it would suspend all food aid to the country, although U.S. officials denied they were using food as a political tool. At issue for the United States and other countries, as well as for aid organizations such as the United Nations World Food Program, is the limited amount of monitoring allowed by North Korea. Questions of whether aid actually reaches the country's neediest people or is intercepted and distributed to military officers has long been a point of contention for those who provide relief. Regardless, the North Korean government will not allow agencies to monitor or report on the progress of their programs within the country.

In Hunger and Human Rights: The Politics of Famine in North Korea (2005), Stephan Haggard and Marcus Noland of the U.S. Committee for Human Rights in North Korea contend that the famine of the mid- to late-1990s was not simply a matter of bad weather patterns devastating crops, as the North Korean government has insisted. Instead, Haggard and Noland believe—along with many other researchers—that the famine was a preventable tragedy that was caused by the failed agricultural and social services system. In essence, the disaster is widely considered to have been a man-made famine. Certainly, North Korea has experienced extreme weather for more than ten years. Aidan Foster-Carter reports in "North Korea's Kim-Made Famine" (May 23, 2001, http://www.atimes.com/koreas/ CE23Dg02.html) that the country has been in a cycle of drought and flood since 1994. However, Foster-Carter explains that a program of ill-advised agricultural techniques, combined with the system of collective farming, have proven disastrous to the country.

North Korea is 80% mountainous. To advance its ideology of complete independence, leaders cut the country off from trade and instead cleared land for farming higher and higher into the mountains. This "terracing" had two consequences: severe deforestation left the valleys vulnerable to landslides, and tenuously arable land was made even less fertile with the overuse of harsh chemical fertilizers. Furthermore, a government-imposed commitment to raise corn and rice, to the exclusion of most other crops, had left much of the population malnourished long before the events of the 1990s brought the situation to its crisis. So when the unusually heavy rains began in 1995, the terraced farms were washed away down the mountains, onto the fields in the valleys, destroying all the crops. This pattern is ongoing.

Haggard and Noland report that during and since the famine the North Korean government has blocked humanitarian relief efforts. When it has allowed aid to filter in, it has diverted its own funding away from feeding its people and instead focused on increasing its militarization program. The roots of the food crisis are, however, in the division of Korea into north and south. Historically, the northern region was devoted to industry and the southern to agriculture. When the peninsula was officially broken up into the two countries after the Korean War, the North developed policies devoted to strict self-reliance, which isolated it from its main source of food in South Korea. The Soviet Union and China stepped in as trading partners to some degree, but the collapse of the former and the economic transformation of the latter further alienated North Korea and left it with even less foreign economic support.

Many observers believe that behind the decade-long food crisis and the general state of poverty in North Korea is the country's pursuit of a nuclear program and the overall attention to increasing military might at all costs. North Korea has sought a nuclear program since the Korean War, when the United States threatened to use nuclear weapons against the North as part of its support of the South (Robert S. Norris and Hans M. Kristensen, "North Korea's Nuclear Program, 2005," May–June 2005, http://www.thebulletin.org/article_nn.php?art_ofn=mj05 norris). The continued U.S. military presence in South Korea, as well as North Korea's allegiance to the Soviet Union throughout the cold war, further spurred the North's nuclear ambitions. It is not known for certain whether or not North Korea has nuclear weapons or enriched uranium, as both North Korean and U.S. leaders claim. However, according to Norris and Kristensen, North Korean leaders may see the sale of weapons and/or components to rogue governments as one way to deal with its people's ongoing impoverishment.

CHAPTER 6
THE POOR IN DEVELOPED COUNTRIES

Although the majority of the world's poor live in underdeveloped and developing countries, a fair number also live in the developed world—some in the wealthiest countries on earth. The economic gap between rich and poor nations has been widening since the 1980s, but the gap between rich and poor within developed countries has also been growing, as it has in transition economies.

CHARACTERISTICS OF POVERTY IN WEALTHY COUNTRIES

Usually in wealthy countries, poverty is not absolute. The poor in these nations do not for the most part experience famine or starvation, and although homelessness does occur, it is a multifaceted phenomenon that can have causes other than poverty. In fact, many poor people in the developed world work full time and earn more money per week than those in the developing world earn per year. However, relative poverty is poverty nonetheless, and in wealthy countries it can have harsh consequences.

Some researchers and aid workers have suggested that the poor in wealthy countries suffer more psychological problems and social isolation than those in low-income countries. In 1999 Mari Marcel-Thekaekara, a renowned international aid worker and founder of ACCORD, a nongovernmental organization that works with tribal people in Tamil Nadu, India, reported in London's *Guardian* ("Poor Relations," February 27, 1999) that in some respects the kind of poverty she witnessed in the Easterhouse slum in Glasgow, Scotland, was worse than anything she had seen working in India for ten years. "[W]e were hit by the reality of the poverty surrounding us in Glasgow. Most of the men in Easterhouse hadn't had a job in twenty years. They were dispirited, depressed, often alcoholic. Their self-esteem had gone. Emotionally and mentally they were far worse off than the poor where we worked in India, even though the physical trappings of poverty were less stark."

In October 2005 another article in the *Guardian* declared that alcoholism and poverty were the primary factors in Russia's rapid population decline ("Population Dip in Russia Blamed on Alcoholism and Poverty," October 24, 2005). According to the article, the life expectancy for Russian women is seventy-two years, but for men it is just fifty-eight years. The psychological aspects of poverty exist worldwide. In the United States poor people suffer disproportionately from mental health problems, according to the American Psychological Association, and are much less likely than their nonpoor counterparts to receive medical help. A study by the University of Alberta in Canada found that children who begin life in poverty experience higher levels of antisocial behavior ("Long-Term Poverty Affects Mental Health of Children," *Science Daily*, February 9, 2006). The United Nations Children's Fund (UNICEF) reported in March 2005 that forty to fifty million children in the world's wealthiest countries will grow up in poverty ("Child Poverty on the Rise in Wealthy Nations," March 1, 2005). Even Japan, known for its relatively low poverty rates, has experienced an alarming increase; the country was stunned when in January 2005 a woman and her three-year-old son were found dead in their Tokyo-area apartment, having starved to death (J. Sean Curtin, "Japan, Land of Rising Poverty," *Asia Times Online*, February 11, 2005).

These examples illustrate the severity of the problem. In nearly all industrialized countries—with the notable exception of those in Scandinavia—poverty is rising, particularly among children, and the depth of poverty is increasing. Reasons include stagnating wages, long-term unemployment, and rising prices of essentials such as food and fuel. More complex reasons include racism, immigration, and increasing numbers of divorces that lead to single parenthood. A decrease or total absence of social safety nets such as day care, elder care, and health care complicates the matter even further.

THE UNITED STATES

At 12.7% in 2004 (up from 12.5% in 2003), the United States has the highest poverty rate in the developed world (U.S. Census Bureau, *Income, Poverty, and Health Insurance Coverage in the United States: 2004*, August 2005). (See Table 6.1.) Poverty in the United States is strongly connected to race and ethnicity. African Americans, Hispanic Americans, and American Indians and Alaska natives were three times more likely to live in poverty than white Americans. (See Table 6.2.)

At the same time, the gap between the rich and the poor continues to grow. Income statistics from the Center on Budget and Policy Priorities show that the poor are separated from the upper class by an especially wide margin in certain U.S. states, including Arizona, New York, Tennessee, and Texas. (See Table 6.3.) The United States is home to the greatest number of billionaires: 374 of the world's 691 billionaires were from the United States, according to *Forbes* magazine's 2005 list of the richest people in the world. Scott Klinger addressed this disparity on the AlterNet Web site in "The Cavernous Divide" (http://www.alternet.org/story/21544 March 21, 2005). Klinger argues that low corporate taxes, government investment of public money into technology that benefits the upper classes, and a stagnant minimum wage help to explain the chasm between rich and poor in the United States, with Wal-Mart serving as a prime example:

> Some billionaires' fortunes rest upon paying their employees poverty wages. Such is the case for the Walton family (numbers 10 through 14 on the *Forbes* list.) Wal-Mart is the largest private employer in the world. Many of its U.S. workers are so poorly paid that they must rely on food stamps and other forms of public assistance to get by. Such forms of government aid represent an indirect government subsidy to corporations whose business model does not include paying employees enough to live on.

In his article "37 Million Hidden in the Land of Plenty" (London *Guardian*, February 19, 2006), Paul Harris observes that the majority of America's poor do work regularly, but low wages and a lack of benefits keep them in relative poverty: "Even families with two working parents are often one slice of bad luck—a medical bill or factory closure—away from disaster. The minimum wage of $5.15 an hour has not risen since 1997 and, adjusted for inflation, is at its lowest since 1956." Harris also points to the social problems associated with being poor in the United States: "In America, to be poor is a stigma. In a country which celebrates individuality and the goal of giving everyone an equal opportunity to make it big, those in poverty are often blamed for their own situation."

Amy K. Glasmeier, a professor of economic geography at Pennsylvania State University and author of *An*

Atlas of Poverty in America: One Nation, Pulling Apart, 1960–2003 (Routledge, 2005), calls poverty America's "dirty little secret":

> The lack of concern about people who fail to make sufficient income to live above the poverty line (which is $19,157 for a family of four) "occurs" because in many ways poverty in America is all but invisible. . . . Poor people do not want to stand out from the general population. Instead, they make every effort to be like the rest of us by working full time and attempting to provide for themselves and their families.

According to Glasmeier, part of the problem is the way poverty is measured in the United States, and many other researchers and economists agree. In "Calculating Poverty in U.S. Fuels Debate" (Associated Press, February 21, 2006), Stephen Ohlemacher explains that because the poverty threshold measurement was created in the 1960s and has only been updated to reflect inflation, "a single parent making $13,000 a year is living above the poverty line, while someone with a $1 million house who takes a year off work to travel the world could be below it." The measurement does not take into consideration such non-cash income factors as food stamps and health and housing benefits, and the calculation is based on income before taxes, not after. Non-income assets such as houses also are not counted, nor are regional cost-of-living differences.

Glasmeier adds that the cost-of-living estimates upon which the poverty threshold depends are inaccurate to begin with. She argues that a family of four can acquire basic necessities on the $19,000 per year poverty cut-off in only a few of the country's 3,100 counties. As an example Glasmeier cites Tunica, Mississippi, considered the poorest city in the United States, claiming that a family of four would need a minimum of $27,000 per year to afford the basics there.

Reporter Anna Bernasek, writing in the *New York Times* ("A Poverty Line That's Out of Date and Out of Favor," March 12, 2006), contends that the main reason the U.S. poverty threshold measurement has not been updated since its inception is that presidents, not economists or statisticians, are responsible for providing the definition of poverty. Changes to the calculation of the poverty threshold being proposed by the National Academy of Sciences would likely add about five million Americans to the ranks of the poor. Bernasek suggests that this new calculation is unpopular in Washington because a rise in the official number of poor Americans may be perceived as a policy failure by the public.

What Poverty Looks Like in the United States

What does it mean to be poor in the United States? In December 2005 the conservative *Economist* magazine published "The Mountain Man and the Surgeon: Reflections on Relative Poverty in North America and

TABLE 6.1

People and families in poverty by selected characteristics, United States, 2003 and 2004

[Numbers in thousands. People as of March of the following year.]

Characteristic	2003 below poverty		2004 below poverty		Change in poverty (2004 less 2003)[a]	
	Number	Percentage	Number	Percentage	Number	Percentage
People						
Total	35,861	12.5	36,997	12.7	1,136	0.3
Family status						
In families	25,684	10.8	26,564	11.0	879	0.3
Householder	7,607	10.0	7,854	10.2	247	0.2
Related children under 18	12,340	17.2	12,460	17.3	120	0.1
Related children under 6	4,654	19.8	4,737	19.9	84	0.1
In unrelated subfamilies	464	38.6	570	45.4	106	6.8
Reference person	191	37.6	235	45.4	44	7.9
Children under 18	271	41.7	314	46.5	43	4.8
Unrelated individual	9,713	20.4	9,864	20.5	151	0.1
Male	4,154	18.0	4,284	18.3	130	0.3
Female	5,559	22.6	5,580	22.5	21	−0.1
Race[b] and Hispanic origin						
White	24,272	10.5	25,301	10.8	1,029	0.4
White, not Hispanic	15,902	8.2	16,870	8.6	968	0.5
Black	8,781	24.4	9,000	24.7	219	0.3
Asian	1,401	11.8	1,209	9.8	−192	−2.0
Hispanic origin (any race)	9,051	22.5	9,132	21.9	81	−0.6
Age						
Under 18 years	12,866	17.6	13,027	17.8	161	0.2
18 to 64 years	19,443	10.8	20,514	11.3	1,071	0.5
65 years and older	3,552	10.2	3,457	9.8	−95	−0.4
Nativity						
Native	29,965	11.8	30,991	12.1	1,027	0.3
Foreign born	5,897	17.2	6,006	17.1	109	−0.1
Naturalized citizen	1,309	10.0	1,328	9.8	19	−0.1
Not a citizen	4,588	21.7	4,678	21.6	91	−0.1
Region						
Northeast	6,052	11.3	6,233	11.6	181	0.3
Midwest	6,932	10.7	7,538	11.6	606	0.9
South	14,548	14.1	14,798	14.1	249	—
West	8,329	12.6	8,429	12.6	100	—
Work experience						
All workers (16 years and older)	8,820	5.8	9,383	6.1	563	0.3
Worked full-time, year-round	2,636	2.6	2,896	2.8	259	0.2
Not full-time, year-round	6,183	12.2	6,487	12.8	304	0.7
Did not work at least one week	15,446	21.5	15,845	21.7	400	0.2
Families						
Total	7,607	10.0	7,854	10.2	247	0.2
Type of family						
Married couple	3,115	5.4	3,222	5.5	107	0.1
Female householder, no husband present	3,856	28.0	3,973	28.4	117	0.4
Male householder, no wife present	636	13.5	658	13.5	22	—

— Represents zero or rounds to zero.

[a]Details may not sum to totals because of rounding.

[b]Federal surveys now give respondents the option of reporting more than one race. Therefore, two basic ways of defining a race group are possible. A group such as Asian may be defined as those who reported Asian and no other race (the race-alone or single-race concept) or as those who reported Asian regardless of whether they also reported another race (the race-alone-or-in-combination concept). This table shows data using the first approach (race alone). The use of the single-race population does not imply that it is the preferred method of presenting or analyzing data. The Census Bureau uses a variety of approaches. About 2.6 percent of people reported more than one race in Census 2000.

SOURCE: "Table 3. People and Families in Poverty by Selected Characteristics: 2003 and 2004," in *Current Population Reports*, U.S. Census Bureau, Bureau of Labor Statistics, 2005, http://www.census.gov/hhes/www/poverty/poverty04/table3.pdf (accessed April 10, 2006)

Africa," which compared the lives of an unemployed truck driver in the coal mining industry of eastern Kentucky's Appalachian region (which has a poverty rate of 24.5%) with a doctor in the Democratic Republic of Congo in Africa. The article noted that, with incomes of $521 and $250–$600 per month respectively, the two men are roughly in the same income bracket, yet the American truck driver is considered desperately poor while the Congolese doctor is viewed as quite well-off relative to the rest of his country. In the United States the

TABLE 6.2

Poverty rates and numbers, by race and Hispanic origin, United States, 2002–04

[Numbers in thousands. People as of March of the following year.]

Race[a] and Hispanic origin	3–year average 2002–2004 Estimate	2–year average 2002–2003 Estimate	2–year average 2003–2004 Estimate	Change in poverty (2003–2004 average less 2002–2003 average)[b] Estimate
Percentage				
All races	12.4	12.3	12.6	0.3*
White	10.5	10.3	10.6	0.3*
White, not Hispanic	8.3	8.1	8.4	0.3*
Black	24.4	24.3	24.6	0.3
American Indian and Alaska Native	24.3	23.9	24.4	0.5
Asian	10.6	10.9	10.8	−0.1
Native Hawaiian and Other Pacific Islander	13.2	14.4	12.9	−1.5
Hispanic origin (any race)	22.1	22.1	22.2	—
Number				
All races	35,809	35,216	36,429	1,214*
White	24,346	23,869	24,786	917*
White, not Hispanic	16,113	15,735	16,386	651*
Black	8,794	8,691	8,891	199
American Indian and Alaska Native	554	540	557	17
Asian	1,257	1,281	1,305	24
Native Hawaiian and Other Pacific Islander	92	106	84	−22
Hispanic origin (any race)	8,913	8,803	9,092	289*

— Represents zero or rounds to zero.

[a]Federal surveys now give respondents the option of reporting more than one race. Therefore, two basic ways of defining a race group are possible. A group such as Asian may be defined as those who reported Asian and no other race (the race-alone or single-race concept) or as those who reported Asian regardless of whether they also reported another race (the race-alone-or-in-combination concept). This table shows data using the first approach (race alone). The use of the single-race population does not imply that it is the preferred method of presenting or analyzing data. The Census Bureau uses a variety of approaches. About 2.6 percent of people reported more than one race in Census 2000.

[b]Details may not sum to totals because of rounding.

SOURCE: "Table 4. Number of Poverty and Poverty Rates by Race and Hispanic Origin Using 2- and 3-Year Averages: 2002 to 2004," in *Current Population Reports*, U.S. Census Bureau, Bureau of Labor Statistics, 2005, http://www.census.gov/hhes/www/poverty/poverty04/table4.pdf (accessed April 10, 2006)

median annual income in 2004 was $44,389, whereas in Congo the annual average income is $673, and even basic utilities like running water and electricity are rare. By contrast, more often than not, impoverished American families have at least one television in their home, their children usually attend school, they typically do not have to grow their own food to survive, and in general they may look like everyone else.

While U.S. poverty is certainly different in nature relative to poverty in the developing world, there are some similarities. For instance, some people in the United States experience persistent poverty, living without basic utilities, safe drinking water, and sanitation even in the twenty-first century. Although the majority of Americans—even many of those living below the poverty threshold—manage to afford items such as televisions, a rising number of households have trouble affording food at least once during a given year. This kind of food insecurity is a major indicator of the state of poverty in the United States. Another more visibly extreme indicator of American poverty is homelessness. As the twenty-first century progresses, both of these situations—food insecurity and homelessness—are occurring with more and more frequency throughout the United States.

FOOD INSECURITY. In developing countries hunger is often extreme enough to cause fatal malnutrition.

Although hunger in the United States is not as visible, it does result in chronic under-nutrition, which can lead to numerous physical and psychological problems as well as learning disabilities in children. According to the non-profit organization Food Research and Action Center (FRAC), 11.9% of households (13.5 million—38.2 million people) in the United States were food insecure in 2004; 4.4 million of those were suffering from hunger. The U.S. Department of Agriculture's Economic Research Service (USDA-ERS) report *Household Food Security in the United States, 2004* (Mark Nord, Margaret Andrews, and Steven Carlson, October 2005) found that 20% of households experiencing food insecurity sought emergency aid from a food pantry at some point during 2004. For about 30% of those experiencing food insecurity with hunger, the condition was chronic, meaning that it occurred in almost every month of the year.

The USDA-ERS reports that, in food-insecure households in the United States in 2004, children appear to have been protected from hunger in most cases, with adults cutting back on their own food intake in order to continue feeding their children. Nonetheless, approximately 274,000 U.S. households reported that they had at least one child who had to go hungry at least one day during the year. Although the overall rate of food insecurity and food insecurity with hunger increased between 2003 and 2004—from 11.2% to 11.9% and from 3.5% to

TABLE 6.3

Top ten U.S. states for selected income inequality measures, early 1980s to early 2000s

Greatest income inequality between the top and the bottom, early 2000s	Greatest income inequality between the top and the middle, early 2000s
1. New York	1. Texas
2. Texas	2. Kentucky
3. Tennessee	3. Florida
4. Arizona	4. Arizona
5. Florida	5. Tennessee
6. California	6. New York
7. Louisiana	7. Pennsylvania
8. Kentucky	8. North Carolina
9. New Jersey	9. New Mexico
10. North Carolina	10. California

Greatest increases in income inequality between the top and the bottom, early 1980s to early 2000s	Greatest increases in income inequality between the top and the middle, early 1980s to early 2000s
1. Arizona	1. Kentucky
2. New York	2. Pennsylvania
3. Massachusetts	3. West Virginia
4. Tennessee	4. Indiana
5. New Jersey	5. Hawaii
6. West Virginia	6. Texas
7. Connecticut	7. Tennessee
8. Hawaii	8. North Carolina
9. Kentucky	9. Arizona
10. South Carolina	10. New York

Greatest increases in income inequality between the top and the bottom, early 1990s to early 2000s	Greatest increases in income inequality between the top and the middle, early 1990s to early 2000s
1. Tennessee	1. Kentucky
2. Connecticut	2. Pennsylvania
3. Washington	3. North Carolina
4. North Carolina	4. Indiana
5. Utah	5. Tennessee
6. Texas	6. Texas
7. West Virginia	7. West Virginia
8. Pennsylvania	8. Vermont
9. Florida	9. New Jersey
10. Maine	10. Connecticut

SOURCE: Jared Bernstein, Elizabeth McNichol, and Karen Lyons, "Table A. Top Ten States for Selected Income Inequality Measures," in *Pulling Apart: A State-by-State Analysis of Income Trends*, Center on Budget and Policy Priorities, Economic Policy Institute, January 2006, http://www.cbpp.org/1-26-06sfp.pdf (accessed April 10, 2006)

3.9%, respectively—the rates for children have remained in the 0.5% to 0.7% range since 1999. Still, households with children had almost twice the rate of food insecurity as households without children: 17.6% versus 8.9%. (See Table 6.4 and Table 6.5 for information on the prevalence of food security, food insecurity, and food insecurity with hunger in 2004; see Figure 6.1 for comparisons of food insecurity during 2003 and 2004.)

Overall, according to the USDA-ERS report, households made up of people older than sixty-five with no children present experienced the lowest rates of food insecurity (6.5%), and households in which all adults were younger than sixty-five and no children were present had the second lowest rate (6.7%). Several household characteristics serve as indicators of high-risk populations—populations with food insecurity and/or hunger rates well above the national average. The report

indicates that families with incomes below the poverty threshold were particularly vulnerable, with 36.8% of them experiencing food insecurity and/or hunger at some point during the year. Single-parent households, especially those headed by women, also saw very high rates of food insecurity: 33% for households headed by a single female and 22.2% for households headed by a single male. African-American and Hispanic households also had rates of about twice the national average, at 23.7% and 21.7%, respectively. (See Figure 6.1.)

HOMELESSNESS. There are many factors that can lead to a person becoming homeless in the United States: unemployment or underemployment, mental illness, drug or alcohol addiction, a lack of family support, poor education, and failed social services are among the most frequent. However, the root cause is poverty. An overwhelming majority of homeless people, for whatever reason, cannot afford adequate permanent housing.

A joint study by the National Coalition on the Homeless and the National Law Center on Homelessness and Poverty (*A Dream Denied: The Criminalization of Homelessness in U.S. Cities*, January 2006) cites a survey from the U.S. Conference of Mayors that reported a 6% increase in requests for emergency shelter in 71% of cities from 2004 to 2005; 14% of these emergency requests could not be met because of a shortage of shelters, and 32% of requests from families were left unmet. Overall, approximately 3.5 million Americans are homeless at some point every year. Nevertheless, the study reports that the enactment of laws "criminalizing" homelessness is also on the rise, including statutes that establish curfews or that outlaw panhandling, public sleeping, loitering, or outdoor feeding (which limits the ability of churches and charities to provide meals).

The National Alliance to End Homelessness's (NAEH) report *Family Homelessness in Our Nation and Community: A Problem with a Solution* (2005) notes that on any given night, approximately 100,000 American families are homeless, and 600,000 families experience homelessness for at least one night every year. About 50% of homeless people live in families; 70% of them live in urban areas, 19% in suburbs, and 11% in rural areas. Characteristics of homeless families include extreme poverty (an average income of about $5,000 annually); low education levels; single parenthood; unemployment; children under the age of five; and a lack of social support from family and friends. Homeless families also tend to be headed by young parents, and nationwide 43% are estimated to be African American.

The NAEH identifies a lack of affordable housing as the primary reason families become homeless, adding that since the 1970s a low-income housing surplus has turned into a severe deficit: "In 1971 there were 300,000 *more* affordable units than there were low-income

TABLE 6.4

Prevalence of food security, food insecurity, and food insecurity with hunger, by selected household characteristics, United States, 2004

Category	Total[a]	Food secure		Food insecure					
				All		Without hunger		With hunger	
	1,000	1,000	Percent	1,000	Percent	1,000	Percent	1,000	Percent
All households	112,967	99,473	88.1	13,494	11.9	9,045	8.0	4,449	3.9
Household composition:									
With children <18	39,990	32,967	82.4	7,023	17.6	5,311	13.3	1,712	4.3
With children <6	17,922	14,606	81.5	3,316	18.5	2,573	14.4	743	4.1
Married-couple families	27,065	23,926	88.4	3,139	11.6	2,509	9.3	630	2.3
Female head, no spouse	9,641	6,459	67.0	3,182	33.0	2,291	23.8	891	9.2
Male head, no spouse	2,693	2,096	77.8	597	22.2	428	15.9	169	6.3
Other household with child[b]	592	487	82.3	105	17.7	83	14.0	22	3.7
With no children <18	72,977	66,506	91.1	6,471	8.9	3,734	5.1	2,737	3.8
More than one adult	43,177	40,278	93.3	2,899	6.7	1,834	4.2	1,065	2.5
Women living alone	17,012	15,010	88.2	2,002	11.8	1,084	6.4	918	5.4
Men living alone	12,788	11,219	87.7	1,569	12.3	816	6.4	753	5.9
With elderly	26,202	24,510	93.5	1,692	6.5	1,227	4.7	465	1.8
Elderly living alone	10,693	9,911	92.7	782	7.3	517	4.8	265	2.5
Race/ethnicity of households:									
White non-Hispanic	81,388	74,383	91.4	7,005	8.6	4,632	5.7	2,373	2.9
Black non-Hispanic	13,509	10,303	76.3	3,206	23.7	2,108	15.6	1,098	8.1
Hispanic[c]	12,014	9,404	78.3	2,610	21.7	1,903	15.8	707	5.9
Other	6,056	5,382	88.9	674	11.1	403	6.7	271	4.5
Household income-to-poverty ratio:									
Under 1.00	13,347	8,438	63.2	4,909	36.8	3,098	23.2	1,811	13.6
Under 1.30	18,367	12,118	66.0	6,249	34.0	3,994	21.7	2,255	12.3
Under 1.85	28,081	19,700	70.2	8,381	29.8	5,443	19.4	2,938	10.5
1.85 and over	63,575	60,138	94.6	3,437	5.4	2,443	3.8	994	1.6
Income unknown	21,311	19,636	92.1	1,675	7.9	1,158	5.4	517	2.4
Area of residence[d]:									
Inside metropolitan area	92,474	81,661	88.3	10,813	11.7	7,246	7.8	3,567	3.9
In principal cities[e]	30,312	25,650	84.6	4,662	15.4	3,114	10.3	1,548	5.1
Not in principal cities	46,444	42,279	91.0	4,165	9.0	2,865	6.2	1,300	2.8
Outside metropolitan area	20,492	17,811	86.9	2,681	13.1	1,799	8.8	882	4.3
Census geographic region:									
Northeast	21,038	19,006	90.3	2,032	9.7	1,430	6.8	602	2.9
Midwest	25,957	23,126	89.1	2,831	10.9	1,889	7.3	942	3.6
South	41,157	35,693	86.7	5,464	13.3	3,605	8.8	1,859	4.5
West	24,815	21,648	87.2	3,167	12.8	2,121	8.5	1,046	4.2

[a]Totals exclude households whose food security status is unknown because they did not give a valid response to any of the questions in the food security scale. In 2004, these represented 404,000 households (0.4 percent of all households).
[b]Households with children in complex living arrangements—e.g., children of other relatives or unrelated roommate or boarder.
[c]Hispanics may be of any race.
[d]Metropolitan area residence is based on 2003 Office of Management and Budget delineation. Prevalence rates by area of residence are not precisely comparable with those of previous years.
[e]Households within incorporated areas of the largest cities in each metropolitan area. Residence inside or outside of principal cities is not identified for about 17 percent of households in metropolitan statistical areas.

SOURCE: Mark Nord, Margaret Andrews, and Steven Carlson, "Table 2. Prevalence of Food Security, Food Insecurity, and Food Insecurity with Hunger by Selected Household Characteristics, 2004," in *Household Food Security in the United States, 2004*, Economic Research Report No. 11, U.S. Department of Agriculture, Economic Research Service, October 2005, http://www.ers.usda.gov/publications/err11/err11.pdf (accessed April 10, 2006)

families who needed them; in 2001 there were 4.7 million *fewer* units than families. Today, for every 100 low-income or poor households that need housing, only 75 units are affordable." Higher-cost housing forces families to choose between paying rent and buying other necessities such as food, which in turn leads to food insecurity.

Another possible consequence of family homelessness is that children may be placed into the state-run foster care system. According to the NAEH report, 30% of children in foster care have parents who are homeless or in an unstable housing situation; in addition, people who have spent time in the foster care system as children are more likely to become homeless as adults, meaning homelessness becomes a continuing cycle over generations.

The National Law Center on Homelessness and Poverty's publication *Educating Homeless Children and Youth: The 2005 Guide to Their Rights* notes that at least 1.35 million school-age American children (representing 10% of all poor children in the United States) are homeless every year. Homelessness presents an especially difficult problem for children, who often have a hard time attending school regularly and performing successfully if they do attend. The U.S. Department of Education reported in 2000 that only 77% of homeless children who are enrolled in school attend regularly, although 87% are enrolled.

TABLE 6.5

Prevalence of food security, food insecurity, and food insecurity with hunger in households with children, by selected household characteristics, United States, 2004

Category	Total[a] 1,000	Food secure 1,000	Food secure Percent	Food insecure All 1,000	Food insecure All Percent	Food insecure Without hunger among children 1,000	Food insecure Without hunger among children Percent	Food insecure With hunger among children 1,000	Food insecure With hunger among children Percent
All households with children	39,990	32,967	82.4	7,023	17.6	6,749	16.9	274	0.7
Household composition:									
With children <6	17,922	14,606	81.5	3,316	18.5	3,240	18.1	76	.4
Married-couple families	27,065	23,926	88.4	3,139	11.6	3,036	11.2	103	.4
Female head, no spouse	9,641	6,459	67.0	3,182	33.0	3,037	31.5	145	1.5
Male head, no spouse	2,693	2,095	77.8	598	22.2	577	21.4	21	.8
Other household with child[b]	592	487	82.3	105	17.7	100	16.9	5	.8
Race/ethnicity of households:									
White non-Hispanic	25,117	21,929	87.3	3,188	12.7	3,077	12.3	111	.4
Black non-Hispanic	5,653	4,001	70.8	1,652	29.2	1,587	28.1	65	1.1
Hispanic[c]	6,708	4,909	73.2	1,799	26.8	1,733	25.8	66	1.0
Other	2,512	2,128	84.7	384	15.3	352	14.0	32	1.3
Household income-to-poverty ratio:									
Under 1.00	5,816	3,138	54.0	2,678	46.0	2,541	43.7	137	2.4
Under 1.30	7,835	4,435	56.6	3,400	43.4	3,229	41.2	171	2.2
Under 1.85	12,334	7,695	62.4	4,639	37.6	4,414	35.8	225	1.8
1.85 and over	21,576	20,037	92.9	1,539	7.1	1,508	7.0	31	.1
Income unknown	6,080	5,235	86.1	845	13.9	827	13.6	18	.3
Area of residence:[d]									
Inside metropolitan area	33,138	27,435	82.8	5,703	17.2	5,473	16.5	230	.7
In principal cities[e]	10,277	7,851	76.4	2,426	23.6	2,337	22.7	89	.9
Not in principal cities	17,462	15,194	87.0	2,268	13.0	2,177	12.5	91	.5
Outside metropolitan area	6,852	5,532	80.7	1,320	19.3	1,276	18.6	44	.6
Census geographic region:									
Northeast	7,229	6,179	85.5	1,050	14.5	1,015	14.0	35	.5
Midwest	8,996	7,532	83.7	1,464	16.3	1,411	15.7	53	.6
South	14,563	11,833	81.3	2,730	18.7	2,619	18.0	111	.8
West	9,202	7,422	80.7	1,780	19.3	1,705	18.5	75	.8
Individuals in households with children:									
All individuals in households with children	158,626	130,875	82.5	27,751	17.5	26,696	16.8	1,055	.7
Adults in households with children	85,587	71,703	83.8	13,884	16.2	13,374	15.6	510	.6
Children	73,039	59,171	81.0	13,868	19.0	13,323	18.2	545	.7

[a]Totals exclude households whose food security status is unknown because they did not give a valid response to any of the questions in the food security scale. In 2004, these represented 144,000 households with children (0.4 percent).
[b]Households with children in complex living arrangements—e.g., children of other relatives or unrelated roommate or boarder.
[c]Hispanics may be of any race.
[d]Metropolitan area residence is based on 2003 Office of Management and Budget delineation. Prevalence rates by area of residence are not precisely comparable with those of previous years.
[e]Households within incorporated areas of the largest cities in each metropolitan area. Residence inside or outside of principal cities is not identified for about 17 percent of households in metropolitan statistical areas.

SOURCE: Mark Nord, Margaret Andrews, and Steven Carlson, "Table 3. Prevalence of Food Security, Food Insecurity, and Food Insecurity with Hunger in Households with Children by Selected Household Characteristics, 2004," in *Household Food Security in the United States, 2004*, Economic Research Report No. 11, U.S. Department of Agriculture, Economic Research Service, October 2005, http://www.ers.usda.gov/publications/err11/err11.pdf (accessed April 10, 2006)

The McKinney-Vento Homeless Assistance Act of 1987 ensures that homeless children have certain rights regarding school enrollment and attendance:

- Homeless children are permitted to stay in their school even if they move.

- They can enroll in a new school with no proof of residency, immunizations, guardianship papers, or records from former schools.

- They are entitled to transportation to and from school along with other children.

- They can receive all necessary school services.

- They have the right to challenge decisions made by schools and districts.

However, even federal legislation cannot fully protect homeless children. The National Coalition for the

FIGURE 6.1

Prevalence of food insecurity, by selected characteristics, United States, 2003 and 2004

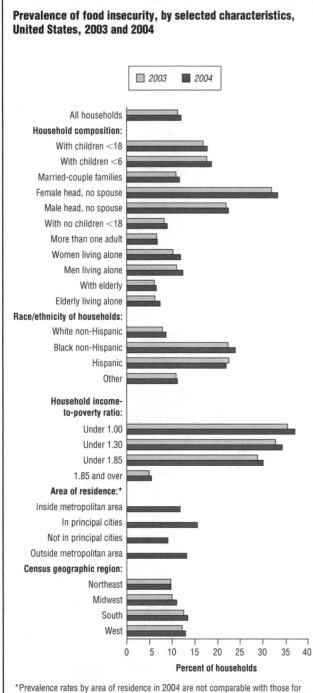

*Prevalence rates by area of residence in 2004 are not comparable with those for 2003 and earlier years because they represent somewhat different geographic areas. The 2004 survey classified metropolitan area residence based on revised metropolitan statistical areas delineated by the Office of Management and Budget in 2003.

SOURCE: Mark Nord, Margaret Andrews, and Steven Carlson, "Figure 3. Prevalence of Food Insecurity, 2003 and 2004," in *Household Food Security in the United States, 2004*, Economic Research Report No. 11, U.S. Department of Agriculture, Economic Research Service, October 2005, http://www.ers.usda.gov/publications/err11/err11.pdf (accessed April 10, 2006)

an estimated three to six months of school time lost with each move. Although the McKinney-Vento Act was strengthened in 2002, the NCH maintains that the program is still underfunded by about $15 million.

Patterns of U.S. Poverty as Reported by the Census Bureau

The U.S. Census Bureau uses the poverty threshold measurement discussed above and in Chapter 1, occasionally adding alternative measurement methods as they become available. As of 2006 the Census measurements still produce the most accurate overview of poverty in the United States, although they are admittedly controversial and do not necessarily tell the whole story of American poverty.

RACE AND ETHNICITY. While overall poverty has risen in the United States, especially among working people, some demographic groups have historically experienced higher rates. According to the U.S. Census Bureau's *Income, Poverty, and Health Insurance Coverage in the United States: 2004* (August 2005), the total poverty rate for all groups is almost 12.7% (thirty-seven million people), but African-Americans have the highest rate of any racial or ethnic group, at 24.7% (nine million); this remained unchanged from 2003 to 2004. (See Table 6.1.) The rate for Hispanics also saw no change during that time, holding at 21.9% (9.1 million). People of Asian descent actually saw a decrease in poverty in the United States, from 11.8% in 2003 to 9.8% (1.4 million) in 2004. The rate for non-Hispanic whites rose from 8.2% to 8.6% (16.9 million). The three-year average rate for Native American and Alaska Natives in 2002–04 was nearly as high as for African-Americans: 24.3%. For Native Hawaiians and Pacific Islanders the three-year average was 13.2%. (See Table 6.2.)

AGE. Of all age groups, children under eighteen have the highest poverty rate in America, at 17.8%. (See Table 6.1.) For people aged eighteen to sixty-four, the rate is markedly lower, at 11.3%. The Census Bureau's report notes that children make up only 25.2% of the total American population but account for 35.2% of people in poverty. Children under six living in a family with a single mother or female householder have the highest poverty rate: 52.6% of them live in poverty, versus 10.1% of children in married-couple families. From 2003 to 2004 the poverty rate for people eighteen to sixty-four increased by about one-half of 1%; for those sixty-five and older it decreased slightly, from 10.2% to 9.8%. (See Table 6.1.)

IMMIGRATION STATUS. Most people in the United States who live in poverty are American-born—87.9%—while 4.6% are foreign-born American citizens, and 7.4% are foreign-born and not citizens, according to *Income, Poverty, and Health Insurance Coverage in the*

Homeless (NCH) fact sheet "Education of Homeless Children and Youth" (June 2005) states that about 42% of homeless children transfer schools at least once each year, and 51% transferred two or more times, resulting in

United States: 2004. American-born citizens experienced an increase in their poverty rate from 2003 to 2004, from 11.8% to 12.1%. The rate for foreign-born naturalized citizens was 10% in 2003 and 9.8% in 2004. Foreign-born noncitizens experienced a poverty rate of 21.6% in 2004. (See Table 6.1.)

DEPTH OF POVERTY. The Census Bureau also calculates how far Americans in poverty fall below the official poverty threshold for their individual situation. This is important information because it allows researchers and legislators to see just how poor the poor are. In 2004, according to *Income, Poverty, and Health Insurance Coverage in the United States: 2004*, 15.6 million Americans (5.4% of the total population) earned less than 50% of the poverty threshold, accounting for 42.3% of the total number of Americans in poverty. These numbers, which count the poorest of the poor, stayed the same from 2003 to 2004. The numbers increased, though, for people in the middle range of poverty—those who earned at least 50% but less than 100% of the poverty threshold for their situation—from 20.6 million (7.2%) in 2003 to 21.4 million (7.4%) in 2004. For the high-range category of poor people—those who earn as much as the threshold or slightly above it (between 100% and 125% of the threshold)—the numbers stayed the same: 12.7 million people, representing 4.4% of the poor.

WESTERN EUROPE: POVERTY IN THE UNITED KINGDOM AND GERMANY

Germany and the United Kingdom (UK) are the two largest economies in the European Union (EU). The United Kingdom has the EU's highest rate of relative poverty and the highest level of income inequality. In Germany unemployment is increasing rapidly, and child poverty in particular is on the rise. According to economics reporter Steve Schifferes of BBC News Online ("Is the UK a Model Welfare State?," August 4, 2005), the Western countries of the European Union address the problems of the poor with three different models of social welfare programs: social democratic, liberal, and corporatist.

The social democratic model exists mainly in Scandinavian countries (Norway, Sweden, Denmark) and is paid for mostly through taxes, which allows it to provide a high level of services for all. The liberal model of the United Kingdom provides a low level of benefits but also lower taxes; it relies on the private sector to aid the poor and encourages the unemployed to take whatever work is available. (This model is similar to the welfare system of the United States.) The corporatist model is used in most other countries in continental Europe, including France and Germany, with benefits coming through employers from individual contributions.

Schifferes emphasizes that the main difference among the three models and the countries in which they are implemented lies in their differing views of poverty and the poor. In the United Kingdom, as in the United States, the poor are considered "deserving" or "undeserving" of government aid depending on their lifestyle. In both the social democratic and corporatist models of welfare, poverty is viewed as either a result of inequality and injustice or a circumstance that can happen to nearly anyone. It is believed, therefore, that everyone deserves the opportunity to receive aid if necessary.

Poverty is a global issue: it exists everywhere to some degree, regardless of what welfare model a country uses. According to Schifferes, about one in five UK households and one in eight German households are poor. Rates of child poverty are even higher, affecting one in four children in Britain and as many as 35% of children in parts of the former East Germany. Even Scandinavian countries have not eradicated poverty entirely, but they do have the lowest poverty rates in the European Union and some of the lowest in the world, averaging around 5% overall and less than 5% for children.

The United Kingdom

By the middle to late 1990s the United Kingdom had one of the highest poverty rates in Europe and among developed countries. An estimated 4.6 million children—one out of every three—were poor. The overall poverty rate was double what it had been in the late 1970s. According to the United Nations Development Program's *Human Development Report 2005*, this was the result of government policies of the 1980s that caused income inequality to increase at a remarkable rate: the wealthiest 20% of British society saw their annual incomes increase ten times more than those of the poorest 20%. In *Making a Difference. Tackling Poverty—A Progress Report* (2006), the United Kingdom's Department for Work and Pensions (DPW) reported that the number of people receiving unemployment benefits had risen 50% between 1979 and 1997; in addition, the number of single parent and disability benefits claims had tripled.

In response, the government initiated a radical anti-poverty campaign in 1999, the main goal of which was to eradicate child poverty in Britain entirely by 2020. The results have been encouraging. As part of the BBC News Online's special series on poverty in the United Kingdom, "Breadline Britain: The Welfare State Sixty Years On," Evan Davis reported in his article "UK Poverty Line Is Moving Target" (March 9, 2006) that the program had successfully moved about 100,000 British children per year out of poverty. However, Britain's relative method of calculating its poverty line meant that if incomes increased across all levels of society the line would likewise rise, resulting in even more people living in relative poverty. The answer, and the challenge for the government, suggests Davis, lies in increasing the incomes of poor people at a faster rate than the incomes of the wealthier members of the society.

Twelve million people—about one in five—in Britain are poor, according to a joint report from the New Policy Institute and the Joseph Rowntree Foundation (Guy Palmer, Jane Carr, and Peter Kenway, *Monitoring Poverty and Social Exclusion 2005*, 2005). Britain's Department for Work and Pensions reports that families with children make up the greatest proportion of poor people in the United Kingdom (33%), and married couples without children represent 11%. Nineteen percent are unmarried people without children, while 18% are single people with children. The remaining number of those living in poverty in the United Kingdom are elderly people, 12% of whom are married and 7% of whom are single. The Luxembourg Income Study, an international cooperative research project that tracks income in thirty countries, reports that in all, 21.8% of British people live below 60% of median income (the typical European poverty measurement), which contrasts sharply with 14.1% in France, 13.1% in Germany, and 12.3% in Sweden.

Germany

Although Germany is one of the largest economies in the world and was extraordinarily successful in recovering from the economic, infrastructural, and social disasters wrought by World War II and the Nazi Party's control, the country fell into economic stagnation in the early 2000s. By early 2005 the unemployment rate was the highest it had been since the 1930s, according to BBC News Online ("German Jobless Rate at New Record," March 1, 2005). In December 2005 the unemployment rate had dropped, from 12.6% to 11.2%, before rising again to 12.2% in February 2006. The country's weak economy caused not only joblessness but, increasingly, outright poverty, especially among families with children.

In September 2005 Sabine Dobel reported on Expatica.com ("Going without in Wealthy Germany") that more and more Germans—the poor, the elderly, children, and the disabled—are suffering from malnutrition as a result of unemployment and cutbacks in government aid. Incidences of middle-class people removing food from dumpsters for their own consumption are on the rise in German cities, according to Dobel. Perhaps most alarming are reports that as many as 20% to 30% of people admitted to hospitals in Germany are malnourished, particularly sick children. In an ironic twist indicative of the urgency of the German situation, in March 2006 the Tawfiq Hospital in Malindi, Kenya—the twenty-sixth poorest country in the world—sent volunteer aid workers to Berlin to distribute coffee and tea to hungry Germans waiting in breadlines during Germany's unusually cold winter. The group Medical Direct Help in Africa was "shocked into action after discovering that even people in a rich country like Germany could lack sustenance" ("Kenya Offers Aid to Third World Germany," *Deutsche Welle*, March 6, 2006).

The Cologne Institute for the German Economy argued that the high unemployment rate had resulted in a drop in the German standard of living, but that relative unemployment was not really rising ("German Think Tank Says Joblessness behind Poverty," *Deutsche Welle*, March 7, 2006). In fact, the Institute maintained that the German method of measuring poverty—setting the poverty line at 60% or less of average monthly income—was the real problem, for much the same reason that British researchers criticize the United Kingdom's poverty line calculation: across-the-board income increases cause the poverty line to rise, meaning that more people fall below it. At the same time, with incomes in the highest economic category rising faster than those in the middle and low categories, income inequality has grown in Germany as it has in other developed countries.

As of March 2006, 16% of Germans lived below the nation's poverty line. *Deutsche Welle* reported in February 2006 ("Germany Serious about Minimum Wage," February 24, 2006) that two million poor Germans have full-time jobs. As of 2006 Germany did not have a minimum wage law—an issue that has stirred up a heated debate across the country. Other European Union countries have a minimum wage, but the idea instituting one in Germany has the nation split: many union leaders are calling for a high minimum wage, while others argue that this would result in the loss of more jobs.

The minimum wage issue is part of a larger controversy across the country regarding the government's proposed labor and social welfare reforms, known as Hartz IV. These reforms would increase the workweek from its traditional thirty-five hours with no pay increase. In addition, Germany's generous unemployment benefits would be strictly limited, and the power of labor unions would be curtailed. Proponents of the reforms argue that the long history of Germany's brand of capitalism—characterized by an extremely high level of social welfare programs—is over, and government guidance of economic markets must give way to an entirely free market system. Opponents of the reforms believe they will only increase the country's rapidly rising poverty rate.

Child poverty in Germany is an especially serious issue. Miles Corak, Michael Fertig, and Marcus Tamm reported in *A Portrait of Child Poverty in Germany* (Institute for the Study of Labor, March 2005) that the

FIGURE 6.2

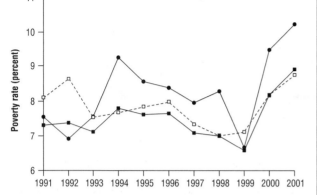

Child poverty rates relative to the overall population and adult households without children, Germany, 1991–2001

Legend:
- Child poverty rate
- Poverty rate for entire population
- Adult poverty rate (no children in household)

SOURCE: Miles Corak, Michael Fertig, and Marcus Tamm, "Figure 3. Child Poverty Rates Relative to the Overall Population and Adult Households without Children," in *A Portrait of Child Poverty in Germany*, IZA DP No. 1528, Forschungsinstitut zur Zukunft der Arbeit Institute for the Study of Labor, March 2005, ftp://repec.iza.org/RePEc/Discussionpaper/dp1528.pdf (accessed April 10, 2006)

FIGURE 6.3

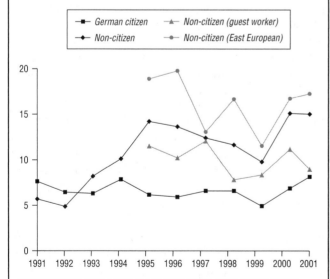

Child poverty rates in West Germany by citizenship status, 1991–2001

Legend:
- German citizen
- Non-citizen (guest worker)
- Non-citizen
- Non-citizen (East European)

Note: The poverty line is defined as 50% of the median country wide individual equivalised income.

SOURCE: Miles Corak, Michael Fertig, and Marcus Tamm, "Figure 4. Child Poverty Rates in West Germany by Citizenship Status," in *A Portrait of Child Poverty in Germany*, IZA DP No. 1528, Forschungsinstitut zur Zukunft der Arbeit Institute for the Study of Labor, March 2005, ftp://repec.iza.org/RePEc/Discussionpaper/dp1528.pdf (accessed April 10, 2006)

FIGURE 6.4

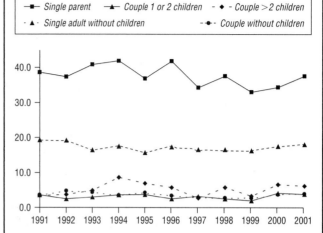

Household poverty rates in Germany, by family type, entire country, 1991–2001

Legend:
- Single parent
- Couple 1 or 2 children
- Couple >2 children
- Single adult without children
- Couple without children

Note: Poverty rates are defined as the proportion of households living in poverty, not the proportion of individuals in poverty. The poverty line is still defined as 50% of the median country wide individual equivalised income.

SOURCE: Miles Corak, Michael Fertig, and Marcus Tamm, "Figure 5. Household Poverty Rates by Family Type (Entire Country)," in *A Portrait of Child Poverty in Germany*, IZA DP No. 1528, Forschungsinstitut zur Zukunftder Arbeit Institute for the Study of Labor, March 2005, ftp://repec.iza.org/RePEc/Discussionpaper/dp1528.pdf (accessed March 28, 2006)

overall child poverty rate in Germany was 10.2% in 2001. However, the rate in the former East Germany was considerably higher than in the West: 12.6% versus 9.8%. Figure 6.2 shows that, since 1994 and with the brief exception of 1999, child poverty in Germany was significantly higher than either overall German poverty or poverty in German households without children. Likewise, Figure 6.3 demonstrates that, between 1991 and 2001, children residing in Germany without German citizenship had a much higher poverty rate than children who were citizens in West Germany. Finally, in Figure 6.4 it is evident that children in single-parent households throughout Germany have suffered from a far higher rate of poverty (approximately 32% or more) since 1991 than those in two-parent households.

EASTERN EUROPE: THE RUSSIAN FEDERATION

The Russian Federation is the largest country by land area in the world, at almost 6.6 million square miles. It is a loose federation of eighty-eight separate republics, territories, and other political subdivisions, each of which has two delegates in the Russian parliament and varying degrees of political and economic autonomy. The Russian Federation's 142.9 million people are extremely diverse culturally and ethnically: there are believed to be about 160 distinct ethnic groups throughout the country.

This diversity has fueled violent conflicts at times since the dissolution of the Soviet Union in 1991. The Russian Federation is more commonly referred to as Russia, but Russia was actually the largest of the republics that made up the Soviet Union. Both as a part of the Soviet Union and as a member of the Russian Federation, Russia accounts for more than half of the country's population and at least 60% of its gross domestic product (GDP).

The Transition from Soviet Control to Free Market

The Russian Federation emerged as an independent nation late in 1991, when the Union of Soviet Socialist Republics (USSR, or Soviet Union) of which it had been a major component collapsed. The Soviet Union was a communist country with a centrally planned and tightly controlled economy. In theory, this system ensured that all citizens received the basic necessities of life, and as such there was no poverty. In reality, however, the Soviet system had been struggling to meet the basic needs of its citizens for years prior to its downfall. Mikhail Gorbachev, who led the Soviet Union from 1985 to 1991, introduced the concepts of *glasnost* (openness) and *perestroika* (reconstruction) in an attempt to reform and repair the Soviet system.

The pace of reform under Gorbachev proved too slow to satisfy critics of the Soviet system, and too fast to be satisfactory to its defenders. Communist hard-liners launched a coup in August 1991 in an attempt to remove Gorbachev and end his reforms. They were resisted and defeated by reformers, most notably Boris Yeltsin, the president of the Russian state within the Soviet Union. Having defeated the hard-line Communists the reformers were left as the most powerful force in the country, and they moved quickly to end the Soviet Union.

The Soviet Union was officially dissolved on December 21, 1991. Boris Yeltsin was now the president of an independent Russia. Yeltsin had already embarked on a program of radical economic reforms, known as "shock therapy," to end the Communist economic system and force the country into a Western-style free-market economy. The result of these major changes, implemented quickly, was massive economic disruption. Inflation soared, wages for average Russians fell, manufacturing output declined, and many Russians became unemployed. Some Russians were able to take advantage of the new system to become quite wealthy, but many more sunk into poverty. In subsequent years the economy recovered somewhat, but poverty remains a serious problem.

Russian Poverty since the 1990s

According to the World Bank report *Russian Federation: Reducing Poverty through Growth and Social Policy Reform* (February 8, 2005), poverty in

TABLE 6.6

Percentage of the poor in Russian Federation by individual types, 1997–2002

Year	Active males	Active females	Elderly	Children 0–6 years	Children 7–15 years	All persons
Percentage of poor						
1997	23.9	22.8	17.9	33.6	29.9	24.2
1998	31.5	29.6	25.4	41.0	38.4	31.4
1999	40.6	39.8	37.7	49.8	48.8	41.6
2000	35.0	33.9	32.5	42.6	43.9	35.9
2001	25.6	24.8	21.5	32.5	33.7	26.2
2002	19.4	18.3	15.1	26.2	26.8	19.6
Percentage change in poverty						
1998	31.9	29.7	42.0	22.1	28.3	29.9
1999	29.0	34.3	48.5	21.6	27.2	32.3
2000	−13.8	−14.7	−13.7	−14.4	−10.0	−13.6
2001	−26.8	−26.9	−33.8	−23.8	−23.2	−27.1
2002	−24.5	−26.3	−29.8	−19.4	−20.4	−25.1
1997–2002	−4.1	−4.3	−3.3	−4.8	−2.1	−4.1

SOURCE: "Table 6.8. Percentage of the Poor by Individual Types, 1997–2002," in *Russian Federation: Reducing Poverty through Growth and Social Policy Reform*, Report No. 28923-RU, World Bank, Poverty Reduction and Economic Management Unit, Europe and Central Asia Region, February 8, 2005, http://194.84.38.65/mdb/upload/PAR_020805_eng.pdf (accessed April 10, 2006)

Russia was reduced by approximately 50% between 1999 (when it was at 41.5%) and 2002 (when it was 19.6%), with an estimated thirty million people lifted above the poverty line during this time. (See Table 6.6.) The unemployment rate has also dropped dramatically, from a high of 13.2% in 1998 to 8.6% in 2002. The report notes that poverty in Russia is "shallow," meaning that most of the poor have incomes somewhere around the poverty line, with many people living just above it. While this makes for less depth of poverty, it also means that a greater number of people are vulnerable to economic fluctuations: the risk of falling into, or deeper into, poverty is greater for far more people.

Certain segments of the Russian population are more likely to be poor than others—in other words, they have more poverty risk factors than others. For children younger than sixteen the poverty rate is quite high, at 26.7%. (See Table 6.7.) People living in rural areas in the central and eastern parts of the Russian Federation have a poverty rate of 30.4%, versus 15.7% for urban dwellers. (See Table 6.8.) However, because there are so many more people living in the western, urban areas of the federation (around Russia's capital city of Moscow), 15.7% of this much greater number actually translates into more people than 30.4% of the smaller population living in rural areas. It makes sense, then, that the majority of impoverished Russians are members of urban households with children. Figure 6.5 shows the geographic distribution of poverty in the Russian Federation, with the highest concentration in the most populous, western areas. In fact, 58.5% of the poor live

TABLE 6.7

Children face greater risk of poverty in Russian Federation, 2002

[In percent]

	Poor, incidence	Depth of poverty	Severity of poverty	"Near poor", incidence	Share of poor	Share of "near poor"	Share of population
Children (below 16)	26.7	7.4	3.0	10.4	24.9	20.4	18.3
Working	18.8	4.9	1.9	8.9	62.0	62.1	64.8
Elderly	15.1	3.5	1.2	9.7	13.0	17.5	16.9
Total	**19.6**	**5.1**	**2.0**	**9.3**	**100.0**	**100.0**	**100.0**

SOURCE: "Table 2.3. Children Face Greater Risk of Poverty (%)," in *Russian Federation: Reducing Poverty through Growth and Social Policy Reform*, Report No. 28923-RU, World Bank, Poverty Reduction and Economic Management Unit, Europe and Central Asia Region, February 8, 2005, http://194.84.38.65/mdb/upload/PAR_020805_eng.pdf (accessed April 10, 2006). Data from the Russian Household Budget Survey.

TABLE 6.8

Poverty in Russian Federation, urban and rural differences, 2002

[In percent]

	Poor, incidence	Depth of poverty	Severity of poverty	"Near poor", incidence	Share of poor	Share of "near poor"	Share of population
Urban	15.7	3.9	1.5	8.5	58.5	67.0	73.2
Moscow	6.6	1.1	0.3	7.4	3.1	7.3	9.2
Other urban	17.0	4.2	1.6	8.7	55.4	59.7	64.0
Rural	30.4	8.6	3.5	11.5	41.5	33.0	26.8
Total	**19.6**	**5.1**	**2.0**	**9.3**	**100.0**	**100.0**	**100.0**

SOURCE: "Table 2.1. In Russia Poverty Has a Rural Face (%)," in *Russian Federation: Reducing Poverty through Growth and Social Policy Reform*, Report No. 28923-RU, World Bank, Poverty Reduction and Economic Management Unit, Europe and Central Asia Region, February 8, 2005, http://194.84.38.65/mdb/upload/PAR_020805_eng.pdf (accessed April 10, 2006). Data from the Russian Household Budget Survey.

in large cities, and—perhaps more surprisingly—89% live in a household in which at least one person is regularly employed. (See Table 6.9.)

The states of the Russian Federation also experience greater disparities in regional income, in part because the country is so large and has such a diversity of geographical features and varying degrees of remoteness, ranging from the huge metropolitan city of Moscow to the most isolated, inhospitable parts of southern Siberia. As Figure 6.6 shows, urban and rural Russians live with very different basic services—an indicator of poverty and standards of living. While at least 60% of all five income categories in urban areas have access to most infrastructural and utilities services, in rural areas access ranges from less than 20% of the poorest with access to hot water to just over 60% of the richest with running water.

The Russian Federation in the post-Soviet years has seen a decline in education equity across income groups. During the Soviet years, literacy was near 100%, and free, compulsory education was open to all. With increasing competition in more recent years, however, the poor have been largely left out of preschool and post-compulsory education. Furthermore, government spending on education has fallen behind that of most other former-Soviet

countries in Central and Eastern Europe: in 2002 Russia spent just 3% of its gross domestic product on education, whereas Estonia had the highest GDP education spending, at more than 7%; the Central and Eastern European average was about 4.5%; and the European Union/North American average was about 5.5%. The World Bank's *Russian Federation: Reducing Poverty through Growth and Social Policy Reform* reports that about 8% of poor children in Russia complete higher education, versus 21% of nonpoor children.

Perhaps most troubling is the decline in overall Russian health and its link to poverty since the economic transition. According to the World Health Organization, life expectancy in the Russian Federation in 2003 was fifty-eight years for men and seventy-two for women. Healthy life expectancy was 52.8 years for men and 64.3 for women. According to Oleksiy Ivaschenko in *Longevity in Russia's Regions: Do Poverty and Low Public Health Spending Kill?* (United Nations University, World Institute for Development Economic Research, June 2004), life expectancy throughout the Russian Federation declined substantially between 1990 and 2000, by as much as seven years in some of the regions hit hardest by the depression of the 1990s. Working-age men accounted for the majority of premature deaths—an estimated 1.3 to 1.6 million between

FIGURE 6.5

Poverty map of the Russian Federation, distribution of the poor, 2002

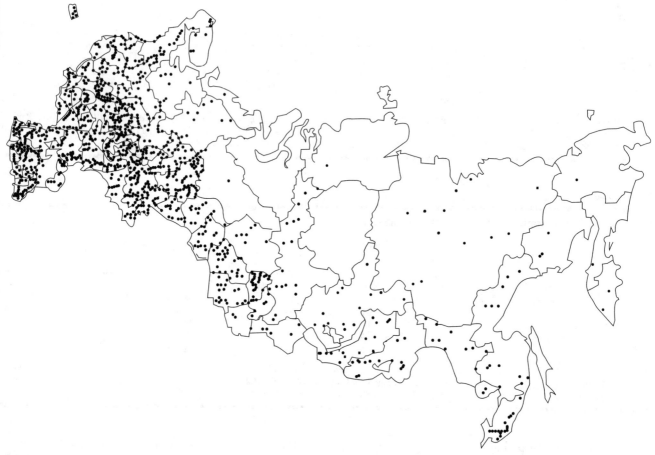

Note: One dot is equal to 20,000 poor individuals.

SOURCE: "Figure 2.2. Poverty Map of the Russian Federation, 2002: Distribution of the Poor," in *Russian Federation: Reducing Poverty through Growth and Social Policy Reform*, Report No. 28923-RU, World Bank, Poverty Reduction and Economic Management Unit, Europe and Central Asia Region, February 8, 2005, http://194.84.38.65/mdb/upload/PAR_020805_eng.pdf (accessed April 10, 2006). Data from the Russian Household Budget Survey.

TABLE 6.9

Poverty in Russian Federation, by household employment status, 2002

[In percent]

Household employment	Poor, incidence	Depth of poverty	Severity of poverty	"Near poor", incidence	Share of poor	Share of "near poor"	Share of population
One member working	22.3	6.2	2.5	9.3	27.6	24.3	24.3
2 or more working	18.0	4.5	1.7	9.1	59.7	63.3	65.0
Jobless households	47.3	15.3	7.0	12.7	6.8	3.9	2.8
Non-working age households	14.7	3.2	1.1	10.2	5.9	8.6	7.9
Total	**19.6**	**5.1**	**2.0**	**9.3**	**100.0**	**100.0**	**100.0**

SOURCE: "Table 2.6. The Majority of the Poor Are Working Households (%)," in *Russian Federation: Reducing Poverty through Growth and Social Policy Reform*, Report No. 28923-RU, World Bank, Poverty Reduction and Economic Management Unit, Europe and Central Asia Region, February 8, 2005, http:// 194.84.38.65/mdb/upload/PAR_020805_eng.pdf (accessed April 10, 2006). Data from the Russian Household Budget Survey.

1990 and 1995. Ivaschenko cites studies linking the rise in premature deaths to stress related to unemployment, low wages, poor diet, increased crime rates, and a dramatic rise in alcoholism, all associated with low income.

Furthermore, Russia has experienced an increase in the incidence of infectious diseases since 1990. In 2004 there were 126 new cases of tuberculosis per 100,000 people, according to the World Health Organization's *Global*

FIGURE 6.6

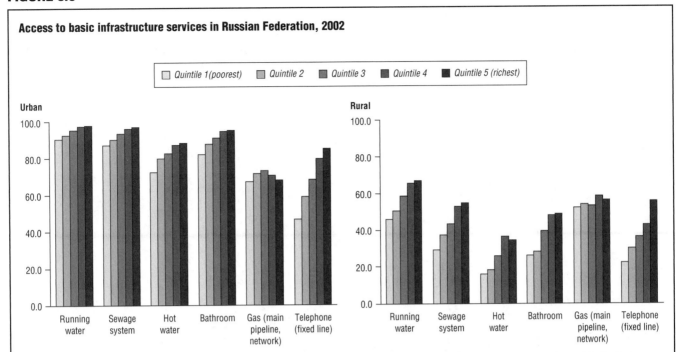

Access to basic infrastructure services in Russian Federation, 2002

☐ Quintile 1(poorest) ☐ Quintile 2 ☐ Quintile 3 ■ Quintile 4 ■ Quintile 5 (richest)

Urban

Rural

SOURCE: "Figure 8. Access to Basic Infrastructure Services, 2002," in *Russian Federation: Reducing Poverty through Growth and Social Policy Reform*, Report No. 28923-RU, World Bank, Poverty Reduction and Economic Management Unit, Europe and Central Asia Region, February 8, 2005, http://194. 84.38.65/mdb/upload/PAR_020805_eng.pdf (accessed April 10, 2006)

Tuberculosis Control. The emergence of drug-resistant strains in particular has caused concern among health care professionals worldwide. These strains accounted for about 8.3% of new cases in 2003. The incidence of HIV and AIDS has also increased since 1990, rising from 10,000 or fewer cases in 1997 to more than 250,000 in 2003. Analysts point to the breakdown of the health care and social services system, along with an increase in stress-related risky behavior, in the post-Soviet era.

ALCOHOLISM IN RUSSIA. Vodka has played an important role in Russian culture for centuries. Even prior to the economic crash of the 1990s and the shaky recovery of the early 2000s, alcoholism was common throughout the country. However, according to the World Health Organization, annual per capita alcohol consumption has increased more or less steadily from 1990, when it was 7.08 liters (6.22 quarts), to 2001, when it was 10.58 liters (9.31 quarts). The Australian Broadcasting Corporation's foreign correspondent Michael Brissenden reported on August 26, 2003, that beer consumption was increasing by 30% per year, largely due to government encouragement because taxes on beer generate much-needed income, and beer is marketed as more of a soft drink than an alcoholic beverage. Periodically the governments of Russian states attempt to curb alcohol consumption by implementing legislation, but these attempts have backfired. Mikhail Gorbachev's anti-alcohol campaign resulted in a huge black market, and

a 2000 attempt to raise taxes on vodka by 40% ended in public rioting.

Beer and vodka are not the only threats to Russians' health. Cheap counterfeit alcohol, homemade moonshine, and even de-icing solvent and cologne contribute to the problem. In December 2005 Alex Rodriguez of the *Chicago Tribune* reported in "Alcohol Destroying Rural Russia" that as many as 40,000 Russians die of alcohol poisoning each year, and one-third of all deaths in the country are related in some way to alcohol abuse. By comparison, U.S. deaths directly attributable to alcohol poisoning alone averaged 317 annually between 1996 and 1998, according to the National Institute of Alcohol Abuse and Alcoholism; about 1,000 more fatalities each year in the United States had alcohol poisoning as a contributing factor, most often in a death that included poisoning from another drug.

In his *Chicago Tribune* article Rodriguez illustrated some of the reasons rural-dwelling Russians turn so often to alcohol:

Fifteen years of post-Soviet capitalism has left rural Russia straggling far behind. Russians in collective farms across the country's eleven time zones could count on a safety net of free housing and health care—and on regular paychecks—during the Soviet era. In today's Russia, those same villagers live day-to-day, shivering through stretches of winter without heat, cringing at the sight of their children in tattered school clothes.

In the extremely harsh winter of 2005–06, with temperatures exceeding twenty degrees below zero, the combination of poverty and alcoholism was particularly deadly.

As of January 2006, 123 homeless people and alcoholics had frozen to death on the streets of Moscow, with the number expected to rise before winter's end (Andrew E. Kramer, "In Frozen Moscow, City Rescues the Homeless and the Drunk," *New York Times*, January 21, 2006).

CHAPTER 7

WOMEN AND CHILDREN IN POVERTY

Women are poorer than men because they are often denied equal rights and opportunities, lack access to assets, and do not have the same entitlements as men. They also carry the burden of reproductive and care work and represent the majority of unpaid labour.

—United Nations Development Program, Gender and Poverty Reduction

The quality of a child's life depends on decisions made every day in households, communities and in the halls of government. . . . As children go, so go nations. It's that simple.

—UNICEF Executive Director Carol Bellamy

Virtually all groups that study poverty—from international organizations like the United Nations and the World Bank to small local charities—agree that the most effective way to reduce it is to improve the social, economic, and political situation of women and, by extension, children. Women's levels of health, education, and security reflect those of their families. When a mother suffers the effects of poverty, future generations of her family do as well, creating a cycle of impoverishment from which it is very difficult to escape.

GLOBAL CONVENTIONS ON THE RIGHTS OF WOMEN AND CHILDREN

UN Convention on the Rights of the Child, 1989

In 1989 the United Nations (UN) adopted a treaty called the Convention on the Rights of the Child (CRC). Considered one of the most wide-ranging and important human rights documents the global community had ever agreed upon, the CRC was charged with establishing "norms" and standards for the lives of children to which all countries could hold themselves accountable, including:

- Protection from violence, abuse, and abduction

- Protection from hazardous employment and exploitation

- Adequate nutrition

- Free compulsory primary education

- Adequate health care

- Equal treatment regardless of gender, race, or cultural background

The CRC became the most widely ratified human rights treaty in history, passed by 192 countries. As of 2006 only two countries had not ratified it: Somalia and the United States. (Ratification by the United States was hampered by the fact that the Convention forbids capital punishment of minors. Before the U.S. Supreme Court outlawed it in *Roper v. Simmons* (2005), several states had allowed the death penalty for those who were between sixteen years old and eighteen years old at the time they committed their crimes.)

Beijing Declaration and Platform for Action, 1995

In September 1995 at the United Nations Fourth World Conference on Women in Beijing, China, representatives of 189 countries unanimously adopted a program intended to promote gender equality around the world, which became known as the Beijing Declaration and Platform for Action. One of the main goals outlined by the Platform was addressing the enormous increase of women living in poverty in the late twentieth century—a trend that has come to be known as the "feminization of poverty." The Platform sought to:

- Review, adopt, and maintain macroeconomic policies and development strategies that address the needs and efforts of women in poverty

- Revise laws and administrative practices in order to ensure women's equal rights and access to economic resources

- Provide women with access to savings and credit mechanisms and institutions

- Develop gender-based methodologies and conduct research to address the feminization of poverty

FIGURE 7.1

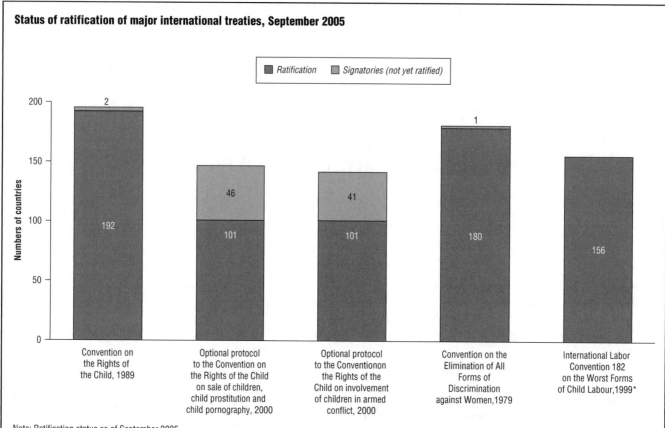

Status of ratification of major international treaties, September 2005

Note: Ratification status as of September 2005.
*The International Labour Organization (ILO) database includes lists of conventions ratified, non-ratified and denounced.

SOURCE: "Figure 4.1. Status of Ratification of Major International Treaties," in *The State of the World's Children 2006*, United Nations Children's Fund, 2005, http://www.unicef.org/sowc06/pdfs/sowc0506_eps_charts.pdf (accessed April 8, 2006). Data from United Nations Treaty Collections Databases and ILOLEX of International Labour Standards. Copyright © 2005, International Labour Organization.

UN Millennium Development Goals and Other Conventions

In 2000 all member countries of the United Nations pledged to meet eight human development goals outlined in the Millennium Campaign, an international effort to eradicate extreme poverty, along with its causes and consequences. These Millennium Development Goals (MDGs) include four that specifically address the needs and challenges of women and children affected by poverty:

• Achieve universal primary education

• Promote gender equality and empower women

• Reduce child mortality

• Improve maternal health

The standards of the CRC, the Beijing Platform, and the Millennium Campaign together have led to a global acknowledgment that the protection of children and the eradication of gender disparities are essential to combating poverty. Figure 7.1 shows how many countries have ratified the Convention on the Rights of the Child, the Convention on the Elimination of All Forms of Discrimination against Women (1979), and the International Convention on the Worst Forms of Child Labour (1999). Also included is information on the Optional Protocols to the Convention on the Rights of the Child on child prostitution and pornography (2000) and on the involvement of children in armed conflict (2000).

PROGRESS TOWARD INTERNATIONAL GOALS

Progress has been made toward many of the development goals outlined by the UN during the 1990s. According to the UNDP (http://hdr.undp.org/reports/global/2005/pdf/presskit/HDR05_PR1E.pdf), since the 1990s more than 135 million people have been lifted out of extreme poverty (having an income of less that one dollar per day per person), 1.2 billion people have gained access to clean water, thirty million more children attend school, and child deaths have been reduced by two million per year. However, as of 2005, 2.5 billion people stilled lived on an income less than two dollars per person per day, more than one billion people still did not have access to safe water, 115 million children were still not in school, and more than ten million children per year still died of preventable causes.

Beijing+10.

In March 2005 during a conference in New York City that became known as Beijing+10, the UN Commission on the Status of Women assessed progress toward the goals outlined in the Beijing Platform (http://daccessdds.un.org/doc/UNDOC/GEN/N04/636/83/PDF/N0463683.pdf?OpenElement). According to the report, as of 2004 women were more likely than men to be poor, and female-headed households were more likely than male-headed households to be poor. Among the statistics cited by the UN, in Malawi a full three-quarters of the poor are women; in Zimbabwe, 72% of female-headed households are poor, compared with 58% of households headed by men. Even in the developed world women fared worse than men; according to the UN report, for instance, women headed 62% of poor households in the Netherlands. Only Burkina Faso reported that men experienced higher poverty rates: 46.9% of households headed by men experienced poverty in that west African country, compared with 36.5% of households headed by women.

Many of the national programs begun since the Beijing Platform focus on increasing women's employment opportunities, ensuring social safety nets, and improving training and education. Some countries instituted minimum wage laws, affecting the poor women who make up the majority of low-income workers. In Portugal, for example, 69% of the people who benefited from the country's minimum wage in 2003 were poor women, according to the UN report. Other countries created lines of credit, loans, and other incentives for self-employment and entrepreneurship. In 2002 Vietnam's program granted loans to more than 20% of poor households headed by women. Some developing countries—including Liberia, Namibia, Zimbabwe, and the Dominican Republic—have changed their laws on inheritance and land ownership to include women.

INFORMAL LABOR. However, implementation of programs consistent with the goals of the Beijing Platform has not been uniform throughout the world. In *Beijing Betrayed: Women Worldwide Report That Governments Have Failed to Turn the Platform into Action* (Women's Environment and Development Organization [WEDO], March 2005, http://www.wedo.org/files/beijingbetrayed.htm), organizations from 150 countries reported on actions taken—or not taken—since 1995.

One of the trends cited by WEDO as having a significant impact on women in poverty is the proliferation of informal paid labor, or work that is outside the formal labor sector and therefore not subject to legal protections such as safety and wage regulations. The WEDO report estimates that at least 60% of women in developing countries are employed in the informal work sector, although precise figures are impossible to obtain because this type of work falls outside government purview. In Figure 7.2 the three

FIGURE 7.2

Segmentation of informal employment by average earnings and sex, poverty risk of households by sources of income, poverty risk of households by primary source of income

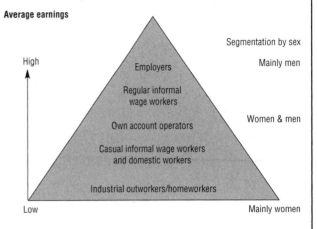

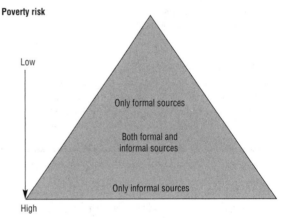

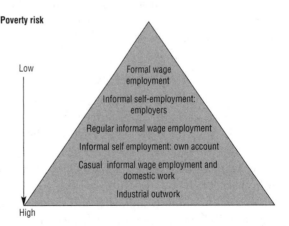

SOURCE: Martha Chen, Joann Vanek, Francie Lund, James Heintz, with Renana Jhabvala, and Christine Bonner, "Figures 3.1–3.3. Segmentation of Informal Employment by Average Earnings and Sex, Poverty Risk of Households by Sources of Income, Poverty Risk of Households by Primary Source of Income," in *Progress of the World's Women 2005: Women, Work, and Poverty,* United Nations Development Fund for Women, 2005, http://www.unifem.org/attachments/products/PoWW2005_eng.pdf (accessed April 8, 2006)

TABLE 7.1

Costs of informal work

Direct costs

1. High costs of running informal businesses, including direct and indirect taxes
2. High costs of informal wage work
   - Long hours and unscheduled overtime
   - Occupational health hazards
3. High costs of accessing capital in informal financial markets and high indebtedness
4. High costs associated with periodic 'shocks' to work

Indirect costs

1. Lack of secure work and income
   - Greater insecurity of work
   - Variability and volatility of income
2. Lack of worker benefits and social protection
   - Few (if any) rights such as paid sick leave, overtime compensation or severance pay
   - No childcare provisions
   - Little (if any) employment-based social protection
   - No health, disability, property, unemployment or life insurance
3. Lack of training and career prospects
4. Lack of capital and other assets
   - Lack of/vulnerability of productive assets
   - Limited (if any) access to formal financial services
5. Lack of legal status, organization and voice
   - Uncertain legal status
   - Lack of organization and voice

SOURCE: Martha Chen, Joann Vanek, Francie Lund, James Heintz, with Renana Jhabvala, and Christine Bonner, "Box 4.1. Costs of Informal Work," in *Progress of the World's Women 2005: Women, Work, and Poverty*, United Nations Development Fund for Women, 2005, http://www.unifem.org/attachments/products/PoWW2005_eng.pdf (accessed April 8, 2006)

pyramids represent the top-to-bottom structure of informal work and poverty according to gender. Employers—the highest paid people in the informal sector—are overwhelmingly male, while those working exclusively in the informal sector and those performing industrial outwork—overwhelmingly female sectors—have the highest risk of living in poverty.

Table 7.1 lists the direct and indirect costs involved in working in the informal sector. Of particular concern to women are the indirect costs related to a lack of child care, health benefits, sick leave, and insurance. With women largely responsible for the care of children and the home, the daily insecurity of having no options for child and health care or time off to care for an ill family member, along with the longer-term problem of having no disability or employment insurance, makes working in the informal economy an extremely difficult task.

POLITICAL REPRESENTATION. Another global issue highlighted by the Beijing Platform is the lack of female representation in governments and public administration. One of the specific goals of the Platform was to increase the proportion of women serving in national parliaments around the world to 30%. In some countries positive results have been realized: in Rwanda gender

quotas led to women comprising 48.8% of the national parliament in 2005. That same year 36% of members of the Cuban parliament were female, and in South Africa 32.8% were female. Still, twelve countries had no female representatives: Bahrain, Kuwait, Micronesia, Nauru, Palau, Saint Kitts and Nevis, Saudi Arabia, Solomon Islands, Tonga, Tuvalu, United Arab Emirates, and Guinea-Bissau. Even in the United States, where women outnumber men in the population 51% to 49%, representation is not equal: women made up only 15.1% of the U.S. Congress in 2006.

In 2005 the African country of Liberia ushered in what international observers believe could be the beginning of change for the entire continent and for the developing world overall, electing Africa's first female president, Ellen Johnson-Sirleaf, a Harvard-educated economist who once headed the United Nations Development Program and advised the World Bank. Chile also elected its first female president, Michelle Bachelet, in 2006, beginning a new era of government in Latin America. With women gaining positions of power and influence, legislation that addresses female poverty should have a better chance of ratification.

The Millennium Development Goals: Five Years Later

In 2005 the United Nations published a five-year review of movement toward the MDGs (http://millenniumindicators.un.org/unsd/mi/pdf/MDG%20Book.pdf). While the UN report found progress, it conceded that the goals are not on track to be fulfilled by the 2015 deadline. For example, the goal to halve extreme poverty between 1990 and 2015 is off track, even though poverty overall has been reduced in most regions. More than 800 million people in developing countries suffer from chronic hunger—an increase since 1990—and about a quarter of children younger than five in the developing world are malnourished. Of the estimated eleven million children who die each year from treatable causes, more than half die as a direct result of malnourishment and disease. Figure 7.3 shows how achievement of the MDGs would improve children's lives. Among children under five years old, 5.5 million lives would be saved in 2015 alone.

Between 1990–91 and 2001–02, enrollment in primary school in developing regions overall increased from 80% to 83%. In five regions—Latin America and the Caribbean (LAC), East Asia, Central Asia, Northern Africa, and Southeast Asia—enrollment reached greater than 90%. While this level of enrollment is considered an impressive advance, the MDG of achieving universal primary school enrollment is moving slowly. More than a third of school-age children in sub-Saharan Africa do not attend school. In South Asia, West Asia, and the Pacific Rim countries, 20% of children do not attend school.

Progress toward the MDGs that specifically address women's issues has been disappointing. The UN's MDG

FIGURE 7.3

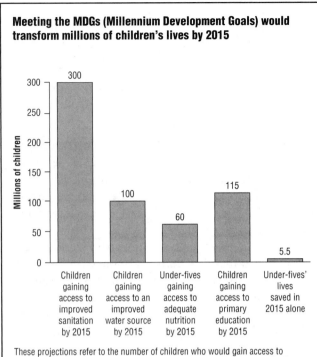

Meeting the MDGs (Millennium Development Goals) would transform millions of children's lives by 2015

Millions of children

- Children gaining access to improved sanitation by 2015: 300
- Children gaining access to an improved water source by 2015: 100
- Under-fives gaining access to adequate nutrition by 2015: 60
- Children gaining access to primary education by 2015: 115
- Under-fives' lives saved in 2015 alone: 5.5

These projections refer to the number of children who would gain access to essential services between now and 2015 if the Millenium Development Goals (MDGs) are met.

SOURCE: "Figure 1.1. Meeting the MDGs Would Transform Millions of Children's Lives in the Next 10 Years," in *The State of the World's Children 2006,* United Nations Children's Fund, 2005, http://www.unicef.org/sowc06/pdfs/sowc0506_eps_charts.pdf (accessed April 8, 2006)

report found that women by far outnumber men in the informal workforce, both paid and unpaid; 62% of unpaid family workers are women. The UN also reported that maternal mortality rates are not dropping in the countries where pregnancy and childbirth are already the most dangerous. While in the developed world the rate was fourteen maternal deaths per 100,000 live births in 2000, in developing regions the rate was 450 deaths per 100,000 live births. At the same time in sub-Saharan Africa, the rate was 920 deaths per 100,000 live births—by far the highest rate in the world. On the other hand, there have been a few significant advances in the goal of improving health services for pregnant women and new mothers. For instance, the proportion of deliveries in the developing world attended by skilled professionals increased from 41% in 1990 to 57% in 2003.

THE FEMINIZATION OF POVERTY

The term the "feminization of poverty" was first used in 1978 by a researcher named Diana Pearce, who had found that two-thirds of poor adults over age sixteen in the United States were female. Although Pearce was referring specifically to U.S. data, the term entered common usage in both poverty research and women's studies.

The feminization of poverty is generally understood to have three main causes:

- The increasing number of female-headed households
- Individual and cultural stereotypes about and discrimination against women and girls
- Macroeconomic trends such as globalization and trade that fail to take into account women's roles in economies

There are many reasons women tend to be poorer than men. Lower wages, failed social safety nets, fewer educational opportunities, substandard health care, and a lack of employee protections and benefits such as paid maternity leave and child care all contribute to the problem. In addition, women typically are the primary caretakers of children and elders, which also makes them more vulnerable to impoverishment as they have less time to earn money outside the home.

Women's Work

The United Nations Development Fund for Women (UNIFEM) explains in its report *Progress of the World's Women 2005: Women, Work, and Poverty* that, although globalization has brought new opportunities for highly educated and skilled workers, it has in many cases had the opposite effect on those with less training and education, who typically come from poor backgrounds in the first place. According to the UNIFEM report:

> Increasingly, rather than informal work becoming formalized as economies grow, work is moving from formal to informal, from regulated to unregulated, and workers lose job security as well as medical and other benefits. What we are seeing is that growth does not automatically "trickle down" to the poor. It can in fact widen the gap between rich and poor. As globalization intensifies, the likelihood of obtaining formal employment is decreasing in many places, with "footloose" companies shifting production from one unregulated zone to an even less regulated one elsewhere, employing workers in informal contract or casual work with low earnings and little or no benefits.

This situation has become common in developing countries, where 50% to 80% of nonagricultural employment is in the informal sector. More than 60% of women in developing countries perform nonagricultural paid informal labor; the figure rises when informal paid agricultural work is factored in. Additionally, many women perform informal unpaid agricultural work on family or community farms. Average wages are lower for both informal and agricultural workers, male and female, and the risk of falling into or remaining in poverty is higher for those workers as well.

In addition to earning lower wages and having a greater risk of poverty, workers in the informal sector

TABLE 7.2

Occupational health and safety hazards

Problems associated with poor health and safety in the workplace vary from job to job and are also heavily dependent on the environment in which each job is undertaken. Some of the common problems associated with different types of informal work include:

1. Garment makers

   - Neck and backache
   - Pain in limbs and joints
   - Poor vision resulting from eye strain
   - Headaches, dizziness and fatigue
   - Respiratory problems associated with dust and textile fibres

2. Street vendors

   - Exposure to weather—extreme temperatures, wind, rain and sun
   - Poor access to clean water
   - Poor sanitation from dirty streets and poor drainage, as well as waste produce from other vendors
   - Diseases transmitted by vermin
   - Lead poisoning and respiratory problems from vehicle fumes
   - Musculoskeletal problems associated with ergonomic hazards at workstations and static postures
   - Risk of physical harm from municipal authorities, members of the public or other traders

3. Waste pickers

   - Exposure to weather—extreme temperatures, wind, rain and sun
   - Poor sanitation and limited or no access to clean water
   - Exposure to dangerous domestic and industrial waste, including toxic substances such as lead and asbestos
   - Exposure to other dangerous matter, including blood, faecal matter, broken glass, needles, sharp metal objects and animal carcasses
   - Back and limb pain, itchy skin/rashes
   - Diseases transmitted by vermin, flies and mosquitoes
   - Specific high risk of tuberculosis, bronchitis, asthma, pneumonia, dysentery and parasites

SOURCE: Martha Chen, Joann Vanek, Francie Lund, James Heintz, with Renana Jhabvala, and Christine Bonner, "Box 4.2. Occupational Health and Safety Hazards," in *Progress of the World's Women 2005: Women, Work, and Poverty*, United Nations Development Fund for Women, 2005, http://www.unifem.org/attachments/products/PoWW2005_eng.pdf (accessed April 8, 2006)

---

are at a higher risk of experiencing human rights abuses, including a lack of access to social services and basic infrastructure (passable roads, clean water, reliable sanitation, etc.); a greater chance of becoming ill or disabled and of losing property; fewer work-related benefits and securities; fewer housing and property rights; and generally worse health, less education, and shorter life spans. Some specific risks for garment workers, street vendors, and waste pickers are outlined in Table 7.2.

Female workers are at a higher risk of poverty not only because average wages are lower for women than for men (see Table 7.3; "own account" workers are those who produce goods for their own use; "private wage" earners are those working in the private sector; "public wage" earners work in the public sector; "domestic" earners work in cleaning, cooking, child care, etc.) but also because women tend to work fewer hours due to their unpaid responsibilities in the home and community. These responsibilities—which include the care of children, elderly, and sick family members; domestic chores such as cooking, cleaning, making clothing, and growing

food; and unpaid work in the community—are referred to as "unpaid care work." This designation helps to distinguish it from paid domestic labor (formal or informal), such as cooking, cleaning, and/or child care in other people's homes or businesses.

UNIFEM identifies four "dimensions" that create the relationship between work—paid and unpaid—and poverty for women:

- The *temporal dimension*: Because women spend more time doing unpaid work within the home, performing housework and child care, they have less time to spend doing paid work outside the home, although studies have shown that, overall, women spend more time working overall than men do. This means that women tend to do more part-time paid work, which in turn means that they earn less money. In developing countries women spend much of their unpaid time performing heavier physical chores such as collecting water and fuel and growing and harvesting crops, leaving them even less time for paid work as well as for child care.

- The *spatial dimension*: Women in both developing and developed countries sometimes are forced to migrate to other areas, regions, or even countries to find paid work. This might mean leaving a rural home to work in a city (or vice versa) or migrating from, for example, a country like Mexico to perform seasonal farm work in a country like the United States. In either case, a woman who migrates for work will have to find someone to care for her family while she is away. At the same time, however, women who have children often are not able to migrate to regions with better work opportunities.

- The *employment segmentation dimension*: Women's traditional role as caretakers within the home has led to a narrow choice of work outside the home. Without specific training or education, women in almost every culture tend to fall into the same occupations: domestic servants, clothing and textile workers, teachers, and care workers. These occupations tend to be relatively unstable, informal, lower-paying, and, in some cases (such as in the textile industry), more dangerous than other jobs.

- The *valuation dimension*: The value placed on work that is seen as traditionally female is related to employment segmentation. "Women's work," meaning the kind of work that women typically do for free within their homes and communities, generally is considered less valuable than work that is perceived to require more training or education. Therefore, it is less regulated and brings in lower pay.

Gender is not the only factor that determines women's greater likelihood of impoverishment and

TABLE 7.3

Women's hourly earnings as a percentage of men's hourly earnings, by selected country and type of employment, 2005

	Costa Rica	Egypt	El Salvador	Ghana	South Africa
Formal					
Non-agricultural					
Employers	56.6	n.a.	78.9	n.a.	n.a.
Own-account	62.1	n.a.	45.1	54.6	n.a.
Private wage	84.6	151.9	87.5	n.a.	89.5
Public wage	87.7	107.6	116.2	84.2	95.6
Agricultural					
Private wage	85.1	n.a.	105.4	n.a.	66.3
Informal					
Non-agricultural					
Employers	97.6	n.a.	83.8	n.a.	83.6
Own-account	50.6	n.a.	65.1	80.2	59.6
All wage	n.a.	263.3	n.a.	69.8	n.a.
Private wage	79.5	317.1	75.4	n.a.	107.0
Public wage	n.a.	n.a.	135.2	88.0	99.2
Domestic	57.4	n.a.	56.2	n.a.	100.0
Agricultural					
Own-account	53.3	n.a.	56.9	65.0	n.a.
Private wage	n.a.	n.a.	86.4	n.a.	98.5
Public wage	n.a.	n.a.	177.6	n.a.	n.a.

Notes: n.a.=data not available or insufficient observations to derive statistically significant estimates. Hourly earnings include all reported employment income. Usual hours worked were used to compute a standard hourly rate. Individuals reporting excessive hours worked (generally, more than 140 per week) were dropped. The value of non-wage benefits and in-kind payments were included in earnings calculations. However, there is a tendency to underestimate these contributions. Also, only employed persons who reported their income are included in the estimations. The computation of self-employment income varies from country to country. For the Egyptian household data, no information on self-employment income is provided. In most cases, self-employment earnings included the value of goods produced in a family enterprise.

SOURCE: Martha Chen, Joann Vanek, Francie Lund, James Heintz, with Renana Jhabvala and Christine Bonner, "Table 3.6. Women's Hourly Earnings as a Percentage of Men's Hourly Earnings," in *Progress of the World's Women 2005: Women, Work, and Poverty*, United Nations Development Fund for Women, 2005, http://www.unifem.org/attachments/products/PoWW2005_eng.pdf (accessed April 8, 2006)

difficulty obtaining and holding on to work. In different cultures religion, race, and especially class play a role. However, as the dimensions of work described above demonstrate, women in general—in nearly every culture—experience living and working conditions that make economic advancement difficult.

Poor women who do work typically find employment in more or less undesirable jobs. Some are degrading; others are dangerous. Some cause health problems, while others are simply monotonous. Women living in extreme poverty tend to fall into the same types of work regardless of where they live in the world: begging, digging for garbage, sweatshop labor, farm work, street vending, and prostitution—voluntary and forced—are some of the most common types of employment for poor women.

Women's Wages and Poverty Rates in the Developed World

According to the Women's Learning Partnership for Rights, Development, and Peace (WLP), a nongovernmental organization (NGO) that works as a consultant group to the United Nations, in every country in the world women's pay is lower than men's, including countries in the developed world. Globally speaking, women earn an average of 30% to 40% of what men earn. Living in a developed country does not guarantee a working woman equity in wages: the WLP reports that in France, Germany, Italy, and the United Kingdom, women earn an average of 75% of what men earn, while in Australia, Sri Lanka, Tanzania, and Vietnam women's wages are 90% of men's.

THE UNITED STATES. Median weekly full-time earnings of American women in 2004 were about 80% of the earnings of men (Bureau of Labor Statistics, *Women in the Labor Force: A Databook*, May 2005). This is in spite of the Equal Pay Act of 1963 (EPA), which outlawed unequal pay for equal work. (American women at that time had median earnings equal to fifty-eight cents for every dollar earned by American men.) The National Women's Law Center reports that as of 2004 African-American women in the United States had median earnings of sixty-five cents for every dollar earned by white men, and Hispanic women earned just fifty-six cents for every dollar earned by white men (http://www.nwlc.org/pdf/PaycheckFairnessActApr06.pdf).

Among U.S. workers active in the labor force for at least twenty-seven weeks during 2004, a slightly higher percentage of women (6.2%) than men (5%) lived in poverty (Bureau of Labor Statistics, *A Profile of the Working Poor, 2004*, May 2006). However, for working families (those with at least one family member in the labor force for half the year or more), the rates displayed a wider gap, with families headed by single women (22.6%) experiencing a significantly higher poverty rate than families headed by single men (13.2%).

According to a joint report by the AFL–CIO (American Federation of Labor–Congress of Industrial Organizations) and the Institute for Women's Policy Research ("Equal Pay for Working Families: National and State Data on Pay Gap and Its Costs," 1999), closing the wage gap between the sexes would increase women's total family income by $4,000 a year and could cut poverty rates in half.

CANADA. According to the Canadian Research Institute for the Advancement of Women (CRIAW), as of 2005 one in seven Canadian women (2.4 million in total) was living in poverty, and women working full-time, year-round earned just 71% of what men earned ("Women in Poverty," 2005 http://www.criaw-icref.ca/). In fact, Canada, which is one of the wealthiest countries in the world, had the fifth-largest wage gap in the developed world in 2004, after Japan, Korea, Portugal, and Spain (*OECD in Figures*, 2004). Statistics Canada reports that as of 2001 (the most recent figures available at the time of publication) the average income of women with a post-secondary degree was Can$29,539; average income for men with less than a ninth-grade education was Can$30,731, indicating that higher levels of education do not necessarily lead to higher pay for Canadian women.

Unmarried women under age sixty-five living alone had a poverty incidence of 38.4% in 2004, according to Statistics Canada (http://www40.statcan.ca/l01/cst01/famil41a.htm). Because many of these single women also headed families, children under age eighteen who lived in households headed by a single woman suffered a higher incidence of poverty (52.1%) than children living in two-parent families (11.6%). Average total income in families headed by single women (Can$34,100) was significantly less than in families headed by men alone (Can$52,900) in 2004 (http://www40.statcan.ca/l01/cst01/famil05a.htm). In fact, 37% of single mothers who work make less than Can$10 an hour, according to the CRIAW. "Women in Poverty," also observes that the highest rates of poverty and the lowest wages for women in Canada occur among Aboriginal (Native Canadian), immigrant, minority, and disabled women. The average annual income of Aboriginal women is Can$13,300, compared with Can$19,350 for non-Aboriginal women. Immigrant women who have college degrees earn an average of Can$14,000 less than Canadian-born women with college degrees. Minority women in Canada earn an average of Can$16,621 annually, while disabled women earn about Can$17,000 a year.

THE EUROPEAN UNION. In the European Union (EU) women's earnings averaged about 16% lower than men's, according to the European Commission's (EC) publication *The Social Situation in the European Union 2004*. This finding was confirmed by the EC's *Report from the Commission to the Council, the European Parliament, the European Economic and Social Committee and the Committee of the Regions on Equality between Women and Men, 2005*, which also noted that the gap had closed slightly—to 15%—with the addition of ten more countries to the Union in 2004 (the Czech Republic, Estonia, Cyprus, Latvia, Lithuania, Hungary, Malta, Poland, Slovenia, and Slovakia).

POOR WOMEN'S HEALTH

It is not surprising that poor people suffer from more health problems and receive a lower quality of health care than their nonpoor counterparts. Women, however, suffer disproportionately, first because there simply are more poor women than poor men in the world, and second because, as the bearers of children, women face a different set of potential diseases, illnesses, and injuries related to their reproductive systems.

The Millennium Development Goal of improving *maternal* health, as opposed to *women's* health, points to the significance of reproduction in the overall picture of women's health, as well as in the social and economic status of their families. A mother's health typically reflects the health of her entire family, just as a mother's education reflects that of her children (see section below). Of the link between poverty and maternal health, United Nations Population Fund (UNFPA) executive director Thoraya Obaid stated in October 2005: "If women are healthy then they can jump start the life of their family and the economy" ("Women's Health Fuelling Poverty," BBC News, October 12, 2005, http://news.bbc.co.uk/2/hi/health/4331996.stm).

Reproductive Health and Poverty

In *State of World Population 2005. The Promise of Equality: Gender Equity, Reproductive Health, and the MDGs* the UNFPA cites illnesses of the reproductive system as the leading cause of death and disability of women globally and the second most common cause of poor health in the world after communicable diseases. According to an estimate by the Alan Guttmacher Institute, women's reproductive health issues result in the loss of as much as 250 million years' worth of productive time each year and a 20% reduction of women's overall productivity ("The Benefits of Investing in Sexual and Reproductive Health," *Issues in Brief*, 2004). The UNFPA reported in 2005 that complications of pregnancy and childbirth kill one woman every minute and injure twenty others—99% of them in developing countries. Figure 7.4 provides a breakdown of the causes of maternal death as reported by the World Health Organization (WHO) in 2005. According to the *State of the World Population*, several aspects of reproductive health have wide-reaching and long-term socioeconomic effects on families, communities, countries, and even entire regions.

Because most maternal deaths occur in already impoverished countries that are clustered together geographically, their regional impact is particularly acute. At the most personal level, children who lose their mothers tend to experience emotional problems that eventually may make them less productive as adults, and households lose valuable income without an adult female wage earner; many families, in fact, are pushed over the brink of poverty as a result of the high cost of health care when a mother becomes sick. (See Table 7.4.) Communities feel the loss because women in developing countries perform so many essential unpaid tasks, such as caring for children and elders, growing and harvesting food, and gathering fuel and water. High rates of maternal deaths affect the overall economic situation in a region in terms of lost productivity and lost potential for economic, cultural, and technological expansion.

WHO's *World Health Report 2005: Make Every Mother and Child Count* warns that if progress on improving maternal health continues at the slow rate it has seen since the 1990s, the Millennium Development Goals will not be met by 2015. Of the 136 million births every year, 529,000 result in the death of the mother; as of 2005, 300 million women were experiencing illnesses brought on by pregnancy or childbirth. WHO maintains that most of those deaths could be prevented with increased access to skilled care during and following childbirth. In 2005, 43% of mothers and newborns received some care at birth, but not enough to prevent the complications that often arise. Additionally, WHO reports that increased public expenditures on health care, higher wages for health care workers, and universal access to medical care are essential to reaching the MDGs, especially those that relate to women and children.

Table 7.5 illustrates the link between reproductive rights and the MDGs. Included in reproductive rights are issues such as violence against women and the rights to marry voluntarily, space children as desired, receive clear and accurate information about the reproductive process, and benefit from scientific progress. For women living in low-income countries, these rights cannot be

FIGURE 7.4

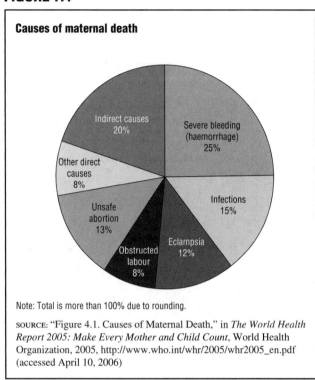

Causes of maternal death

Note: Total is more than 100% due to rounding.

SOURCE: "Figure 4.1. Causes of Maternal Death," in *The World Health Report 2005: Make Every Mother and Child Count*, World Health Organization, 2005, http://www.who.int/whr/2005/whr2005_en.pdf (accessed April 10, 2006)

TABLE 7.4

Economic effects of fatal illness in the household, 1992

	Timing of impact			
Type of effect	Before illness	During illness	Immediate effect of death	Long term effect of death
Effect on production and earnings	Organization of economic activity Residential location	Reduced productivity of ill adult Reallocation of labor	Lost output of deceased	Lost output of deceased Reallocation of land and labor
Effect on investment and consumption	Insurance Medical costs of prevention Precautionary savings Transfer to other households	Medical cost of treatment Dissaving Changes in consumption and investment	Funeral costs Transfers Legal fees	Changes in type and quantity of investment and consumption
Effect on household health and composition	Extended family Fertility	Reduced allocation of labor to health maintaining activities	Loss of deceased	Poor health of surviving household members Dissolution or reconstitution of household
Psychic costs		Disutility of ill person	Disutility to person Grief of loved ones	

SOURCE: Margaret E. Greene and Thomas Merrick, "Table 1. Economic Effects of Fatal Illness in the Household," in *Poverty Reduction: Does Reproductive Health Matter?*, HNP Discussion Paper 33399, The World Bank, The International Bank for Reconstruction and Development, July 2005, http://www-wds.worldbank.org/servlet/WDSContentServer/WDSP/IB/2005/08/22/000012009_20050822094645/Rendered/PDF/333990HNP0Gree1tyReduction01public1.pdf (accessed April 10, 2006). Data based on Over et al., 1992.

TABLE 7.5

Reproductive rights and the MDGs (Millennium Development Goals)

Elements of reproductive rights	Examples of rights-based actions	Relevance to specific Millennium Development Goals (MDGs)
Right to life and survival	Prevent avoidable maternal and infant deaths End neglect of and discrimination against girls that can contribute to premature deaths Ensure access to information and methods to prevent sexually transmitted infections, including HIV	Promote gender equality and empower women (MDG 3) Reduce child mortality (MDG 4) Improve maternal health (MDG 5) Combat HIV/AIDS, malaria and other diseases (MDG 6)
Right to liberty and security of the person	Take measures to prevent, punish and eradicate all forms of gender-based violence Enable women, men and adolescents to make reproductive decisions free of coercion, violence and discrimination Eliminate female genital mutilation/cutting Stop sexual trafficking	Eradicate extreme poverty and hunger (MDG 1) Promote gender equality and empower women (MDG 3) Reduce child mortality (MDG 4) Improve maternal health (MDG 5) Combat HIV/AIDS, malaria and other diseases (MDG 6)
Right to seek, receive and impart information	Make information about reproductive health and rights issues and related policies and laws widely and freely available Provide full information for people to make informed reproductive health decisions Support reproductive health and family life education both in and out of schools	Promote gender equality and empower women (MDG 3) Combat HIV/AIDS, malaria and other diseases (MDG 6)
Right to decide the number, timing and spacing of children	Provide people with full information that enables them to choose and correctly use a family planning method Provide access to a full range of modern contraceptive methods Enable adolescent girls to delay pregnancy	Eradicate extreme poverty and hunger (MDG 1) Achieve universal primary education (MDG 2) Promote gender equality and empower women (MDG 3) Ensure environmental stability (MDG 7)
Right to voluntarily marry and establish a family	Prevent and legislate against child and forced marriages Prevent and treat sexually transmitted infections that cause infertility Provide reproductive health services, including for HIV prevention, to married adolescent girls and their husbands	Achieve universal primary education (MDG 2) Promote gender equality and empower women (MDG 3) Reduce child mortality (MDG 4) Improve maternal health (MDG 5) Combat HIV/AIDS, malaria and other diseases (MDG 6)
Right to the highest attainable standard of health	Provide access to affordable, acceptable, comprehensive and quality reproductive health information and services Allocate available resources fairly, prioritizing those with least access to reproductive health education and services	Eradicate extreme poverty and hunger (MDG 1) Promote gender equality and empower women (MDG 3) Reduce child mortality (MDG 4) Improve maternal health (MDG 5) Combat HIV/AIDS, malaria and other diseases (MDG 6)
Right to the benefits of scientific progress	Fund contraceptive research, including female-controlled methods, microbicides and male methods Offer a variety of contraceptive options Provide access to emergency obstetric care that can prevent maternal deaths and obstetric fistula	Promote gender equality and empower women (MDG 3) Reduce child mortality (MDG 4) Improve maternal health (MDG 5) Combat HIV/AIDS, malaria and other diseases (MDG 6)
Right to non-discrimination and equality in education and employment	Prohibit discrimination in employment based on pregnancy, proof of contraceptive use or motherhood Establish programmes to keep girls in schools Ensure pregnant and married adolescent girls, and young mothers, are able to complete their education	Eradicate extreme poverty and hunger (MDG 1) Achieve universal primary education (MDG 2) Promote gender equality and empower women (MDG 3) Combat HIV/AIDS, malaria and other diseases (MDG 6)

SOURCE: "Reproductive Rights and the MDGs," in *State of World Population 2005*, United Nations Population Fund, 2005, http://www.unfpa.org/swp/2005/pdf/en_swp05.pdf (accessed April 8, 2006)

taken for granted. In fact, many are prohibited from using contraception—or from even receiving information about it—and must marry whomever their families choose for them. In some cultures, going against these conventions can place the woman in a position that results in physical and emotional violence. The inability to decide how many children to have or how many years apart to have them can easily overwhelm a family's finances, particularly a family that is already poor. There are also health considerations: a woman who can control her reproductive choices is more likely to receive adequate health care, and thus less likely to die in childbirth.

In *Poverty Reduction: Does Reproductive Health Matter?* (World Bank Health, Nutrition and Population, July 2005), Margaret E. Greene and Thomas Merrick argue that controversy over reproductive rights—namely, abortion and birth control—has hit poor women particularly hard. According to Greene and Merrick, the issue

has actually harmed poor women's health: governments have been pressured to cut funding for medical care and family planning, and the United Nations was forced to drop the goal of achieving universal reproductive health care from the Millennium Declaration. The United Nations Population Fund reports in *State of the World Population 2005* that as of 2005 the world's women suffered disproportionately from sexual and reproductive health problems—nearly 35% of women globally versus less than 20% of men.

Figure 7.5 shows the percentages of the poorest and wealthiest women who give birth with the attendance of skilled medical personnel in selected low-income countries. Poor women are far less likely to have a skilled attendant present during the births of their children. In Vietnam, where 100% of the richest women have access to medical personnel during childbirth, only 58% of the poorest women do. In Ethiopia just 1% of the poorest

FIGURE 7.5

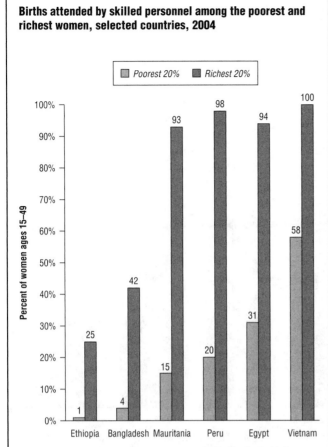

Births attended by skilled personnel among the poorest and richest women, selected countries, 2004

Note: Skilled personnel defined to include a doctor, nurse or trained midwife.

SOURCE: "Figure 2. Births Attended by Skilled Personnel among the Poorest and Richest Women," in *State of World Population 2005*, United Nations Population Fund, 2005, http://www.unfpa.org/swp/2005/pdf/en_swp05.pdf (accessed April 8, 2006). Data from World Bank, 2004, *Round II Country Reports on Health, Nutrition, and Population Conditions among the Poor and the Better-Off in 56 Countries*.

FIGURE 7.6

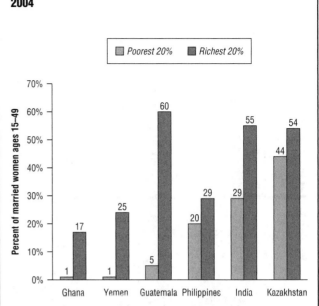

Contraceptive use according to wealth, selected countries, 2004

SOURCE: "Figure 3. Contraceptive Use according to Wealth," in *State of World Population 2005*, United Nations Population Fund, 2005, http://www.unfpa.org/swp/2005/pdf/en_swp05.pdf (accessed April 8, 2006). Data from World Bank, 2004, *Round II Country Reports on Health, Nutrition, and Population Conditions among the Poor and the Better-Off in 56 Countries*.

women receive medical attendance at childbirth, versus 25% of the wealthiest women. These numbers demonstrate that the world's poorest women do not have reproductive rights equal to those of their nonpoor counterparts.

Lack of family planning options most strongly affects poor young women, who may not be prepared for pregnancy and parenthood physically, emotionally, or financially. Figure 7.6 shows the disparity of contraceptive use among the poorest and richest women in Ghana, Yemen, Guatemala, the Philippines, India, and Kazakhstan. In Guatemala, for example, only 5% of the nation's poorest women use contraceptives compared with 60% of wealthy women. Figure 7.7 compares childbearing among the poorest and richest women under age eighteen in Niger, Nicaragua, Nepal, Tanzania, Kenya, Bolivia, and Turkey. In Niger nearly three-quarters (72%) of poor women had given birth by age eighteen,

compared with two-fifths (39%) of wealthy women. In reviewing economic and sociological publications on the link between poverty and early childbearing, Greene and Merrick cite the following points of connection:

- Poor health outcomes for the young mother and her child: higher risk of obstetric complications, leading to higher maternal mortality and morbidity (illness or disease) if she survives; increased risk of abortion and abortion complications if the abortion is unsafe; and low birth weight and other problems for the newborn

- Poor educational outcomes for both the mother and her child, including dropping out of school and less schooling for the child

- Lower and/or altered investment and spending patterns in the mother's immediate and extended family (costs of medical care and child care, for example, can make it difficult or impossible to save money)

- Possibly lower labor force participation by the young mother, with less opportunity to contribute to household income

- Reduced community participation and greater chances of divorce or single parenthood

Early childbearing tends to occur more often in poor countries but even in wealthier countries the highest rates of fertility among adolescents are found among the

FIGURE 7.7

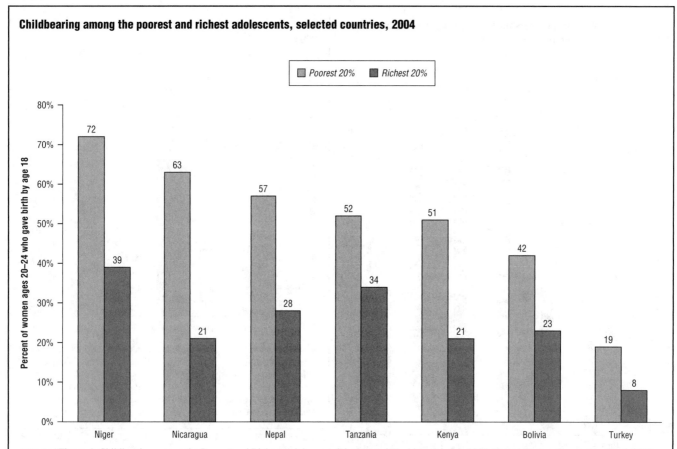

Childbearing among the poorest and richest adolescents, selected countries, 2004

SOURCE: "Figure 4. Childbearing among the Poorest and Richest Adolescents," in *State of World Population 2005*, United Nations Population Fund, 2005, http://www.unfpa.org/swp/2005/pdf/en_swp05.pdf (accessed April 8, 2006). Data from Rani, M. and E. Lule, 2004, "Exploring the Socioeconomic Dimension of Adolescent Reproductive Health: A Multicountry Analysis" *International Family Planning Perspectives*, 30 (3): 112.

poorest groups. Greene and Merrick reported that in 2004, for example, out of a sample of fifty-five countries, the average adolescent fertility rate (the number of women who had given birth before age twenty) for the richest group was 62.6 per 100,000 population, versus 148.6 per 100,000 population for the poorest group. The highest regional rates for adolescent poor women were in Latin America and the Caribbean (172.6 births per 100,000 population), followed by sub-Saharan Africa (169.6). The sampled region with the lowest adolescent fertility rate was East Asia, at forty-six births per 100,000, but it is important to note that in that region only four countries were sample, compared with twenty-nine countries in sub-Saharan.

According to Greene and Merrick, studies have shown that poor women of all ages experience more difficulties with pregnancy and childbearing, but adolescent mothers have more extreme problems because their bodies may not be developed enough to sustain the physical challenges of giving birth. In developing countries women aged fifteen to nineteen are twice as likely to die from complications of childbirth than women in their twenties. Women in poor countries tend to marry and

begin having children earlier than women in wealthier countries. This is partly the cause of the significantly higher number of maternal deaths in underdeveloped and developing regions. (See Table 7.6.) In fact, as Table 7.6 illustrates, the total number of maternal deaths increased annually from 515,000 in 1995 to 529,000 in 2000. Developing regions overall saw an increase from 512,000 in 1995 to 527,000 in 2000, with Asia experiencing the greatest increase. Figure 7.8 shows the various factors that link early pregnancy with poverty. Factors such as a lack of education, childhood and adult illness and malnutrition, a lack of access to natural resources and involvement in the global economy, and high mortality rates can all be linked to higher fertility rates, which in turn lead to lower per capita income.

OBSTETRIC FISTULA. One of the most serious health and social consequences of childbirth in poor countries—particularly in sub-Saharan Africa and South Asia—is the development of obstetric fistula. This childbirth-related injury is caused by exceptionally long labor, often as long as five to seven days, that cuts off blood flow to the vagina, bladder, and/or rectum. The resulting holes in the tissue leave women unable to control the flow of

TABLE 7.6

Comparison of 1995 and 2000 regional and global totals of maternal mortality

Region	2000 Maternal mortality ratio	2000 Maternal deaths (in thousands)	1995 Maternal mortality ratio	1995 Maternal deaths (in thousands)
World total	**400**	**529,000**	**400**	**515,000**
Developed regions*	20	2,500	21	2,800
Europe	28	2.2	36	3.2
Developing regions	440	527,000	440	512,000
Africa	830	251,000	1,000	273,000
Northern Africa	130	4,600	200	7,200
Sub-Saharan Africa	920	247,000	1,100	265,000
Asia	330	253,000	280	217,000
Eastern Asia	55	11,000	60	13,000
South-central Asia	520	207,000	410	158,000
South-eastern Asia	210	25,000	300	35,000
Western Asia	190	9,800	230	11,000
Latin America & the Caribbean	190	22,000	190	22,000
Oceania	240	530	260	560

*Developed regions include Canada, United States of America, Japan, Australia and New Zealand, which are excluded from the regional averages.

SOURCE: Margaret E. Greene and Thomas Merrick, "Table 5. Comparison of 1995 and 2000 Regional and Global Totals," in *Poverty Reduction: Does Reproductive Health Matter?*, HNP Discussion Paper 33399, The World Bank, The International Bank for Reconstruction and Development, July 2005, http://www-wds.worldbank.org/servlet/WDSContentServer/WDSP/IB/2005/08/22/000012009_200508220 94645/Rendered/PDF/333990HNP0Gree1tyReduction01public1.pdf (accessed April 10, 2006). Data from AbouZahr and Wardlaw, 2004.

FIGURE 7.8

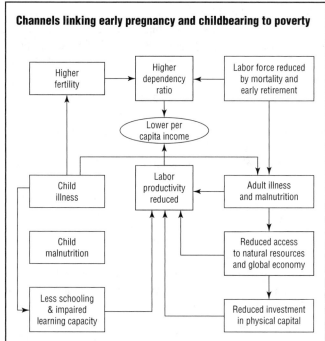

Channels linking early pregnancy and childbearing to poverty

SOURCE: Margaret E. Greene and Thomas Merrick, "Figure 2. Channels Linking Early Pregnancy and Childbearing to Poverty," in *Poverty Reduction: Does Reproductive Health Matter?*, HNP Discussion Paper 33399, The World Bank, The International Bank for Reconstruction and Development, July 2005, http://www-wds.worldbank.org/servlet/WDSContentServer/WDSP/IB/2005/08/22/000012009_20050822094645/Rendered/PDF/333990HNP0Gree1tyReduction01public1.pdf (accessed April 10, 2006). Data from Ruger et al., 2001.

urine and feces, which leak out constantly. Nerve damage to the legs, severe infections, and kidney disease are also common among fistula sufferers.

According to the Fistula Foundation (www.fistulafoundation.org/) and the United Nations Population Fund (UNFPA), more than two million women in the developing world are known to suffer from obstetric fistula, which was virtually eradicated in wealthier countries when caesarian sections became commonplace in the late nineteenth century. The actual number of women who live with the condition is believed to be much higher, since it is rarely discussed and most women who suffer from it never get medical help. WHO estimates that in Nigeria alone, for example, as many as 800,000 women have fistulas, with 20,000 more developing the condition every year ("545 Women Operated on during 'Fistula Fortnight,'" March 7, 2005). Globally, obstetric fistula is believed to occur in 50,000 to 100,000 women per year, most of them under the age of twenty.

According to UNFPA's Campaign to End Fistula (www.endfistula.org/):

> Poverty, malnutrition, poor health services, early marriage, and gender discrimination are interlinked root causes of obstetric fistula. Poverty is the main social risk factor because it is associated with early marriage and malnutrition and because poverty reduces a woman's chances of getting timely obstetric care.

Obstetric fistula is a cause of poverty among women as well as a consequence. Sufferers are often abandoned by their husbands and families and ostracized by their communities because of the stigma attached to their condition. Many are driven from their homes and left to survive or die on their own. The condition can, however, be repaired with surgery, which has about a 93% cure rate, according to the Fistula Foundation. However, few women in affected regions either know about the surgery, which costs from $100 to $400, or have access to it, and most cannot afford it.

In 2003 the first major report on fistula—*Obstetric Fistula Needs Assessment Report: Findings from Nine African Countries*—was published jointly by the UNFPA and the nonprofit organization EngenderHealth. Focusing on the countries most affected by obstetric fistula, the report identified seven critical needs of regions with the highest numbers of fistula sufferers, including education about the physical dangers of early marriage and pregnancy, family planning and maternal health; increased medical care in the form of prevention and treatment; social support services to address the physical and psychological needs of fistula sufferers.

EDUCATION: A TOOL TO LIFT WOMEN OUT OF POVERTY

The Beijing Platform declared that education is an essential human right that contributes to economic development at all levels of society—a declaration that has been supported by the UN, UN Educational, Scientific, and Cultural Organization (UNESCO), the World Bank, and most nongovernmental organizations. However, according to the *Education for All Global Monitoring Report 2006: Literacy for Life* (2005, http://portal.unesco.org/education/en/ev.php-URL_ID=43283&URL_DO=DO_TOPIC&URL_SECTION=201.html), at least 771 million adults over the age of fifteen—one-fifth of the world's adult population—cannot read or write at a functional level; at least two-thirds of them are women.

In its *State of the World Population 2002: People, Poverty, and Possibilities* (2002, http://www.unfpa.org/swp/2002/english/ch1/), the United Nations Population Fund (UNFPA) reports that 31% of women had no formal education in 2000, versus 18% of men. There are many reasons for this disparity, and poverty is chief among them: although women are almost universally less likely to attain high levels of education, being female and poor is, according to the UNFPA report, a "double disadvantage." In rural areas the long walking distances to schools discourage families from sending girls because they fear girls will be sexually assaulted on the way. Fees for attendance, books, and uniforms can also affect whether girls are sent to school. Again, girls in some regions are vulnerable to sexual exploitation from wealthier men who offer to pay for girls' schooling in exchange for sex. Early marriage and pregnancy also cause millions of girls to drop out of school every year. Many families decide to keep daughters at home to help tend and harvest crops, do housework, and care for elders and young siblings. The costs associated with educating girls are generally not seen as worthwhile because girls are not expected to continue

their education or earn a living when they grow up. More simply, in many cultures girls are not valued in the same way that boys are, so to many impoverished families educating them seems like a waste of time and money—and in some places it is altogether forbidden.

Barbara Herz and Gene B. Sperling report in *What Works in Girls' Education: Evidence and Policies from the Developing World* (2004, http://www.cfr.org/content/publications/attachments/Girls_Education_full.pdf) that education for girls in developing countries is essential for economic success at all levels of society. The benefits of educating girls are seen from families to nations, in the forms of higher wages, faster economic growth, and more productive farming. This in turn results in decreased levels of malnutrition; women having smaller, healthier, more educated families; reducing the spread of HIV/AIDS; reducing rates of violence against women; and fostering democratic participation in society.

According to Herz and Sperling, when girls attend school just one year beyond the average, they eventually earn 10% to 20% more than average as adults. On the macroeconomic level, even modest increases in the number of women receiving a secondary education can lead to an increase in annual per capita income of 0.3%; likewise, as per capita growth continues, more girls achieve higher levels of education—a cycle that is beneficial, ultimately, for everyone. Similarly, the more education women have, the lower their rates of fertility will be. In Brazil, for example, illiterate women have an average of six children each, whereas literate women average 2.5 children each. Lower overall fertility rates lead to healthier, better-educated children. In fact, infant mortality rates are between 5% and 10% lower among girls who stay in school just one year longer than average. In countries where girls receive as many years of schooling as boys, infant mortality rates are 25% lower than in countries that do not have educational gender parity (equality).

Herz and Sperling conclude that governments of low-income countries can encourage families to educate their daughters and increase overall educational gender parity by eliminating school fees, providing local schools with flexible schedules that are safe for girls, and focusing on providing a quality education that realistically takes into account the needs of girls and their families.

Table 7.7 shows which countries achieved the Millennium Development Goal of gender parity in education as of 2002, those that are likely to achieve the goal by 2005, those that are likely to achieve the goal by 2015, and those countries that are in danger of not achieving the goal by 2015.

VIOLENCE AGAINST WOMEN

Violence against women happens in every economic class of every culture around the world. While it is a

TABLE 7.7

Country prospects for the achievement of gender parity in primary and secondary education by 2005 and 2015

	Gender parity in secondary education				Number of countries
	Achieved in 2002	Likely to be achieved in 2005	Likely to be achieved in 2015	At risk of not achieving goal the by 2015	
Achieved in 2002	Albania, Anguilla, Armenia, Australia, Azerbaijan, Bahamas, Barbados, Belarus, Bulgaria, Canada, Chile, China, Croatia, Cyprus, Czech Republic, Ecuador, France, Georgia, Germany, Greece, Hungary, Indonesia, Israel, Italy, Jamaica, Japan, Jordan, Kazakhstan, Kyrgyzstan, Latvia, Lithuania, Malta, Mauritius, Netherlands, Norway, Oman, Republic of Korea, Republic of Moldova, Romania, Russian Federation, Serbia and Montenegro, Seychelles, Slovakia, Slovenia, The former Yugoslav Republic of Macedonia, Ukraine, United Arab Emirates, United States, Uzbekistan \n49	Austria, Bolivia, Guyana, Kenya \n4	Switzerland, Argentina, Belize, Botswana \n4	Gambia, Mauritania, Myanmar, Peru, Poland, Rwanda, Uganda, Zimbabwe, Bahrain, Bangladesh, Belgium, Brunei Darussalam, Colombia, Costa Rica, Denmark, Dominican Republic, Finland, Iceland, Ireland, Kuwait, Lesotho, Luxembourg, Malaysia, Maldives, Mexico, Mongolia, Namibia, Netherlands Antilles, New Zealand, Nicaragua, Palestinian Autonomous Territories, Philippines, Qatar, Saint Lucia, Saint Vincent and the Grenadines, Samoa, Spain, Suriname, Tonga, Trinidad and Tobago, United Kingdom, Vanuatu, Venezuela \n43	100
Likely to be achieved in 2005	Estonia \n1	Islamic Republic of Iran \n1	Ghana, Saudi Arabia \n2	India, Syrian Arab Republic, Lebanon, Panama, Tunisia \n5	9
Likely to be achieved in 2015	Cuba \n1	Egypt \n1		Nepal, Senegal, Tajikistan, Togo, Zambia, Brazil, Portugal \n7	9
At risk of not achieving the goal by 2015	El Salvador, Swaziland, Paraguay \n3		Cameroon, Macao (China), South Africa, Viet Nam \n4	Benin, Burkina Faso, Burundi, Cambodia, Chad, Comoros, Côte d'Ivoire, Djibouti, Eritrea, Ethiopia, Guatemala, Lao People's Democratic Republic, Malawi, Mali, Morocco, Mozambique, Niger, Papua New Guinea, Sudan, Turkey, Yemen, Algeria, Aruba, British Virgin Islands \n24	31
Number of countries	54	6	10	79	149

Note: Where countries are shown in white, enrollment disparities at the expense of boys are observed in secondary education.

SOURCE: "Table 2. 10. Country Prospects for the Achievement of Gender Parity in Primary and Secondary Education by 2005 and 2015," in *Education for All Global Monitoring Report 2006: Literacy for Life*, United Nations Educational, Scientific and Cultural Organization, 2005, http://www.unesco.org/education/GMR2006/full/chapt2_eng.pdf (accessed April 8, 2006). Copyright © UNESCO, 2005

multifaceted social problem, many experts consider it to be largely a health issue because of the physical and emotional havoc it wreaks on its victims; the other dimension of violence against women is that it is a human rights issue. Amnesty International calls it "a major human rights scandal and a public health crisis" ("Women, Violence, and Health," March 2004, http://www.web.amnesty.org/library/Index/ENGACT770012005?open&of=ENG-366). Although hard data are difficult to obtain because of the covert nature of the problem, there is a known link between violence against women and poverty. Figure 7.9 shows percentages of women in selected low-income countries who believed wife-beating was justified as of 2004. The reasons given—presented in the graph's "Note"—are indicative of the status of women in these cultures.

In *Addressing Violence against Women and Achieving the Millennium Development Goals* (2005, http://www.who.int/gender/documents/MDGs&VAWSept05.pdf), the WHO cites two main reasons poor women are more vulnerable to violence than their nonpoor counterparts: fewer resources—in terms of both money and support services—to help women avoid or escape violence; and

the stressors of poverty, such as hunger, unemployment, and lack of education, that may lead some men to become violent or exacerbate an already violent situation. In addition, women who work in unregulated, informal employment are often subject to physical, sexual, or psychological abuse by their employers. In both developing and developed countries, social standards and enforced gender roles contribute to the incidence of violence.

The WHO report recommends several global economic actions that can affect women who are routine victims of violence:

- Promote increased access to postprimary, vocational and technical education for women

- Address gender gaps in earnings as well as barriers to accessing credit for women

- Extend and upgrade childcare benefits to enable women's full participation in the paid labor market

- Address issues of occupational segregation that often translate into inferior conditions of employment for women

FIGURE 7.9

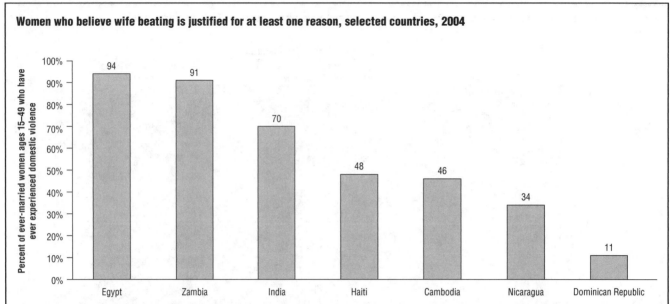

Women who believe wife beating is justified for at least one reason, selected countries, 2004

Note: Reasons for justification include neglecting the children, going out without telling partner, arguing with partner, refusing to have sex, not preparing food properly/on time, talking to other men.

SOURCE: "Figure 5. Women Who Believe Wife Beating Is Justified for at Least One Reason," in *State of World Population 2005*, United Nations Population Fund, 2005, http://www.unfpa.org/swp/2005/pdf/en_swp05.pdf (accessed April 8, 2006). Data from Kishor, S. and K. Johnson, 2004, *Profiling Domestic Violence: A Multicountry Study*, Calverton, MD: ORC Macro, Measure DHS+:66.

- Ensure social protection and benefits for women in precarious employment situations—often those involved in informal employment

The WHO report notes, however, that increasing women's economic and social opportunities can actually put them at greater risk of violence, as such opportunities can breed resentment from the men in their lives. The WHO emphasizes that a well-funded and developed social support system is essential if poor women are to permanently escape violence. Educational programs are particularly important, for both women and men, if perceived gender roles are to be expanded to include advancement for women without the danger of violence.

Exact figures for incidences of violence are almost impossible to obtain, because most violent acts committed against women—especially in developing countries—go unreported. However, it is estimated that 10% to 50% of women around the world have been assaulted by their husbands or male partners at some point. The numbers rise when brothers and other male relatives who perpetrate the violence are counted. In fact, physical and sexual assaults committed by male family members are the most common type of violence against women. In developing countries this type of violence is largely the result of traditional gender norms, most of which have evolved out of men's social and economic dominance over women.

The connection between poverty and violence against women lies primarily in that dominance. In many cultures women are completely dependent on their husbands and male relatives for survival. Amnesty International cites laws that prohibit women from owning or inheriting property and from divorcing abusive husbands; hierarchies that allow fathers, brothers, and husbands to withhold access to food, clothing, and shelter; and customs, such as "wife inheritance" and honor crimes, that force women to obey male relatives or risk exile or death.

In addition, violent conflicts at the village, tribal, and national level reduce millions of women and children to refugee status, leaving them vulnerable to unemployment, disease, starvation, rape, and kidnapping. Millions more women and children (the UN estimates thirty million worldwide) end up as victims of international sex trafficking; the U.S. Department of Health and Human Services' Administration for Children and Families reports that poor women may be lured into the sex trade by promises of a good job in another country, or they may be sold into the trade by their parents, brothers, husbands, or male partners. Others are abducted and forced into the trade. Taken together, these factors leave poor women especially vulnerable to physical, sexual, and psychological violence.

Furthermore, a woman who has suffered domestic violence is more likely to become impoverished. Globally, with as many as one in three women being violently assaulted in her lifetime, the chances of severe, debilitating injury to a large number of abused women are high. In a November 2005 address before the U.S.

Congressional Human Rights Caucus, S. K. Guha of UNIFEM noted that violence against women is increasingly acknowledged to be both a consequence and a cause of poverty among women and children. Severely abused women are generally unable to work, especially if they are also responsible for performing the physical labor of harvesting food and gathering fuel and water for their families.

Violence against Women in the United States

In the United States domestic violence is conclusively linked to homelessness among women and children. The American Civil Liberties Union (ACLU) reports that domestic violence was cited by 50% of U.S cities surveyed in 2005 as a primary cause of homelessness (http://www.aclu.org/pdfs/dvhomelessness032106.pdf). Further, the ACLU notes that 50% of homeless women in San Diego, California, reported being the victims of domestic violence, and that in Minnesota, one-third of homeless women indicated that they left their homes to escape domestic violence. Overall, according to the National Network to End Domestic Violence, Domestic Violence (September 2004; http://www.nnedv.org/pdf/ Homelessness.pdf), 92% of homeless women in the United States have at some point been the victims of severe physical and/or sexual abuse.

VIOLENCE AGAINST WOMEN ACT 2005. In December 2005 both the U.S. Senate and House of Representatives passed the Violence against Women Act 2005 (VAWA), which was part of the larger Department of Justice authorization bill. The VAWA 2005 is a reauthorization of an earlier act passed in 1994. The 2005 version of VAWA enhanced the provisions of its earlier version, with increased funding for violence-prevention programs, emergency shelter for women and children, and long-term housing solutions for low-income women and their children. The act also mandates that abused women be allowed to take ten days off from work each year to attend court or to look for housing, and it provides greater access to law enforcement and the justice system for abused immigrant woman who would otherwise have no legal recourse and might have to leave the country with abusive partners. Because violent relationships tend to affect poor women disproportionately in the United States, the provisions of the VAWA that allow time off from work and help for immigrant women mean that more poor women will be able to keep their jobs and remain in the country while they make arrangements to leave and/or prosecute their abusers.

POVERTY'S YOUNGEST VICTIMS

According to the report *State of the World's Children 2006: Excluded and Invisible* (2005, http://www.unicef. org/egypt/sowc06_fullreport.pdf) by the United Nations Children's Fund's (UNICEF), the least developed

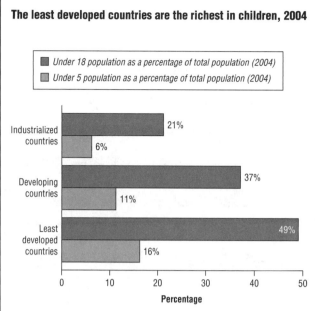

FIGURE 7.10

The least developed countries are the richest in children, 2004

- ■ Under 18 population as a percentage of total population (2004)
- ■ Under 5 population as a percentage of total population (2004)

SOURCE: "Figure 2.1 The Least Developed Countries Are the Richest In Children," in *The State of the World's Children 2006*, United Nations Children's Fund, 2005, http://www.unicef.org/sowc06/pdfs/sowc0506_eps_charts.pdf (accessed April 8, 2006). Data based on calculations from United Nations Population Division.

countries in the world are home to the greatest number of children—49% of the total population of least developed countries was under eighteen years old in 2004; in developing countries children under eighteen made up 37% of the total population. (See Figure 7.10.)

Children are more vulnerable to the effects of poverty than any other demographic group, and because their numbers in poor countries are so high, they suffer disproportionately from the disease, hunger, abuse, and exploitation that so often go hand in hand with poverty. UNICEF reports that "more than one billion children suffer from one or more extreme forms of deprivation in adequate nutrition, safe drinking water, decent sanitation facilities, health-care services, shelter, education and information." As Figure 7.11 shows, 30.7% of children in developing countries have no access to a toilet, while 33.9% live in homes with more than five people per room. For 21.1%, there is access only to untreated, potentially hazardous, water sources. Furthermore, 13.1% have never been to school. Underdeveloped and developing countries overall have the highest rates of children not attending school, as shown in Figure 7.12. Whereas 96% of girls and 95% of boys in developed countries are enrolled in primary school, just 65% of girls and 71% of boys in underdeveloped ("least developed") countries are enrolled in primary school. Even fewer poor children are enrolled in secondary school: 26% of girls and 30% of boys in underdeveloped countries, versus 92% of girls and 91% of boys in developed countries.

FIGURE 7.11

Severe deprivation among children in the developing world, by different deprivations, 2003

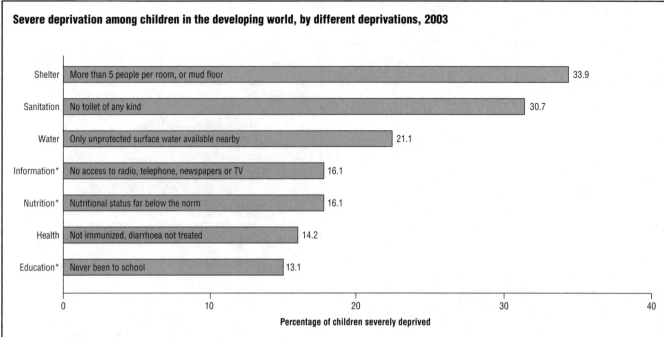

*Age ranges: Education: 7–18 years old; Information: over 3 years old; Nutrition: under 5 years old.
Note: The data used in the original study have been updated using Demographic and Health Surveys (DHS) and Multiple Indicator Cluster Surveys (MICS).

SOURCE: "Figure 2.1. Severe Deprivation among Children in the Developing World, by Different Deprivations," in *The State of the World's Children 2006*, United Nations Children's Fund, 2005, http://www.unicef.org/sowc06/pdfs/figure2_1_2005.pdf (accessed April 8, 2006). Data from Gordon, David, et al., *Child Poverty in the Developing World*, The Policy Press, Bristol, UK, October 2003.

FIGURE 7.12

Children living in the poorest countries are most at risk of missing out on primary and secondary school, 2000–04

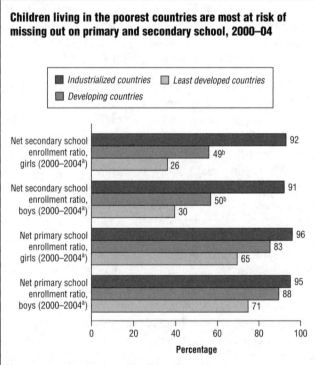

[a]Data refer to the most recent year available during the period specified.
[b]Excludes China.

SOURCE: "Figure 2.2. Children Living in the Poorest Countries Are Most at Risk of Missing Out on Primary and Secondary School," in *The State of the World's Children 2006*, United Nations Children's Fund, 2005, http://www.unicef.org/sowc06/pdfs/sowc0506_eps_charts.pdf (accessed April 8, 2006). Data from Demographic and Health Surveys (DHS) and Multiple Indicator Cluster Surveys (MICS).

Table 7.8 lists each country's rank according to its under-five mortality rate, as well as each country's infant and under-five mortality rates, life expectancy, literacy and education rates, and gross national per capita income. In general, life expectancy at birth increases as gross national income per capita increases. Infant and under-five mortality rates improved overall between 1990 and 2004 in least developed, developing, and industrialized countries.

Table 7.9 shows the status of child protection in countries around the world. Western and Central African countries have the overall highest percentage of children involved in child labor (41% of both girls and boys). At 46%, South Asia has the highest rate of child marriage of any geographic region, followed closely by Western and Central Africa, at 45%.

Child poverty is not limited to low-income countries. In eleven out of the fifteen countries belonging to the Organization for Economic Cooperation and Development (OECD), child poverty increased from the period of the late 1980s–early 1990s through the late 1990s–early 2000s. In this group, Mexico had the highest rate of child poverty, rising from 24.7% in the earlier period to 27.7% in the later period. The United States had the second highest rate; even with a drop from 24.3% to 21.9%, the U.S. child poverty rate far exceeded the rate of all other OECD countries except Mexico. In the United Kingdom the drop from 18.5% to 15.4% was due in large part to the commitment

TABLE 7.8

Under-five mortality rank and other development indicators, by country, 1990–2004

Countries and territories	Under-5 mortality rank	Under-5 mortality rate 1990	Under-5 mortality rate 2004	Infant mortality rate (under 1)[a] 1990	Infant mortality rate (under 1)[a] 2004	Total population (thousands) 2004	Annual number of births (thousands) 2004	Annual number of under-5 deaths (thousands) 2004	Gross national income per capita (US$)[b] 2004	Life expectancy at birth (years)[c] 2004	Total adult literacy rate[d] 2000–2004	Net primary school enrolment/attendance (percent)[e] 1996–2004[g]	Percent share of household income[f] 1993–2003[g] Lowest 40%	Percent share of household income[f] 1993–2003[g] Highest 20%
Afghanistan	4	260	257	168	165	28,574	1,395	359	250[m]	46	—	53[i]	—	—
Albania	125	45	19	37	17	3,112	53	1	2,080	74	99	95	23	37
Algeria	79	69	40	54	35	32,358	671	27	2,280	71	70	94[i]	19	43
Andorra	159	—	7	—	6	67	1	0	—[k]	—	—	89	—	—
Angola	2	260	260	154	154	15,490	749	195	1,030	41	67	58[i]	—	—
Antigua and Barbuda	143	—	12	—	11	81	2	0	10,000	—	—	—	—	56
Argentina	127	29	18	26	16	38,372	685	12	3,720	75	97	97[i]	10	45
Armenia	90	60	32	52	29	3,026	34	1	1,120	72	99	97	18	41
Australia	162	10	6	8	5	19,942	249	1	26,900	81	—	97	18	39
Austria	172	10	5	8	5	8,171	75	0	32,300	79	—	90	21	45
Azerbaijan	51	105	90	84	75	8,355	132	12	950	67	99	91[i]	19	45
Bahamas	140	29	13	24	10	319	6	0	14,920[m]	70	—	86	—	—
Bahrain	148	19	11	15	9	716	13	0	10,840[m]	75	88	86[i]	—	—
Bangladesh	58	149	77	100	56	139,215	3,738	288	440	63	41	79[i]	22	41
Barbados	143	16	12	14	10	269	3	0	9,270[m]	75	100	100	—	—
Belarus	148	17	11	13	9	9,811	91	1	2,120	68	100	94	21	39
Belgium	172	10	5	8	4	10,400	111	1	31,030	79	—	100	22	37
Belize	81	49	39	39	32	264	7	0	3,940	72	77	99	—	—
Benin	23	185	152	111	90	8,177	341	52	530	54	34	54[i]	—	—
Bhutan	56	166	80	107	67	2,116	64	5	760	63	—	78[i]	—	—
Bolivia	62	125	69	89	54	9,009	265	18	960	64	87	86[i]	13	49
Bosnia and Herzegovina	131	22	15	18	13	3,909	37	1	2,040	74	95	84[i]	24	36
Botswana	41	58	116	45	84	1,769	46	5	4,340	35	79	95[i]	7	70
Brazil	88	60	34	50	32	183,913	3,728	127	3,090	71	88	90	8	63
Brunei Darussalam	150	11	9	10	8	366	8	0	24,100[m]	77	93	32[i]	—	—
Bulgaria	131	18	15	15	12	7,780	67	1	2,740	72	98	47[i]	20	39
Burkina Faso	16	210	192	113	97	12,822	601	115	360	48	13	47[i]	12	61
Burundi	17	190	190	114	114	7,282	330	63	90	44	59	65[i]	15	48
Cambodia	26	115	141	80	97	13,798	422	60	320	57	74	75[i]	18	48
Cameroon	25	139	149	85	87	16,038	562	84	800	46	68	100	15	51
Canada	162	8	6	7	5	31,958	328	2	28,390	80	—	99	20	40
Cape Verde	86	60	36	45	27	495	15	1	1,770	71	76	43[i]	—	—
Central African Republic	15	168	193	102	115	3,986	149	29	310	39	49	39[i]	7	65
Chad	12	203	200	117	117	9,448	456	91	260	44	26	85	10	62
Chile	152	21	8	17	8	16,124	249	2	4,910	78	96	99	14	50
China	93	49	31	38	26	1,307,989	17,372	539	1,290	72	91	93[i]	9	62
Colombia	113	36	21	30	18	44,915	970	20	2,000	73	94	31[i]	—	—
Comoros	61	120	70	88	52	777	28	2	530	64	56	54	—	—
Congo	44	110	108	83	81	3,883	172	19	770	52	83	52[i]	—	—
Congo, Democratic Republic of the	8	205	205	129	129	55,853	2,788	572	120	44	65			

TABLE 7.8

Under-five mortality rank and other development indicators, by country, 1990–2004 [CONTINUED]

Countries and territories	Under-5 mortality rank	Under-5 mortality rate 1990	Under-5 mortality rate 2004	Infant mortality rate (under 1)[a] 1990	Infant mortality rate (under 1)[a] 2004	Total population (thousands) 2004	Annual number of births (thousands) 2004	Annual number of under-5 deaths (thousands) 2004	Gross national income per capita (US$)[b] 2004	Life expectancy at birth (years)[c] 2004	Total adult literacy rate[d] 2000–2004[g]	Net primary school enrolment/attendance (percent)[e] 1996–2004[g]	Percent share of household income[f] 1993–2003[g] Lowest 40%	Percent share of household income[f] 1993–2003[g] Highest 20%
Cook Islands	113	32	21	26	18	18	0	0	—	—	—	—	—	—
Costa Rica	140	18	13	16	11	4,253	79	1	4,670	78	96	90	13	52
Côte d'Ivoire	14	157	194	103	117	17,872	661	128	770	46	48	58[l]	14	51
Croatia	159	12	7	11	6	4,540	41	1	6,590	75	98	89	21	40
Cuba	159	13	7	11	6	11,245	136	1	1,170[m]	78	100	93	—	—
Cyprus	172	12	5	10	5	826	10	0	17,580	79	97	96	—	—
Czech Republic	185	13	4	11	4	10,229	91	0	9,150	76	—	87	25	36
Denmark	172	9	5	8	4	5,414	63	0	40,650	77	—	100	23	36
Djibouti	31	163	126	122	101	779	27	3	1,030	53	—	36	—	—
Dominica	135	17	14	15	13	79	2	0	3,650	—	—	81	—	—
Dominican Republic	90	65	32	50	27	8,768	211	7	2,080	68	88	92[l]	14	53
Ecuador	104	57	26	43	23	13,040	296	8	2,180	75	91	100	11	58
Egypt	86	104	36	76	26	72,642	1,890	68	1,310	70	56	83[l]	21	44
El Salvador	98	60	28	47	24	6,762	166	5	2,350	71	80	90	10	57
Equatorial Guinea	9	170	204	103	122	492	21	4	—	43	84	62[l]	—	—
Eritrea	54	147	82	88	52	4,232	166	14	180	54	—	63[l]	—	—
Estonia	152	16	8	12	6	1,335	13	0	7,010	72	100	95	18	44
Ethiopia	20	204	166	131	110	75,600	3,064	509	110	48	42	31[l]	22	39
Fiji	120	31	20	25	16	841	19	0	2,690	68	93	100	—	—
Finland	185	7	4	6	3	5,235	55	0	32,790	79	—	100	24	37
France	172	9	5	7	4	60,257	744	4	30,090	80	—	99	20	40
Gabon	49	92	91	60	60	1,362	42	4	3,940	54	—	94[l]	—	—
Gambia	36	154	122	103	89	1,478	52	6	290	56	—	53[l]	14	53
Georgia	75	47	45	43	41	4,518	50	2	1,040	71	—	89	18	44
Germany	172	9	5	7	4	82,645	687	3	30,120	79	—	83	22	37
Ghana	42	122	112	75	68	21,664	679	76	380	57	54	61[l]	16	47
Greece	172	11	5	10	4	11,098	102	1	16,610	78	91	99	19	44
Grenada	113	37	21	30	18	102	2	0	3,760	—	—	84	—	—
Guatemala	75	82	45	60	33	12,295	433	19	2,130	68	69	78[l]	9	64
Guinea	22	240	155	145	101	9,202	383	59	460	54	—	57[l]	17	47
Guinea-Bissau	10	253	203	153	126	1,540	77	16	160	45	—	41[l]	14	53
Guyana	67	88	64	64	48	750	16	1	990	64	—	97[l]	—	—
Haiti	40	150	117	102	74	8,407	253	30	390	52	52	54[l]	—	—
Holy See	—	—	—	—	—	—	—	—	—	—	—	—	—	—
Honduras	78	59	41	44	31	7,048	206	8	1,030	68	80	87	9	59
Hungary	152	17	8	15	7	10,124	95	1	8,270	73	99	91	23	37
Iceland	192	7	3	6	2	292	4	0	38,620	81	—	100	—	—
India	52	123	85	84	62	1,087,124	26,000	2,210	620	64	61	77[l]	21	43
Indonesia	83	91	38	60	30	220,077	4,513	171	1,140	67	88	94[l]	20	43

TABLE 7.8

Under-five mortality rank and other development indicators, by country, 1990–2004 [CONTINUED]

Countries and territories	Under-5 mortality rank	Under-5 mortality rate 1990	Under-5 mortality rate 2004	Infant mortality rate (under 1)[a] 1990	Infant mortality rate (under 1)[a] 2004	Total population (thousands) 2004	Annual number of births (thousands) 2004	Annual number of under-5 deaths (thousands) 2004	Gross national income per capita (US$)[b] 2004	Life expectancy at birth (years)[c] 2004	Total adult literacy rate[d] 2000–2004[g]	Net primary school enrolment/attendance (percent)[e] 1996–2004[g]	Percent share of household income[f] 1993–2003[g] Lowest 40%	Percent share of household income[f] 1993–2003[g] Highest 20%
Iran (Islamic Republic of)	83	72	38	54	32	68,803	1,308	50	2,300	71	77	86	15	50
Iraq	33	50	125	40	102	28,057	972	122	2,170[m]	59	—	78[i]	—	43
Ireland	162	10	6	8	5	4,080	63	0	34,280	78	—	96	19	44
Israel	162	12	6	10	5	6,601	134	1	17,380	80	97	99	18	42
Italy	172	9	5	9	4	58,033	531	3	26,120	80	—	99	19	46
Jamaica	120	20	20	17	17	2,639	52	1	2,900	71	88	95	17	36
Japan	185	6	4	5	3	127,923	1,169	5	37,180	82	—	100	25	44
Jordan	101	40	27	33	23	5,561	150	4	2,140	72	90	99[i]	19	40
Kazakhstan	60	63	73	53	63	14,839	237	17	2,260	63	100	91[i]	20	40
Kenya	37	97	120	64	79	33,467	1,322	159	460	48	74	78[i]	16	49
Kiribati	66	88	65	65	49	97	2	0	970	—	—	—	—	—
Korea, Democratic People's Republic of	71	55	55	42	42	22,384	349	19	[h]	63	—	100	—	—
Korea, Republic of	162	9	6	8	5	47,645	467	3	13,980	77	—	—	22	38
Kuwait	143	16	12	14	10	2,606	50	1	16,340[m]	77	83	83[i]	—	43
Kyrgyzstan	64	80	68	68	58	5,204	116	8	400	67	99	89[i]	20	—
Lao People's Democratic Republic	53	163	83	120	65	5,792	204	17	390	55	69	62[i]	19	45
Latvia	143	18	12	14	10	2,318	21	0	5,460	72	100	86	20	41
Lebanon	93	37	31	32	27	3,540	66	2	4,980	72	—	97[i]	—	—
Lesotho	54	120	82	84	61	1,798	50	4	740	35	81	65[i]	6	67
Liberia	5	235	235	157	157	3,241	164	39	110	42	56	70	—	—
Libyan Arab Jamahiriya	120	41	20	35	18	5,740	133	3	4,450	74	82	—	—	—
Liechtenstein	172	10	5	9	4	34	0	0	[k]	—	—	—	—	—
Lithuania	152	13	8	10	8	3,443	31	0	5,740	73	100	91	21	40
Luxembourg	162	10	6	7	5	459	6	0	56,230	79	—	90	—	—
Madagascar	35	168	123	103	76	18,113	704	87	300	56	71	76[i]	13	54
Malawi	19	241	175	146	110	12,608	550	96	170	40	64	76[i]	13	56
Malaysia	143	22	12	16	10	24,894	549	7	4,650	73	89	93	13	54
Maldives	74	111	46	79	35	321	10	0	2,510	67	96	92	—	—
Mali	7	250	219	140	121	13,124	647	142	360	48	19	39[i]	13	56
Malta	162	11	6	9	5	400	4	0	12,250	79	88	96	—	—
Marshall Islands	69	92	59	63	52	60	0	0	2,370	—	—	84	—	—
Mauritania	33	133	125	85	78	2,980	123	15	420	53	51	44[i]	17	46
Mauritius	131	23	15	21	14	1,233	20	0	4,640	72	84	97	—	—
Mexico	98	46	28	37	23	105,699	2,201	62	6,770	75	90	99	10	59
Micronesia (Federated States of)	110	31	23	26	19	110	3	0	1,990	68	—	—	—	—
Moldova, Republic of	98	40	28	30	23	4,218	43	1	710[k]	68	96	98[i]	18	44
Monaco	172	9	5	7	4	35	0	0	[k]	—	—	—	—	—

TABLE 7.8

Under-five mortality rank and other development indicators, by country, 1990–2004 [CONTINUED]

Countries and territories	Under-5 mortality rank	Under-5 mortality rate 1990	Under-5 mortality rate 2004	Infant mortality rate (under 1)[a] 1990	Infant mortality rate (under 1)[a] 2004	Total population (thousands) 2004	Annual number of births (thousands) 2004	Annual number of under-5 deaths (thousands) 2004	Gross national income per capita (US$)[b] 2004	Life expectancy at birth (years)[c] 2004	Total adult literacy rate[d] 2000–2004[g]	Net primary school enrolment/attendance (percent)[e] 1996–2004[g]	Percent share of household income[f] 1993–2003[g] Lowest 40%	Percent share of household income[f] 1993–2003[g] Highest 20%
Mongolia	72	108	52	78	41	2,614	58	3	590	65	98	79[j]	16	51
Morocco	77	89	43	69	38	31,020	713	31	1,520	70	51	89[j]	17	47
Mozambique	23	235	152	158	104	19,424	769	117	250	42	46	60[j]	17	47
Myanmar	45	130	106	91	76	50,004	992	105	220[m]	61	90	80[j]	—	79
Namibia	68	86	63	60	47	2,009	56	4	2,370	47	85	78[j]	4	—
Nauru	95	—	30	—	25	13	0	0	—	—	—	81	—	—
Nepal	59	145	76	100	59	26,591	786	60	260	62	49	74[j]	19	45
Netherlands	162	9	6	7	5	16,226	190	0	31,700	79	—	99	21	39
New Zealand	162	11	6	8	5	3,989	55	0	20,310	79	—	100	18	44
Nicaragua	83	68	38	52	31	5,376	153	6	790	70	77	80[j]	15	49
Niger	3	320	259	191	152	13,499	734	190	230	45	14	30[j]	10	53
Nigeria	13	230	197	120	101	128,709	5,323	1,049	390	43	67	62[j]	13	56
Niue	—	9	4	7	1	1	0	—	—	—	—	99	—	—
Norway	185	9	4	7	4	4,598	55	0	52,030	80	—	100	24	37
Occupied Palestinian territory	107	40	24	34	22	3,587	136	3	1,110[m]	73	92	91	—	—
Oman	140	32	13	25	10	2,534	64	1	7,830[m]	74	74	72	—	—
Pakistan	47	130	101	100	80	154,794	4,729	478	600	63	49	56[j]	21	42
Palau	101	34	27	28	22	20	0	0	6,870	—	—	96	—	—
Panama	107	34	24	27	19	3,175	70	2	4,450	75	92	100	9	60
Papua New Guinea	48	101	93	74	68	5,772	176	16	580	56	57	74	12	57
Paraguay	107	41	24	33	21	6,017	175	4	1,170	71	92	89	9	61
Peru	97	80	29	60	24	27,562	627	18	2,360	70	88	96[j]	11	53
Philippines	88	62	34	41	26	81,617	2,026	69	1,170	71	93	88[j]	14	52
Poland	152	18	8	19	7	38,559	365	3	6,090	75	—	98	20	42
Portugal	172	14	5	11	4	10,441	112	1	14,350	78	—	100	17	46
Qatar	113	26	21	21	18	777	14	0	12,000[m]	73	89	94	17	46
Romania	120	31	20	27	17	21,790	213	4	2,920	72	97	89	20	41
Russian Federation	113	29	21	23	17	143,899	1,511	32	3,410	65	99	90	21	39
Rwanda	10	173	203	103	118	8,882	365	74	220	44	64	75[j]	23[m]	39[m]
Saint Kitts and Nevis	113	36	21	30	18	42	1	0	7,600	—	—	95	—	—
Saint Lucia	135	21	14	20	13	159	3	0	4,310	73	90	99	—	—
Saint Vincent and the Grenadines	112	25	22	22	18	118	2	0	3,650	71	—	90	—	—
Samoa	95	50	30	40	25	184	5	0	1,860	71	99	98	—	—
San Marino	185	14	4	13	3	28	0	0	[k]	71	—	—	—	—
Sao Tome and Principe	38	118	118	75	75	153	5	1	370	63	—	78[j]	—	—
Saudi Arabia	101	44	27	35	21	23,950	665	18	10,430	72	79	54	—	—
Senegal	29	148	137	90	78	11,386	419	57	670	56	39	48[j]	17	48
Serbia and Montenegro	131	28	15	24	13	10,510	122	2	2,620	74	96	96	—	—

TABLE 7.8

Under-five mortality rank and other development indicators, by country, 1990–2004 [CONTINUED]

Countries and territories	Under-5 mortality rank	Under-5 mortality rate 1990	Under-5 mortality rate 2004	Infant mortality rate (under 1)a 1990	Infant mortality rate (under 1)a 2004	Total population (thousands) 2004	Annual number of births (thousands) 2004	Annual number of under-5 deaths (thousands) 2004	Gross national income per capita (US$)b 2004	Life expectancy at birth (years)c 2004	Total adult literacy rate d 2000–2004	Net primary school enrolment/attendance (percent)e 1996–2004g	Percent share of household income f 1993–2003g Lowest 40%	Highest 20%
Seychelles	135	19	14	17	12	80	3	0	8,090	—	92	100	—	—
Sierra Leone	1	302	283	175	165	5,336	245	69	200	41	30	41 l	3 m	63 l
Singapore	192	9	3	7	3	4,273	40	0	24,220	79	93	—	14	49
Slovakia	150	14	9	12	6	5,401	51	0	6,480	74	100	86	24	35
Slovenia	185	10	4	8	4	1,967	17	0	14,810	77	100	93	23	36
Solomon Islands	70	63	56	38	34	466	15	1	550	63	—	—	—	—
Somalia	6	225	225	133	133	7,964	359	81	130 m	47	—	11 l	—	—
South Africa	65	60	67	45	54	47,208	1,093	73	3,630	47	82	89 l	10	62
Spain	172	9	5	8	3	42,646	447	2	21,210	80	—	100	20 m	40 m
Sri Lanka	135	32	14	26	12	20,570	330	5	1,010	74	90	—	21	42
Sudan	49	120	91	74	63	35,523	1,163	106	530	57	59	53 l	—	—
Suriname	81	48	39	35	30	446	9	0	2,250	69	88	90 l	—	—
Swaziland	21	110	156	78	108	1,034	30	5	1,660	31	79	72 l	9	64
Sweden	185	7	4	6	3	9,008	95	0	35,770	80	—	100	23	37
Switzerland	172	9	5	7	5	7,240	68	0	48,230	81	—	99	20 m	40 m
Syrian Arab Republic	130	44	16	35	15	18,582	526	8	1,190	74	83	98	—	—
Tajikistan	38	128	118	99	91	6,430	186	22	280	64	99	81 l	20	41
Tanzania, United Republic of	31	161	126	102	78	37,627	1,403	177	330	46	69	82 l	18	46
Thailand	113	37	21	31	18	63,694	1,015	21	2,540	70	93	85	16	50
The former Yugoslav Republic of Macedonia	135	38	14	33	13	2,030	23	0	2,350	74	96	91	22	37
Timor-Leste	56	172	80	130	64	887	45	4	550	56	—	—	—	—
Togo	27	152	140	88	78	5,988	233	33	380	55	53	64 l	—	—
Tonga	105	32	25	26	20	102	2	0	1,830	72	99	100	—	—
Trinidad and Tobago	120	33	20	28	18	1,301	19	0	8,580	70	98	96 l	16 m	46 m
Tunisia	105	52	25	41	21	9,995	166	4	2,630	74	74	97	16	47
Turkey	90	82	32	67	28	72,220	1,505	48	3,750	69	88	88 l	17	47
Turkmenistan	46	97	103	80	80	4,766	107	11	1,340	63	99	85 l	16	48
Tuvalu	73	56	51	40	36	10	0	0	—	—	—	79 l	—	—
Uganda	28	160	138	93	80	27,821	1,412	195	270	48	69	84	16	50
Ukraine	127	26	14	19	14	46,989	391	7	1,260 m	66	99	83	22	38
United Arab Emirates	152	14	8	12	7	4,284	67	1	18,060 m	78	77	83	—	—
United Kingdom	162	10	6	8	5	59,479	663	4	33,940	79	—	100	18	44
United States	152	12	8	9	7	295,410	4,134	33	41,400	78	—	92	16	46
Uruguay	129	25	17	20	15	3,439	57	1	3,950	76	98	90	14	50
Uzbekistan	62	79	69	65	57	26,209	611	42	460	67	99	80 l	23	36
Vanuatu	79	62	40	48	32	207	6	0	1,340	69	74	94	—	—
Venezuela	125	27	19	24	16	26,282	590	11	4,020	73	93	94 l	11	53
Vietnam	110	53	23	38	17	83,123	1,644	38	550	71	90	96 l	19	45
Yemen	43	142	111	98	82	20,329	826	92	570	61	49	72 l	20	41
Zambia	18	180	182	101	102	11479	468	85	450	38	68	68 l	11	57
Zimbabwe	30	80	129	53	79	12936	384	50	480 m	37	90	79 l	13	56

TABLE 7.8

Under-five mortality rank and other development indicators, by country, 1990–2004 [CONTINUED]

Countries and territories	Under-5 mortality rank	Under-5 mortality rate 1990	Under-5 mortality rate 2004	Infant mortality rate (under 1)[a] 1990	Infant mortality rate (under 1)[a] 2004	Total population (thousands) 2004	Annual number of births (thousands) 2004	Annual number of under-5 deaths (thousands) 2004	Gross national income per capita (US$)[b] 2004	Life expectancy at birth (years)[c] 2004	Total adult literacy rate[d] 2000–2004[g]	Net primary school enrolment/attendance (percent)[e] 1996–2004[g]	Percent share of household income[f] 1993–2003[g] Lowest 40%	Percent share of household income[f] 1993–2003[g] Highest 20%
Summary indicators														
Sub-Saharan Africa		188	171	112	102	697,561	28,263	4,833	611	46	60	60	12	57
Eastern and Southern Africa	167	149	105	95		348,833	13,371	1,992		46	65	60	59	
Western and Central Africa	209	191	119			348,728	14,892	2,844	46		55		53	43
Middle East and North Africa	81	56	59			371,384	9,620	539	600	67	79	13	46	47
South Asia		129	92	89	67	1,459,305	37,052	3,409	68	63	58	17	21	41
East Asia and Pacific		58	36	43	29	1,937,058	29,932	1,078	1,686	71	90	74	16	42
Latin America and Caribbean[h]	54	31	43	26	32	548,273	11,674	362	72	67	93	96	59	50
CEE/CIS[n]		54	38	44	5	404,154	5,570	212	2,667	67	97	88	20	41
Industrialized countries		10	6	9		956,315	10,839	65	32,232	79	—	95	19	42
Developing countries		105	87	72	59	5,166,574	119,663	10,411	1,524	65	77	80	15	50
Least developed countries		182	155	115	98	741,597	27,823	4,313	345	52	54	60	18	46
World		95	79	65	54	6,374,050	132,950	10,503	6,298	67	78	82	18	43

Notes: "—" indicates data not available.

a Probability of dying between birth and exactly one year of age expressed per 1,000 live births.

b Gross national income (GNI) is the sum of value added by all resident producers plus any product taxes (less subsidies) not included in the valuation of output plus net receipts of primary income (compensation of employees and property income) from abroad. GNI per capita is gross national income divided by mid-year population. GNI per capita in US dollars is converted using the World Bank Atlas method.

c The number of years newborn children would live if subject to the mortality risks prevailing for the cross-section of population at the time of their birth.

d Percentage of persons aged 15 and over who can read and write.

e Derived from net primary school enrolment rates as reported by UNESCO/UIS (UNESCO Institute of Statistics) and from national household survey reports of attendance at primary school or higher. The net primary school attendance ratio is defined as the percentage of children in the age group that officially corresponds to primary schooling who attend primary school or higher.

f Percentage of income received by the 20 percent of households with the highest income and by the 40 percent of households with the lowest income.

g Data refer to the most recent year available during the period specified in the column heading.

h Range $825 or less.

i Range $826 to $3,255.

j Range $3,256 to $10,065.

k Range $10,066 or more.

l National household survey.

m Indicates data that refer to years or periods other than those specified in the column heading or refer to only part of a country.

n Central and Eastern Europe/Commonwealth of Independent States (formerly the USSR).

SOURCE: "Table 1. Basic Indicators," in *The State of the World's Children 2006*, United Nations Children's Fund, 2005, http://www.unicef.org/sowc06/pdfs/sowc06_tables.pdf (accessed April 8, 2006). Data from the United Nations, The World Bank and the World Health Organization.

TABLE 7.9

Child protection by selected characteristics, selected years 1986–2004

| Countries and territories | Child labour (5–14 years) 1999–2004[a, g] | | | Child marriage 1986–2004[b, g] | | | Birth registration 1999–2004[c, g] | | | Female genital mutilation/cutting 1998–2004[d, g] | | | |
| | | | | | | | | | | Women[e] (15–49 years) | | | Daughters[f] |
	Total	Male	Female	Total	Urban	Rural	Total	Urban	Rural	Total	Urban	Rural	Total
Afghanistan	34[h]	31[h]	38[h]	43	—	—	6	12	4	—	—	—	—
Albania	23	26	19	—	—	—	99	99	99	—	—	—	—
Angola	22	21	23	—	—	—	29	34	19	—	—	—	—
Armenia	—	—	—	19	12	31	97	100	94	—	—	—	—
Azerbaijan	8	9	7	—	—	—	97	98	96	—	—	—	—
Bahrain	5	6	3	—	—	—	—	—	—	—	—	—	—
Bangladesh	7	10	4	65	44	72	7	9	7	—	—	—	—
Benin	26[h]	23[h]	29[h]	37	25	45	70	78	66	17	13	20	6
Bolivia	21	22	20	26	22	37	82	83	79	—	—	—	—
Bosnia and Herzegovina	11	12	10	—	—	—	98	98	99	—	—	—	—
Botswana	—	—	—	10	13	9	58	66	52	—	—	—	—
Brazil	7[h]	9[h]	4[h]	24	22	30	76	—	—	—	—	—	—
Burkina Faso	57[h]	—	—	52	22	62	—	—	—	77	75	77	32
Burundi	24	26	23	17[h]	36[h]	17[h]	75	71	75	—	—	—	—
Cambodia	—	—	—	25	19	26	22	30	21	—	—	—	—
Cameroon	51	52	50	43	30	51	79	94	73	1.4	1	2	—
Central African Republic	56	54	57	57	54	59	73	88	63	36	29	41	—
Chad	57	60	55	71	65	74	25	53	18	45	43	46	—
Colombia	5	7	4	21	18	34	91	95	04	—	—	—	—
Comoros	28	27	29	30	23	33	83	87	83	—	—	—	—
Congo, Democratic Republic of the	28[h]	26[h]	29[h]	—	—	—	34	30	36	—	—	—	—
Costa Rica	50[h]	71[h]	29[h]	—	—	—	—	—	—	—	—	—	—
Cote d'Ivoire	35	34	36	33	24	43	72	88	60	45	39	48	24
Cuba	—	—	—	—	—	—	100	100	100	—	—	—	—
Dominican Republic	9	11	6	41	37	51	75	82	66	—	—	—	—
Ecuador	6[h]	9[h]	4[h]	26[h]	21[h]	34[h]	—	—	—	—	—	—	—
Egypt	6	6	5	19	11	24	—	—	—	97	95	99	47
El Salvador	—	—	—	27	—	—	—	—	—	—	—	—	—
Equatorial Guinea	27	27	27	—	—	—	32	43	24	—	—	—	—
Eritrea	—	—	—	47	31	60	—	—	—	89	86	91	63
Ethiopia	43[h]	47[h]	37[h]	49	32	53	—	—	—	80	80	80	48
Gabon	—	—	—	34	30	49	89	90	87	—	—	—	—
Gambia	22	23	22	—	—	—	32	37	29	—	—	—	—
Georgia	—	—	—	—	—	—	95	97	92	—	—	—	—
Ghana	57[h]	57[h]	58[h]	28	18	39	21	—	—	5	4	7	—
Guatemala	24[h]	—	—	34	25	44	—	—	—	—	—	—	—
Guinea	—	—	—	65	46	75	67	88	56	99	98	99	54
Guinea-Bissau	54	54	54	—	—	—	42	32	47	—	—	—	—
Guyana	19	21	17	—	—	—	97	99	96	—	—	—	—
Haiti	—	—	—	24	18	31	70	78	66	—	—	—	—
India	14	14	15	46	26	55	35	54	29	—	—	—	—
Indonesia	4[h]	5[h]	4[h]	24	15	33	55	69	43	—	—	—	—
Iraq	8	11	5	—	—	—	98	99	97	—	—	—	—
Jamaica	2	3	1	—	—	—	96	95	96	—	—	—	—
Jordan	—	—	—	11	11	12	—	—	—	—	—	—	—
Kazakhstan	—	—	—	14	12	17	—	—	—	—	—	—	—
Kenya	26	27	25	25	19	27	48[h]	64[h]	44[h]	32	21	36	21
Korea, Democratic People's Republic of	—	—	—	—	—	—	99	99	99	—	—	—	—
Kyrgyzstan	—	—	—	21	19	22	—	—	—	—	—	—	—
Lao People's Democratic Republic	24	23	25	—	—	—	59	71	56	—	—	—	—
Lebanon	6	8	4	11	—	—	—	—	—	—	—	—	—

of the government to eliminating child poverty by entirely by 2020 (see Chapter 6).

UNICEF's 2000 publication *Poverty Reduction Begins with Children* (http://www.unicef.org/publications/files/pub_poverty_reduction_en.pdf) emphasizes the special challenges of children who live in poverty and discusses how child poverty differs from poverty in general. Because childhood—particularly the first few months of a person's life—is a time of key developmental changes physically, emotionally, and intellectually, neglect in any of these areas can be a permanent detriment to future well-being. According to UNICEF, impoverished children become "transmitters" of poverty to the next generation when they become parents themselves. The report maintains that this cycle can be broken only when poverty is considered a human rights violation instead of simply a matter of income deprivation.

TABLE 7.9

Child protection by selected characteristics, selected years 1986–2004 [CONTINUED]

Countries and territories	Child labour (5–14 years) 1999–2004[a, g]			Child marriage 1986–2004[b, g]			Birth registration 1999–2004[c, g]			Female genital mutilation/cutting 1998–2004[d, g] Women[e] (15–49 years)			Daughters[f]
	Total	Male	Female	Total	Urban	Rural	Total	Urban	Rural	Total	Urban	Rural	Total
Lesotho	17	19	14	—	—	—	51	41	53	—	—	—	—
Liberia	—	—	—	48[h]	38[h]	58[h]	—	—	—	—	—	—	—
Madagascar	30	35	26	39	29	42	75	87	72	—	—	—	—
Malawi	17	18	16	47	32	50	—	—	—	—	—	—	—
Maldives	—	—	—	—	—	—	73	—	—	—	—	—	—
Mali	30	33	28	65	46	74	48	71	41	92	90	93	73
Mauritania	10[h]	—	—	37	32	42	55	72	42	71	65	77	66
Mexico	16[h]	15[h]	16[h]	28[h]	31[h]	21[h]	—	—	—	—	—	—	—
Moldova, Republic of	28	29	28	—	—	—	98	98	98	—	—	—	—
Mongolia	30	30	30	—	—	—	98	98	97	—	—	—	—
Morocco	11[h]	—	—	16	12	21	85	92	80	—	—	—	—
Mozambique	—	—	—	56	41	66	—	—	—	—	—	—	—
Myanmar	—	—	—	—	—	—	65[h]	66[h]	64[h]	—	—	—	—
Pakistan	—	—	—	32	21	37	—	—	—	—	—	—	—
Namibia	—	—	—	10	9	10	71	82	64	—	—	—	—
Nepal	31	30	33	56	34	60	34	37	34	—	—	—	—
Nicaragua	10[h]	—	—	43	36	55	81	90	73	—	—	—	—
Niger	66	69	64	77	46	86	46	85	40	5	2	5	4
Nigeria	39[h]	—	—	43	27	52	30	53	20	19	28	14	10
Occupied Palestinian territory	—	—	—	—	—	—	98	98	97	—	—	—	—
Pakistan	—	—	—	32	21	37	—	—	—	—	—	—	—
Paraguay	8[h]	10[h]	6[h]	24	18	32	—	—	—	—	—	—	—
Peru	—	—	—	19	12	35	93	93	92	—	—	—	—
Philippines	11	12	10	14	10	22	83	87	78	—	—	—	—
Romania	1[h]	—	—	—	—	—	—	—	—	—	—	—	—
Rwanda	31	31	30	20	21	19	65	61	66	—	—	—	—
Sao Tome and Principe	14	15	13	—	—	—	70	73	67	—	—	—	—
Senegal	33	36	30	36	15	53	62	82	51	—	—	—	—
Sierra Leone	57	57	57	—	—	—	46	66	40	—	—	—	—
Somalia	32	29	36	—	—	—	—	—	—	—	—	—	—
South Africa	—	—	—	8	5	12	—	—	—	—	—	—	—
Sri Lanka	—	—	—	14[h]	10[h]	15[h]	—	—	—	—	—	—	—
Sudan	13	14	12	27[h]	19[h]	34[h]	64	82	46	90	92	88	58
Suriname	—	—	—	—	—	—	95	94	94	—	—	—	—
Swaziland	8	8	8	—	—	—	53	72	50	—	—	—	—
Syrian Arab Republic	8[h]	10[h]	6[h]	—	—	—	—	—	—	—	—	—	—
Tajikistan	18	19	17	—	—	—	75	77	74	—	—	—	—
Tanzania, United Republic of	32	34	30	39	23	48	6	22	3	18	10	20	7
Thailand	—	—	—	21[h]	13[h]	23[h]	—	—	—	—	—	—	—
Timor-Leste	4[h]	4[h]	4[h]	—	—	—	22	32	20	—	—	—	—
Togo	60	62	59	31	17	41	82	93	78	—	—	—	—
Trinidad and Tobago	2	3	2	34[h]	37[h]	32[h]	95	—	—	—	—	—	—
Tunisia	—	—	—	10[h]	7[h]	14[h]	—	—	—	—	—	—	—
Turkey	—	—	—	23	19	30	—	—	—	—	—	—	—
Turkmenistan	—	—	—	9	12	7	—	—	—	—	—	—	—
Uganda	34	34	33	54	34	59	4	11	3	—	—	—	—
Uzbekistan	15	18	12	13	16	11	100	100	100	—	—	—	—
Venezuela	7	9	5	—	—	—	92	—	—	—	—	—	—
Viet Nam	23	23	22	11	5	13	72	92	68	—	—	—	—
Yemen	—	—	—	48	39	53	—	—	—	23	26	22	20
Zambia	11	10	11	42	32	49	10	16	6	—	—	—	—
Zimbabwe	26[h]	—	—	29	21	36	42	56	35	—	—	—	—

Children's Health and Mortality

Improving children's health and reducing rates of child mortality is an implicit factor of the Convention on the Rights of the Child and is explicitly listed as one of the Millennium Development Goals. The most fundamental and important indicators of poverty among children are the state of their health and their rates of mortality. Child mortality rates are also a major indicator of the overall social and economic stability of nations. How much a country invests—or does not invest—in measures to cut back preventable deaths and diseases of children is ultimately indicative of its commitment to its own economic development.

Table 7.10 and Table 7.11 show basic human development indicators in industrialized and developing countries, respectively. Notice that in industrialized countries the percentage of moderately or severely underweight children under five is negligible, while in developing countries the rate is high, at 27%. Additionally, rates of childhood immunization differ markedly in the two income categories. In industrialized countries at least

TABLE 7.9

Child protection by selected characteristics, selected years 1986–2004 [CONTINUED]

Countries and territories	Child labour (5–14 years) 1999–2004[a, g]			Child marriage 1986–2004[b, g]			Birth registration 1999–2004[c, g]			Female genital mutilation/cutting 1998–2004[d, g]				
										Women[e] (15–49 years)			Daughters[f]
	Total	Male	Female	Total	Urban	Rural	Total	Urban	Rural	Total	Urban	Rural	Total
Summary indicators													
Sub-Saharan Africa	36	37	34	40	25	48	38	55	33	38	31	42	24
Eastern and Southern Africa	32	34	29	36	21	43	32	44	28	—	—	—	—
Western and Central Africa	41	41	41	45	28	56	41	59	35	29	29	29	19
Middle East and North Africa	9	9	7	—	—	—	—	—	—	—	—	—	—
South Asia	14	14	15	46	27	54	30	47	25	—	—	—	—
East Asia and Pacific	10[i]	11[i]	10[i]	20[i]	12[i]	25[i]	65[h]	77[i]	56[i]	—	—	—	—
Latin America and Caribbean	11	11	8	25	24	31	82	92	80	—	—	—	—
CEE/CIS[j]	—	—	—	—	—	—	—	—	—	—	—	—	—
Industrialized countries	—	—	—	—	—	—	—	—	—	—	—	—	—
Developing countries	18[i]	18[i]	17[i]	36[i]	22[i]	45[i]	45[h]	62[i]	35[i]	—	—	—	—
Least developed countries	28	29	26	50	33	57	32	44	28	—	—	—	—
World	18[i]	18[i]	17[i]	36[i]	22[i]	45[i]	45[h]	62[i]	35[i]	—	—	—	—

Notes: "—" indicates data not available.

[a]Percentage of children aged 5 to 14 years of age involved in child labour activities at the moment of the survey. A child is considered to be involved in child labour activities under the following classification: (a) children 5 to 11 years of age that during the week preceding the survey did at least one hour of economic activity or at least 28 hours of domestic work, and (b) children 12 to 14 years of age that during the week preceding the survey did at least 14 hours of economic activity or at least 42 hours of economic activity and domestic work combined. Child labour background variables: Sex of the child; urban or rural place of residence; poorest 20% or richest 20% of the population constructed from household assets; mother's education, reflecting mothers with and without some level of education.

[b]Percentage of women 20–24 years of age that were married or in union before they were 18 years old.

[c]Percentage of children less than five years of age that were registered at the moment of the survey. The numerator of this indicator includes children whose birth certificate was seen by the interviewer or whose mother or caretaker says the birth has been registered. MICS data refer to children alive at the time of the survey.

[d]Female genital mutilation/cutting (FGM/C) involves the cutting or alteration of the female genitalia for social reasons. Generally, there are three recognized types of FGM/C: clitoridectomy, excision and infibulation. Clitoridectomy is the removal of the prepuce with or without excision of all or part of the clitoris. Excision is the removal of the prepuce and clitoris along with all or part of the labia minora. Infibulation is the most severe form and consists of removal of all or part of the external genitalia, followed by joining together of the two sides of the labia minora using threads, thorns or other materials to narrow the vaginal opening.

[e]The percentage of women aged 15 to 49 years of age who have been mutilated/cut.

[f]The percentage of women aged 15 to 49 with at least one mutilated/cut daughter.

[g]Data refer to the most recent year available during the period specified in the column heading.

[h]Indicates data that differ from the standard definition or refer to only part of a country but are included in the calculation of regional and global averages.

[i]Excludes China.

[j]Central and Eastern Europe/Commonwealth of Independent States (formerly the USSR).

SOURCE: "Table 9. Child Protection," in *The State of the World's Children 2006*, United Nations Children's Fund, 2005, http://www.unicef.org/sowc/pdfs/sowc06_tables.pdf (accessed April 8, 2006). Data from Multiple Indicator Cluster Survey (MICS) and Demographic and Health Surveys (DHS).

92% of children are immunized against measles, diphtheria/pertussis/tetanus, polio, and *haemophilus influenzae*, while, at most, 79% of children in developing countries have been immunized against these common illnesses.

INFANT MORTALITY. The WHO's *World Health Report 2005* states that of the approximately 136 million babies born each year, at least 3.3 million are stillborn, more than four million die before they are twenty-eight days old, and 6.6 million die before their fifth birthday. The WHO estimates that 98% of all newborn deaths happen in the developing world—28% in sub-Saharan Africa and 36% in Southeast Asia. As of 2005, newborn deaths accounted for more than half of all infant deaths and 40% of all deaths of children under five. As a region, Southeast Asia had the highest overall number of still-births and newborn deaths—1.3 million and 1.4 million, respectively—but sub-Saharan Africa had the highest newborn death rate, at about forty-five newborn deaths per 1,000 live births in that region.

By comparison, in the United States the infant death rate (counting all infants under twelve months old) was 6.84 per 1,000 live births in 2003, down slightly from the 2002 rate of 6.95, according to the Centers for Disease Control (CDC) in "Infant Mortality Statistics from the 2003 Period Linked Birth/Infant Death Data Set" (*National Vital Statistics Reports*, vol. 54, no. 16, May 3, 2006). Wide disparities in infant death rates exist among racial and ethnic groups in the United States, ranging from a low of 4.83 per 1,000 live births for Asians and Pacific Islanders to a high of 13.6 per 1,000 live births for African-Americans. In addition, infants born to teenagers and women over forty have higher rates of mortality than those in the middle years of childbearing age. Likewise, infant death rates decrease among women with higher levels of education, and rates tend to be higher among unmarried women. According to the CDC report, all of these risk factors may be linked to a mother's socioeconomic status, which is in itself a major risk factor in infant death. Lower-income women are less likely to have the financial means to get early prenatal care, and their babies are also less likely to receive quality health care.

TABLE 7.10

Basic indicators of human development in industrialized countries, selected years 1986–2004

Indicator	Region	World
Demographic indicators		
Total population (2004)	956,315,000	6,374,050,000
Population under 18 (2004)	205,133,000	2,181,991,000
Population under 5 (2004)	54,200,000	614,399,000
Survival		
Life expectancy at birth (2004)	79	67
Infant mortality rate (under 1), per 1,000 live births (2004)	5	54
Under-5 mortality rate, per 1,000 live births (2004)	6	79
Under-5 mortality rate, average annual rate of reduction (1990–2004)	3.6	1.3
Maternal mortality ratio, per 100,000 live births (2000, adjusted)	13	400
Health and nutrition		
Percentage of infants with low birthweight (1998–2004[a])	7	16
Percentage of under-5s who are moderately or severely underweight (1996–2004[a])	—	26
Percentage of population using improved drinking water sources (2002)	100	83
Urban	100	95
Rural	100	72
Percentage of population using adequate sanitation facilities (2002)	100	58
Percentage of 1-year-old children immunized (2004) against:		
Tuberculosis (BCG) (bacillus of Calmette and Guerin)	—	84
Diphtheria/pertussis/tetanus (DPT3)	96	78
Polio (polio3)	94	80
Measles	92	76
Hepatitis B (hepB3)	63	49
Haemophilus influenzae (Hib3)	92	—
Education		
Percentage of primary school entrants reaching grade 5 (administrative data; 2000–2004[a])	—	79
Net primary school attendance ratio (1996–2004[a])		
Male	—	76
Female	—	72
Net secondary school attendance ratio (1996–2004[a])		
Male	—	40[b]
Female	—	37[b]
Adult literacy rate (2000–2004[a])	—	78

Indicator	Region	World
Economic indicators		
Gross national income per capita (US$, 2004)	32,232	6,298
Percentage of population living on less than $1 a day (1993–2003[a])	—	21
Percentage share of central government expenditure (1993–2004[a]) allocated to:		
Health	16	13
Education	4	5
Defence	11	11
Percentage share of household income (1993–2003[a]):		
Lowest 40 percent	19	18
Highest 20 percent	42	43
Human Immunodeficiency Virus (HIV)/ Acquired Immunodeficiency Syndrome (AIDS)		
Adult prevalence rate (15–49 years, end 2003)	0.4	1.1
Estimated number of adults and children (0–49 years) living with HIV/AIDS (2003)	1,600,000	37,800,000
Estimated number of children (0–14 years) living with HIV/AIDS (2003)	17,000	2,100,000
Estimated number of children (0–17 years) orphaned by HIV/AIDS (2003)	—	—
Child protection		
Birth registration (1999–2004[a])	—	45[b]
Urban	—	62[b]
Rural	—	35[b]
Child marriage (1986–2004[a])	-	36[b]
Urban	—	22[b]
Rural	—	45[b]
Child labour (5–14 years, 1999–2004[a])	—	18[b]
Male	—	18[b]
Female	—	17[b]
Women		
Adult literacy parity rate (females as a percentage of males, 2000–2004[a])	—	86
Antenatal care coverage (percentage, 1996–2004[a])	—	71
Skilled attendant at delivery (percentage, 1996–2004[a])	99	63
Lifetime risk of maternal death (2000) 1 in . . .	4,000	74

[a]Data refer to the most recent years available during the period specified.
[b]Excludes China.
SOURCE: "Industrialized Countries," in *The State of the World's Children 2006*, United Nations Children's Fund, 2005, http://www.unicef.org/sowc06/pdfs/regional_stat_sum_s21_ic.pdf (accessed April 8, 2006)

Although the overall U.S. infant mortality rate is significantly lower than rates in developing countries, the U.S. rate is more than double that of the countries with the lowest infant mortality. According to statistics reported by the UNDP in its *Human Development Report 2005*, Hong Kong, Singapore, Iceland, Japan and Sweden had the lowest rates in 2003 at three per 1,000 live births, and Sierra Leone had the highest with 182 deaths per 1,000 live births in 2003.

MORTALITY OF CHILDREN UNDER FIVE. Children's health programs begun in the 1970s and 1980s have significantly reduced certain diseases and illnesses.

Incidence of polio, for example, went from 350,000 cases reported in 1988 to 1,185 cases reported in 2005, thanks to the success of polio vaccination programs (*World Health Report 2005*). However, approximately 10.6 million children per year still die before their fifth birthday. Table 7.12 ranks countries according to their under-five mortality rate ("value" refers to the number of deaths per 1,000 live births; countries are listed in worst-to-best order).

Figure 7.13 shows that progress has been made since 1970 in reducing the mortality rate of children under five years old. In 1970 the worldwide mortality rate for young

TABLE 7.11

Basic indicators of human development in developing countries, selected years 1986–2004

Indicator	Region	World	Indicator	Region	World
Demographic indicators			**Economic indicators**		
Total population (2004)	5,166,574,000	6,374,050,000	Gross national income per capita (US$, 2004)	1,524	6,298
Population under 18 (2004)	1,925,281,000	2,181,991,000	Percentage of population living on less than $1 a day (1993–2003[a])	22	21
Population under 5 (2004)	548,486,000	614,399,000	Percentage share of central government expenditure (1993–2004[a]) allocated to:		
Survival			Health	4	13
Life expectancy at birth (2004)	65	67	Education	11	5
Infant mortality rate (under 1), per 1,000 live births (2004)	59	54	Defence	10	11
Under-5 mortality rate, per 1,000 live births (2004)	87	79	Percentage share of household income (1993–2003[a]):	15	18
Under-5 mortality rate, average annual rate of reduction (1990–2004)	1.3	1.3	Lowest 40 percent		
Maternal mortality ratio, per 100,000 live births (2000, adjusted)	440	400	Highest 20 percent	50	43
Health and nutrition			**Human Immunodeficiency Virus (HIV)/ Acquired Immunodeficiency Syndrome (AIDS)**		
Percentage of infants with low birthweight (1998–2004[a])	17	16	Adult prevalence rate (15–49 years, end 2003)	1.2	1.1
Percentage of under-5s who are moderately or severely underweight (1996–2004[a])	27	26	Estimated number of adults and children (0–49 years) living with HIV/AIDS (2003)	34,900,00	37,800,000
Percentage of population using improved drinking water sources (2002)	79	83	Estimated number of children (0–14 years) living with HIV/AIDS (2003)	2,100,000	2,100,000
Urban	92	95	Estimated number of children (0–17 years) orphaned by HIV/AIDS (2003)	—	—
Rural	70	72	**Child protection**		
Percentage of population using adequate sanitation facilities (2002)	49	58	Birth registration (1999–2004[a])	45[b]	45[b]
Percentage of 1-year-old children immunized (2004) against:			Urban	62[b]	62[b]
Tuberculosis (BCG) (bacillus of Calmette and Guerin)	84	84	Rural	35[b]	35[b]
Diphtheria/pertussis/tetanus (DPT3)	76	78	Child marriage (1986–2004[a])	36[b]	36[b]
Polio (polio3)	79	80	Urban	22[b]	22[b]
Measles	74	76	Rural	45[b]	45[b]
Hepatitis B (hepB3)	76	49	Child labour (5–14 years, 1999–2004[a])	18[b]	18[b]
Haemophilus influenzae (Hib3)	—	—	Male	18[b]	18[b]
Education			Female	17[b]	17[b]
Percentage of primary school entrants reaching grade 5 (administrative data; 2000–2004[a])	78	79	**Women**		
Net primary school attendance ratio (1996–2004[a])			Adult literacy parity rate (females as a percentage of males, 2000–2004[a])	84	86
Male	76	76	Antenatal care coverage (percentage, 1996–2004[a])	71	71
Female	72	72	Skilled attendant at delivery (percentage, 1996–2004[a])	59	63
Net secondary school attendance ratio (1996–2004[a])			Lifetime risk of maternal death (2000) 1 in . . .	61	74
Male	40[b]	40[b]			
Female	37[b]	37[b]			
Adult literacy rate (2000–2004[a])	77	78			

[a]Data refer to the most recent years available during the period specified.
[b]Excludes China.

SOURCE: "Developing Countries," in *The State of the World's Children 2006*, United Nations Children's Fund, 2005, http://www.unicef.org/sowc06/pdfs/regional_stat_sum_s21_ic.pdf (accessed April 8, 2006)

children was 146 per 1,000 live births; by 2003 it was 79 per 1,000. Still, more than 70% of child deaths in 2003 occurred in just two regions: Africa and Southeast Asia. The WHO further notes in *World Health Report 2005* that half of all deaths of children under five in 2003 occurred in just six countries: China, the Democratic Republic of the Congo, Ethiopia, India, Nigeria, and Pakistan.

According to the WHO, just six illnesses account for 70% to 90% of the deaths of young children: 19% are from acute lower respiratory infections (typically pneumonia), 17% from diarrhea, 8% from malaria, 4% from measles, 3% from HIV/AIDS, and 37% from neonatal conditions. Africa by far accounts for the most deaths of children from malaria and HIV/AIDS (90%), measles (more than 50%), and pneumonia and diarrhea (40%). (See Figures 7.14 and 7.15.)

Child Labor

Children from poor families frequently must go to work to contribute income to their household, and of all the poverty-related abuses and deprivations children suffer, child labor is among the worst, resulting in physical and psychological damage and, frequently, premature

TABLE 7.12

Mortality rankings, children under five, 2004

	Under-5 mortality rate (2004)			Under-5 mortality rate (2004)			Under-5 mortality rate (2004)	
	Value	Rank		Value	Rank		Value	Rank
Sierra Leone	283	1	Kiribati	65	66	Bulgaria	15	131
Angola	260	2	Guyana	64	67	Mauritius	15	131
Niger	259	3	Namibia	63	68	Serbia and Montenegro	15	131
Afghanistan	257	4	Marshall Islands	59	69	Dominica	14	135
Liberia	235	5	Solomon Islands	56	70	Saint Lucia	14	135
Somalia	225	6	Korea, Democratic	55	71	Seychelles	14	135
Mali	219	7	People's Republic of			Sri Lanka	14	135
Congo, Democratic Republic of the	205	8	Mongolia	52	72	The former Yugoslav Republic of Macedonia	14	135
Equatorial Guinea	204	9	Tuvalu	51	73			
Guinea-Bissau	203	10	Maldives	46	74	Bahamas	13	140
Rwanda	203	10	Georgia	45	75	Costa Rica	13	140
Chad	200	12	Guatemala	45	75	Oman	13	140
Nigeria	197	13	Morocco	43	77	Antigua and Barbuda	12	143
Côte d'Ivoire	194	14	Honduras	41	78	Barbados	12	143
Central African Republic	193	15	Algeria	40	79	Kuwait	12	143
Burkina Faso	192	16	Vanuatu	40	79	Latvia	12	143
Burundi	190	17	Belize	39	81	Malaysia	12	143
Zambia	182	18	Suriname	39	81	Bahrain	11	148
Malawi	175	19	Indonesia	38	83	Belarus	11	148
Ethiopia	166	20	Iran (Islamic Republic of)	38	83	Brunei Darussalam	9	150
Swaziland	156	21	Nicaragua	38	83	Slovakia	9	150
Guinea	155	22	Cape Verde	36	86	Chile	8	152
Benin	152	23	Egypt	36	86	Estonia	8	152
Mozambique	152	23	Brazil	34	88	Hungary	8	152
Cameroon	149	25	Philippines	34	88	Lithuania	8	152
Cambodia	141	26	Armenia	32	90	Poland	8	152
Togo	140	27	Dominican Republic	32	90	United Arab Emirates	8	152
Uganda	138	28	Turkey	32	90	United States	8	152
Senegal	137	29	China	31	93	Andorra	7	159
Zimbabwe	129	30	Lebanon	31	93	Croatia	7	159
Djibouti	126	31	Nauru	30	95	Cuba	7	159
Tanzania, United Republic of	126	31	Samoa	30	95	Australia	6	162
Iraq	125	33	Peru	29	97	Canada	6	162
Mauritania	125	33	El Salvador	28	98	Ireland	6	162
Madagascar	123	35	Mexico	28	98	Israel	6	162
Gambia	122	36	Moldova, Republic of	28	98	Korea, Republic of	6	162
Kenya	120	37	Jordan	27	101	Luxembourg	6	162
Sao Tome and Principe	118	38	Palau	27	101	Malta	6	162
Tajikistan	118	38	Saudi Arabia	27	101	Netherlands	6	162
Haiti	117	40	Ecuador	26	104	New Zealand	6	162
Botswana	116	41	Tonga	25	105	United Kingdom	6	162
Ghana	112	42	Tunisia	25	105	Austria	5	172
Yemen	111	43	Occupied Palestinian Territory	24	107	Belgium	5	172
Congo	108	44	Panama	24	107	Cyprus	5	172
Myanmar	106	45	Paraguay	24	107	Denmark	5	172
Turkmenistan	103	46	Micronesia (Federated States of)	23	110	France	5	172
Pakistan	101	47	Viet Nam	23	110	Germany	5	172
Papua New Guinea	93	48	Saint Vincent and the Grenadines	22	112	Greece	5	172
Gabon	91	49	Colombia	21	113	Italy	5	172
Sudan	91	49	Cook Islands	21	113	Liechtenstein	5	172
Azerbaijan	90	51	Grenada	21	113	Monaco	5	172
India	85	52	Qatar	21	113	Portugal	5	172
Lao People's Democratic Republic	83	53	Russian Federation	21	113	Spain	5	172
			Saint Kitts and Nevis	21	113	Switzerland	5	172
			Thailand	21	113	Czech Republic	4	185
Eritrea	82	54	Fiji	20	120	Bhutan	80	56
Lesotho	82	54	Bosnia and Herzegovina	15	131	Timor-Leste	80	56

death. The United Nations, the International Labor Organization (ILO), and other NGOs distinguish, however, between "child work" (economic activity by children at least twelve years old that is not hazardous and does not interfere with their education) and "child labor" (all work by children under age twelve; hazardous work by children aged twelve to fourteen; and all work defined as "worst forms of child labor"). "Worst forms of child labor," as defined by the ILO, include:

- All forms of slavery or practices similar to slavery, such as the sale and trafficking of children, debt bondage and serfdom and forced or compulsory labor, including forced or compulsory recruitment, of children for use in armed conflict

- The use, procuring or offering a child for prostitution, for the production of pornography or for pornographic performances

TABLE 7.12

Mortality rankings, children under five, 2004 [CONTINUED]

	Under-5 mortality rate (2004)			Under-5 mortality rate (2004)			Under-5 mortality rate (2004)	
	Value	Rank		Value	Rank		Value	Rank
Bangladesh	77	58	Romania	20	120	Norway	4	185
Nepal	76	59	Trinidad and Tobago	20	120	San Marino	4	185
Kazakhstan	73	60	Albania	19	125	Slovenia	4	185
Comoros	70	61	Venezuela	19	125	Sweden	4	185
Bolivia	69	62	Argentina	18	127	Iceland	3	192
Uzbekistan	69	62	Ukraine	18	127	Singapore	3	192
Kyrgyzstan	68	64	Uruguay	17	129	Holy See	No data	—
South Africa	67	65	Syrian Arab Republic	16	130	Niue	No data	—
Jamaica	20	120	Finland	4	185			
Libyan Arab Jamahiriya	20	120	Japan	4	185			

SOURCE: "Under–Five Mortality Rankings," in *The State of the World's Children 2006*, United Nations Children's Fund, 2005, http://www.unicef.org/sowc06/pdfs/sowc06_tables.pdf (accessed April 8, 2006)

FIGURE 7.13

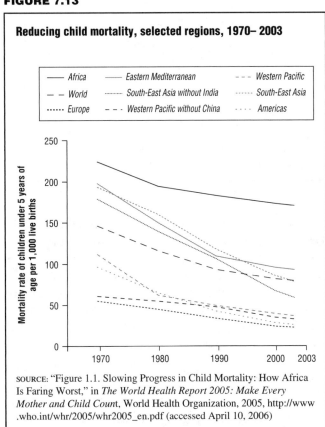

Reducing child mortality, selected regions, 1970– 2003

— Africa
— — World
······ Europe
— Eastern Mediterranean
········ South-East Asia without India
— — Western Pacific without China
— — — Western Pacific
······ South-East Asia
···· Americas

Mortality rate of children under 5 years of age per 1,000 live births

SOURCE: "Figure 1.1. Slowing Progress in Child Mortality: How Africa Is Faring Worst," in *The World Health Report 2005: Make Every Mother and Child Count*, World Health Organization, 2005, http://www.who.int/whr/2005/whr2005_en.pdf (accessed April 10, 2006)

- The use, procuring or offering of a child for illicit activities, in particular for the production and trafficking of drugs

According to the ILO in *Every Child Counts: New Global Estimates on Child Labor* (April 2002, http://www.ilo.org/public/english/standards/ipec/simpoc/others/globalest.pdf), approximately 352 million children aged five to seventeen (about 23% of the total 1.5 billion children in the world) were working in 2000. Of this number,

approximately 246 million children under age seventeen were counted as child laborers; 186.3 million of them were younger than fifteen years old, and 110 million were younger than age twelve.

Child labor occurs everywhere in the world. According to UNICEF in *Child Protection from Violence, Exploitation, and Abuse* (http://www.unicef.org/protection/index_childlabour.html), East Asia and the Pacific have the highest number of child laborers: an estimated 19% of children in the region work, with 127.3 million of them in the five-to-fourteen age group. Sub-Saharan Africa has approximately forty-eight million child laborers (29% of all children under age fifteen in the region). In Latin America and the Caribbean about 17.4 million children work (16% of all children in the region). In the Middle East and North Africa about 15% of children work. In the developed world (including Europe and the United States) about 2.5 million children work, and in transition economies about 2.4 million work. Figure 7.16 shows the percent of male and female child workers in different world regions between 1999 and 2004.

According to the ILO, as of 2000 approximately 171 million children aged five to seventeen were involved in "hazardous work." Hazardous work as defined for children includes occupations that result in physical deformities of young, undeveloped bodies; chronic illnesses such as respiratory diseases in children who work in mines and factories; injuries that can include severe burns, disfigurement, and amputated limbs; vision and hearing impairment; and chronic headaches and gastrointestinal illnesses. UNICEF's *State of the World's Children 2006* reports that as many as 70% of laboring children work in agriculture, an industry that puts children at high risk of accidents and exposure to pesticides.

Injuries and impairments of individual children are not the only risks of child labor, however, which also

FIGURE 7.14

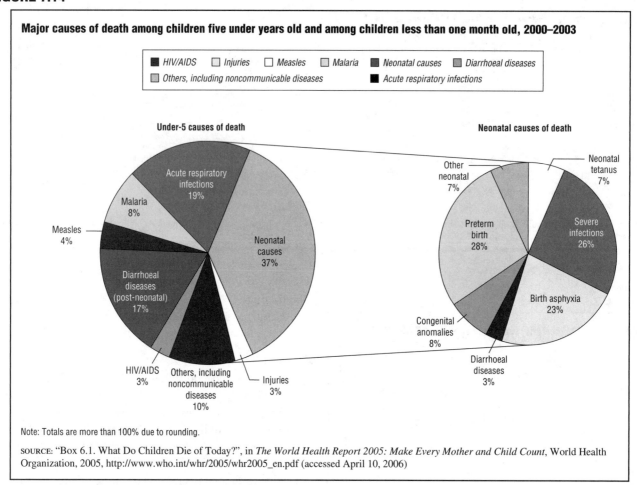

Major causes of death among children five under years old and among children less than one month old, 2000–2003

Legend: HIV/AIDS · Injuries · Measles · Malaria · Neonatal causes · Diarrhoeal diseases · Others, including noncommunicable diseases · Acute respiratory infections

Under-5 causes of death

- Acute respiratory infections 19%
- Malaria 8%
- Measles 4%
- Diarrhoeal diseases (post-neonatal) 17%
- HIV/AIDS 3%
- Others, including noncommunicable diseases 10%
- Injuries 3%
- Neonatal causes 37%

Neonatal causes of death

- Other neonatal 7%
- Preterm birth 28%
- Congenital anomalies 8%
- Diarrhoeal diseases 3%
- Birth asphyxia 23%
- Severe infections 26%
- Neonatal tetanus 7%

Note: Totals are more than 100% due to rounding.

SOURCE: "Box 6.1. What Do Children Die of Today?", in *The World Health Report 2005: Make Every Mother and Child Count*, World Health Organization, 2005, http://www.who.int/whr/2005/whr2005_en.pdf (accessed April 10, 2006)

has long-term global economic consequences. The more hours children spend working, the less time they spend in school, which in turn affects their ability to improve their economic status later in life. This in effect traps these children—and later their children—in the cycle of poverty and prolongs the economic instability of poor countries. According to the *State of the World's Children 2006*, the total international economic benefit of ending child labor would be $5,106.4 billion. Even after subtracting the cost of eliminating child labor—estimated at $760.3 billion—the net benefits would still total $4,132.5 billion. (See Table 7.13.)

Both children's economic activity and child labor can be direct results of poverty. Child labor, however, is far more insidious, dangerous, and disturbing. Experts often comment that child labor robs children of their childhood, not only because it usually means exceptionally long hours performing difficult, often crippling, work for very little pay but also because it exploits children—typically to satisfy the needs or desires of adults. Children sometimes are abducted, sold, or drawn into prostitution or pornography, armed conflict, forced or bonded labor, drug trafficking, and other illicit activities.

The ILO estimates that about 8.4 million children are employed in the unconditional worst forms of child labor. As of 2000 about 5.7 million children worked in forced or bonded labor (in other words, forms of slavery); 1.8 million were in prostitution and pornography; 1.2 million were trafficked; 300,000 were involved in armed conflict; and 600,000 were engaged in other illicit activities. (See Figure 7.17 and Table 7.14.)

Child Trafficking

Poor children are especially vulnerable to child trafficking—the illegal moving of children across cities, countries, or borders for the purpose of using them in various kinds of labor. Children may be abducted, sold, or coerced into the underground world of trafficking. Or they may go willingly, believing that a better life awaits them elsewhere. While exact numbers are impossible to ascertain because of the secretive nature of trafficking, UNICEF and other agencies believe approximately 1.2 million children are trafficked each year. Usually, they are forced into the commercial sex trade (prostitution and/or pornography); are sold as child brides; work as domestic slaves or in mines, factories, or sweatshops; or serve in one of the many instances of ongoing armed conflict across the globe.

FIGURE 7.15

Major causes of death among children under five years old, by region, 2000–2003

[By World Health Organization (WHO) region]

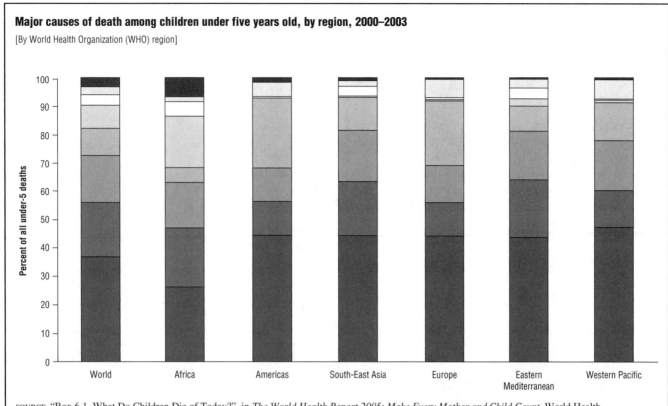

SOURCE: "Box 6.1. What Do Children Die of Today?", in *The World Health Report 2005: Make Every Mother and Child Count*, World Health Organization, 2005, http://www.who.int/whr/2005/whr2005_en.pdf (accessed April 10, 2006)

The ILO report *Facts on Trafficking of Children* (March 2003, http://www.ilo.org/public/english/standards/ipec/publ/download/factsheets/fs_trafficking_0303.pdf) notes that trafficked children typically come from poor, usually rural, areas and have parents who are uneducated and illiterate. The majority are from marginalized ethnic groups. The ILO identifies the following "supply factors" in the trafficking of children, meaning that they are factors that perpetuate the supply of children for trafficking:

• Poverty and the need to earn a living or to support the family

• The desire for a better life

• Ignorance or lack of understanding of the children, parents, or other caregivers of the negative consequences that may be associated with children leaving their homes to work

• Lack of schools or means to pay for education

• Lack of appreciation on the part of parents or children on the value of education

• Family violence or other dysfunction

• Political conflict or natural disasters that devastate local economies

• Traditions of migration for labor, land, or fodder

• Traditions of placement of rural children with urban-based relatives (particularly in Africa);

• Gender discrimination

• Being a member of a marginalized ethnic group or subservient caste

CHILDREN AT WAR. One of the less common but most horrific uses of trafficked children is as soldiers in armed combat. Children as young as nine have been kidnapped and forced to participate in the world's many conflicts and civil wars. Or children may willingly join in combat to escape poverty or abuse at home. Exact numbers are unknown, but it is thought that tens of thousands of children in regions all over the world are trafficked for the purposes of combat. According to the *Child Soldiers Global Report 2004* (2004, http://www.child-soldiers.org/document_get.php?id=966), from 2001 to 2004 children under age eighteen were used as soldiers in ongoing armed conflicts in Afghanistan, Angola, Burundi, Colombia, the Democratic Republic of the Congo (DRC), Côte d'Ivoire, Guinea, India, Iraq, Israel and the Occupied Palestinian Territories, Indonesia, Liberia, Myanmar, Nepal, Philippines, the Russian Federation, Rwanda, Sri Lanka, Somalia, Sudan, and Uganda. Children are used in armed combat, to lay mines and explosives, as spies and decoys, for cooking and domestic labor, and as sex slaves for older soldiers. As of August 2004, seventy-seven countries had

FIGURE 7.16

Percentage of children ages 5–14 involved in child labor activities, 1999–2004

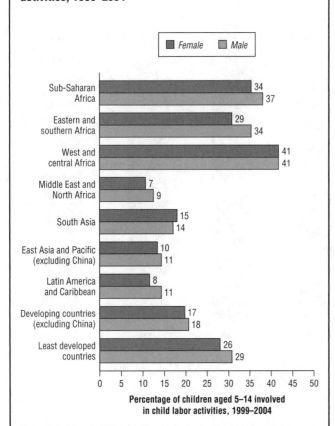

Percentage of children aged 5–14 involved in child labor activities, 1999–2004

Notes: Child labor: A child is considered to be involved in child labor activities under the following classification: (a) children 5 to 11 years of age that during the week preceding the survey did at least one hour of economic activity or at least 28 hours of domestic work; (b) children 12 to 14 years of age that during the week preceding the survey did at least 14 hours of economic activity or at least 42 hours of economic activity and domestic work combined. Regional averages: These aggregates do not include all countries in each region. However, sufficient data was available for more than 50 percent of the target population to generate the averages for the regions shown. Averages for East Asia and Pacific and the developing countries do not include China. Data range: Data refer to the most recent year available during the period specified.

SOURCE: "Figure 3.6. Child Labor in the Developing World," in *The State of the World's Children 2006*, United Nations Children's Fund, 2005, http://www.unicef.org/sowc06/pdfs/sowc0506_eps_charts.pdf (accessed April 8, 2006). Data from Multiple Indicator Cluster Surveys (MICS) and Demographic and Health Surveys (DHS).

TABLE 7.13

Total economic costs and benefits of eliminating child labor over the period 2000–20

	US$ billion, at purchasing power parity
Economic costs	
Education supply	493.4
Transfer implementation	10.7
Interventions	9.4
Opportunity costs	246.8
Total costs	**760.3**
Economic benefits	
Education	5,078.4
Health	28.0
Total benefits	**5,106.4**
Net economic benefit (total benefits − total costs)	4,346.1
Transfer payments	213.6
Net financial benefit (net economic benefit − transfer payments)	**4,132.5**

SOURCE: "Figure 3.4. Total Economic Costs and Benefits of Eliminating Child Labor over the Period 2000–2020," in *The State of the World's Children 2006*, United Nations Children's Fund, 2005, http://www.unicef.org/sowc06/pdfs/sowc0506_eps_charts.pdf (accessed April 8, 2006). Data from International Labour Organization, *Investing in Every Child: An Economic Study on the Costs and Benefits of Eliminating Child Labour*, International Programme on the Elimination of Child Labour, ILO, Geneva, 2004. Copyright © 2005, International Labour Organization.

FIGURE 7.17

Children in unconditional worst forms of child labour and exploitation, 2002

[Thousands; 2000]

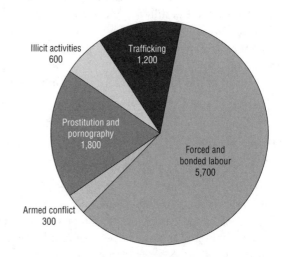

Note: Unconditional worst forms of child labour correspond to those outlined in Article 3 of the International Labour Organization Convention No. 182.

SOURCE: "Figure 3.7. Children in Unconditional Worst Forms of Child Labour and Exploitation," in *The State of the World's Children 2006*, United Nations Children's Fund, 2005, http://www.unicef.org/sowc06/pdfs/sowc0506_eps_charts.pdf (accessed April 8, 2006). Data from International Labour Organization, *Every Child Counts: New Global Estimates on Child Labour*, ILO, International Programme on the Elimination of Child Labour, Statistical Informational and Monitoring Programme on Child Labour, April 2002. Copyright © 2005, International Labour Organization.

ratified the 2002 Optional Protocol to the UN Convention on the Rights of the Child that sets eighteen as the legal age at which people are eligible to participate in combat operations. The International Criminal Court's Rome Statute defines all recruitment of children under age eighteen a war crime.

THE SEX INDUSTRY. Also illegal under international law is trafficking in children for the commercial sex industry, which has grown significantly since the 1980s. In fact, according to *Trafficking in Women, Girls, and Boys. Key Issues for Population and Development Programmes* (October 2002, http://www.unfpa.org/upload/lib_pub_file/266_filename_Trafficking.pdf), the UNFPA reports that

TABLE 7.14

Estimated number of children in the worst forms of child labor, 2000

Unconditional worst form of child labor	Global estimate (in thousands)
Trafficked children	1,200
Children in forced & bonded labor	5,700
Children in armed conflict	300
Children in prostitution & pornography	1,800
Children in illicit activities	600
Total	**8,400***

*The total excludes the category of trafficked children because of the risk of double-counting.

SOURCE: "Estimated Number of Children in Unconditional Worst Forms of Child Labour," in *Every Child Counts: New Global Estimates on Child Labour*, International Labour Organization, International Programme on the Elimination of Child Labour/Statistical Information and Monitoring Programme on Child Labour, International Labour Office, April 2002, http://www.ilo.org/public/english/standards/ipec/simpoc/others/globalest.pdf (accessed April 8, 2006)

FIGURE 7.18

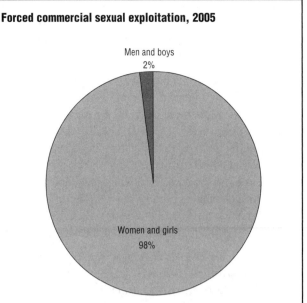

Forced commercial sexual exploitation, 2005

Men and boys 2%

Women and girls 98%

SOURCE: "Figure 3.5. Forced Commercial Sexual Exploitation, 2005," in *The State of the World's Children 2006*, United Nations Children's Fund, 2005, http://www.unicef.org/sowc06/pdfs/sowc0506_eps_charts .pdf (accessed April 8, 2006). Data from International Labour Organization, "A Global Alliance against Forced Labour," ILO, Geneva, 2005. Copyright © 2005, International Labour Organization.

70% of trafficked women and children end up working in the sex industry, and those working in other industries are also at risk of sexual exploitation. Children who end up forced into prostitution are usually girls between the ages of twelve and eighteen, but children as young as five have been found working as sex slaves. According to UNICEF in*State of the World's Children 2006*, trafficking children for the commercial sex industry is most common in East Asia and the Pacific, South Asia, Europe, and Latin America and the Caribbean. Many of the trafficked children who end up working as prostitutes are poor and go willingly with their traffickers because they are offered legitimate-sounding work as waitresses or maids. By the time they have been moved to unfamiliar cities or countries, where they may not speak the language, they have no choice but to work as prostitutes. Of those forced into commercial sexual exploitation worldwide, 98% are women or girls and 2% are men or boys. (See Figure 7.18.)

International tourism and the widening poverty gap are at least partly responsible for the rise in trafficking and child prostitution in the early twenty-first century. Developing countries are heavily dependent on their tourism industries for economic growth, and demand for prostitutes is typically high in tourist regions. *Trafficking in Women, Girls, and Boys* cites studies from Japan, Sweden, the United States, the Ukraine, and Moldova that find that most customers of trafficked prostitutes are married men of all races, nationalities, and ages. The common thread in the studies was the ability to pay for services—meaning that a relatively stable economic situation was necessary to maintain the market for prostitutes. The UNFPA reports that countries that have experienced expanding economies and growing middle classes—along with growing lower classes—have seen the greatest increase in prostitution. However, the demand for younger and younger "prostitutes"—some just four or five years old—is due to men's fears and superstitions about HIV/AIDS: men who frequent prostitutes are willing to pay for sex with children so young they cannot possibly give them AIDS.

IN THE UNITED STATES. In January 2006 President George W. Bush signed into law the Trafficking Victims Protection Reauthorization Act of 2005, which expanded and strengthened the Trafficking Victims Protection Act (TVPA) of 2000. According to the U.S. Department of State's *Trafficking in Persons Report 2005* (June 2005, http://www.state.gov/documents/organization/47255.pdf), an estimated 18,000 to 20,000 people, most of them women and children, are trafficked to the United States annually.

Debt Bondage and Forced Labor

Debt bondage (also called bonded labor, forced labor, or indentured servitude), is a way for people to pay off their debts to others with labor instead of money. This definition, however, fails to express the true nature of debt bondage, which is essentially a form of modern slavery, according to the UN and other international agencies. It is not unusual for very poor families—particularly in underdeveloped and developing countries—to place their children into debt bondage to pay off money they owe. Families also may sell a child into bonded labor for an advance of money, believing that they will be able to buy the child back when they earn enough money or when the child performs enough work to cover the cash advance. However, poor families can rarely buy their children back, and often debt bondage crosses generations—with children sold into labor to pay off the debts or loans of their grandparents or great-grandparents.

The reason debt bondage is common in the developing world is that poor countries generally lack systems of credit and bankruptcy, so there may be no other way for poor families to repay debts. The ILO includes any kind of work done by children under debt bondage in its classification of unconditional worst forms of child labor. Debt bondage sometimes overlaps with trafficking, as people performing debt bondage—again, usually women and children—may be trafficked to other countries or overseas; conversely, trafficking victims may later be sold into debt bondage.

The study *Forced and Bonded Child Labor* (2006, http://www.dol.gov/ILAB/media/reports/iclp/sweat2/bonded.htm) by the U.S. Department of Labor's International Labor Affairs Bureau (ILAB) names Asia and Latin America as the regions where debt bondage and forced labor of children are most common and most extreme. In South Asia as many as one million children are bonded to work in the carpet-making industry of India, Pakistan, and Nepal. Children from age five to fifteen are forced to work up to twenty hours a day, seven days a week. They are not allowed to go outside, and they may be made to sleep and eat in the same room in which they work. They are punished brutally for any transgressions, from crying to making mistakes in weaving to trying to escape. Reports of children being chained to carpet looms are not uncommon.

Millions of children also perform forced and bonded labor in South Asia's glass-making factories, stone quarries, silk manufacturers, lock-making factories, brass industry, fireworks industry, brick kilns, and cigar makers. Children in Thailand and the Philippines are forced to labor in sweatshops, although number estimates are uncertain. In China the numbers of children being kidnapped and bonded to work in textile factories and mines are believed to be on the rise.

According to the ILAB in *Forced and Bonded Child Labor*, in Latin American countries entire families—including children of all ages—are bonded in Brazil's charcoal manufacturing industry and Peru's gold mines. As with all bonded labor, working conditions for these families are essentially those of slavery. Families working in Brazil's charcoal operations are commonly shipped hundreds of miles from their homes, to remote areas with no schools or medical facilities, and they may be kept at the charcoal plants by armed guards. They are also forced to buy food and supplies from their employers, who inflate the prices to keep the families in debt. Injuries and malnourishment are common among these families. In Peru malaria is one of the many ailments suffered by the children who pan for gold in the Madre de Dios riverbed. Recruiters use deception to convince Peruvian children to go to work at the gold mines; when the children agree to work, the gold mine employers break their promises, knowing the children have no labor rights, and the children become indentured.

FORCED LABOR IN THE UNITED STATES. According to *Hidden Slaves: Forced Labor in the United States* (September 2004, http://www.hrcberkeley.org/download/hiddenslaves_report.pdf), the University of California–Berkeley's Human Rights Center notes that at any given time there are at least 10,000 people—particularly young women and girls—being forced to labor against their will in the United States. The majority are from China, Mexico, and Vietnam, although victims are known to have been brought to the United States from at least thirty-eight countries (see Table 2.3 in Chapter 2), and there have been cases of young U.S. citizens being held captive and forced to labor, particularly in prostitution rings. Once in the United States, most victims end up in large states with many immigrants; forced laborers and/or people in debt bondage have been discovered in at least ninety U.S. cities. (See Figure 2.4 in Chapter 2.) The most common sectors forced laborers work in are prostitution and sex services (46%), domestic service (27%), agriculture (10%), sweatshop/factory (5%), and restaurant and hotel work (4%). Others become involved in the sexual exploitation of children (as victims or perpetrators; 3.1%), the entertainment industry (3.1%), or become mail-order brides (0.8%).

CHAPTER 8
POVERTY AND ENVIRONMENTAL HAZARDS

Conditions in the environment that have a negative impact on the health and well-being of a population are known as environmental hazards. These can be natural events, such as an overabundance of insects that destroys crops; a weather pattern that causes a drought or flood; or a sudden, violent disaster such as an earthquake or volcanic eruption. Environmental hazards can also be human-caused problems such as air and water pollution, chemical toxicity, or a poor use of resources that brings about environmental degradation. These events can have an immediate, devastating impact, or they can have more extended consequences. A famine, for example, might cause hundreds of thousands of people to starve to death over a number of months, or exposure to pollution might be associated with long-term health effects over several generations.

THE EFFECTS OF ENVIRONMENTAL
HAZARDS ON THE POOR

Throughout the world, the poor are more often and more severely affected by environmental hazards, including both daily pollutants and large-scale disasters. In a study published in the *Annual Review of Public Health* (vol. 23, 2002, http://publhealth.annualreviews.org/cgi/reprint/23/1/303.pdf), Gary W. Evans and Elyse Kantrowitz found that low-income Americans are more likely to be exposed, and exposed at higher levels, to pollutants and other risks in their homes, schools, and workplaces. For example, flaking, lead-based paint, which is a particular danger to children, is more prevalent in the poorly maintained, older houses of low-income neighborhoods than in newly constructed homes or those that are carefully maintained. In underdeveloped and developing countries environmental risks are generally many times greater because health and safety regulations are less stringent.

Natural disasters affect the poor disproportionately because they so often occur in rural regions and high-risk zones where poor people live out of tradition or necessity. In addition, high-income countries are often better prepared for emergencies than low-income countries. As researchers for the World Bank pointed out in "Natural Disasters: Counting the Cost," (March 2004), developed countries tend to have early warning systems and emergency response plans, as well as emergency medical care and insurance coverage. In low-income countries and remote areas, communication systems are less reliable, if they exist at all, making it difficult to implement early warning systems. After a disaster, victims must often wait for outside help from international organizations, and any money targeted for local development plans must be diverted to relief and rebuilding efforts, which is often a significant setback to human development projects.

WHICH AREAS ARE MOST VULNERABLE
TO NATURAL DISASTERS?

In the e-book *Natural Disaster Hotspots: A Global Risk Analysis* (March 2005), researchers for the World Bank reported that more than half the global population, 3.4 billion people, are vulnerable to natural disasters, especially in Bangladesh, Nepal, the Dominican Republic, Burundi, Haiti, Taiwan, Malawi, El Salvador, and Honduras, where more than 90% of the population of each country is at risk of death from two or more hazards. The regions that statistically face the greatest risks are Central America, East and South Asia, parts of the Mediterranean, and the Middle East. In March 2004 the World Bank reported that two billion people had been affected by natural disasters since the mid-1990s. During the 1990s, 800,000 people were killed in disasters that resulted in direct financial losses of $63 billion annually, not including the cost of emergency relief, cleanup, and rebuilding.

THE NATURAL AND HUMAN-MADE DISASTER OF FAMINE

Famine is the phenomenon of large-scale starvation in a population because of a severe shortage of food or a lack of access to food. It can be caused by natural occurrences such as drought, flooding, or pestilence, or it can be the result of war, in which food is used as a weapon, or even unwise government policies. It is, overall, one of the most devastating events human beings can experience and one of the most dramatic and emotional from the point of view of spectators worldwide. For centuries, periodic famines were a more or less normal part of human existence, mostly because of crop failure. However, within the past 200 years or so famines have occurred as a result of economic and political manipulations. For example, the Irish Potato Famine of 1845 to 1849, which killed an estimated 500,000 to one million people, was caused by a combination of factors, including a naturally occurring potato fungus that ruined crops, Irish property law, and British import-export practices that had some Irish food producers actually exporting crops to England while the Irish were literally starving to death.

Famines in modern times almost exclusively afflict the poor, and in general they afflict those who are the most poor with greatest frequency and most serious effect. Modern, developed countries have sufficient wealth and infrastructure that they do not suffer from famines except under the most extraordinary of circumstances. The most recent famine in a developed country was in the Netherlands in 1944, when an exceptionally difficult winter combined with the destruction caused by World War II caused at least 30,000 Dutch people to starve to death. Poorer, underdeveloped regions have suffered many famines since that time, however. People in these areas may have difficulty meeting their basic needs during the best of times, and when disaster strikes it can become impossible for them to find enough food to eat. This is especially true for the poorest members of these societies.

International relief organizations use a five-level scale to categorize the severity and magnitude of famines: food secure; food insecure; food crisis, famine; severe famine; and extreme famine. A famine that results in fewer than 1,000 deaths is considered a minor famine; one that results in one million or more deaths is a catastrophic famine.

Ethiopia: The "Face of Famine"

The Ethiopian famine in 1984–85 was the result of nearly all the contributing factors to famine—drought, war, politics, and pestilence—coalescing in a single country. By 1986 at least one million people had starved to death. Perhaps the most remarkable thing about Ethiopia's famine was the international outrage it provoked and the public response it elicited, ushering in a period of international charitable donation that continues more than twenty years later.

WAR AND POLITICS IN ETHIOPIA. Engaged in a civil war with its northern province of Eritrea since 1960, Ethiopia was taken over in 1974 by a pro-Soviet military junta called the Derg. In the early 1970s the country had experienced a drought and subsequent famine, from which it had not fully recovered by the end of the decade. With the Derg focusing on insurgencies that had sprung up in all of Ethiopia's regions by 1976, government spending was directed toward increasing military power rather than addressing crop failure. By the late 1970s another drought was beginning, and by the early 1980s famine was inevitable. The war with Eritrea cut off relief supplies through the north, and anti-Soviet Eritrean rebels, backed by the United States, took control of all of Ethiopia's sea ports, further isolating the country's hungry citizens and damaging its economy. Further complicating matters was Ethiopia's agricultural economy, which had focused for many years on growing crops for export, especially coffee, rather than for its own subsistence.

IMAGES OF DEATH BROADCAST AROUND THE WORLD. By March 1984 the Ethiopian government appealed to the international community for aid, but Western leaders were reluctant to send money to a pro-Soviet country that was known for its military spending. In the summer of 1984 European countries had surplus crops, but none of the food was sent to Ethiopia. Then in October 1984, with 200,000 people already dead and eight million more at risk of starvation, a Canadian Broadcasting Corporation news crew in Tigray province in northern Ethiopia covered the story, taking photographs and footage of the dead and dying and broadcasting them to the world. One image in particular, of a little girl named Birhan Woldu who was apparently about to die, caught the public's attention and became known as the "face of famine." Although the girl survived and has become an international symbol for hope, the image of her emaciated face, delirious from hunger, motivated people around the world to donate to emergency relief funds for the country. According to BBC News Online's Kate Milner ("Flashback 1984: Portrait of a Famine," April 6, 2000, http://news.bbc.co.uk/1/hi/world/africa/703958.stm), relief agencies received donations totaling nearly £5 million in just three days from the United Kingdom alone.

THE ETHIOPIAN GOVERNMENT'S SOLUTION. In December 1984 the situation had become completely chaotic. Although international aid was beginning to enter the country, Ethiopian leaders were intercepting the supplies, first to keep them away from insurgents in the regions fighting for independence, and second to divert them to their own soldiers. Thousands of starving

Ethiopians—refugees from both the war and the famine—were fleeing to Sudan every day. The arrival of relief supplies in villages set off riots, with people desperate to get food for their children. In 1985–86 the government imposed a policy of resettlement, with the military forcibly moving those in the northern portions of the country south and relocating peasants into planned villages around such services as water, utilities, medical care, and schools. However, the services promised by Ethiopian leaders were rarely provided, and food production throughout the country actually declined. In 1985–86 Ethiopian crops were hit with a wave of locusts, which destroyed much of the harvest.

BAND AID AND LIVE AID. On October 23, 1984, BBC journalist Michael Buerk reported on the famine from Ethiopia. Among his television audience was Irish pop singer Bob Geldof of the post–punk-era band Boomtown Rats. That night Geldof telephoned another British pop musician, Midge Ure of the band Ultravox, with a plan to record a song about the famine and donate all the proceeds to relief efforts. Just over a month later, on November 25, more than forty of the United Kingdom's most famous pop musicians—including U2's lead singer Bono, who would go on to become one of the most visible celebrities to campaign for poverty relief—were assembled under the name Band Aid in a recording studio to produce the single "Do They Know It's Christmas?" Released on December 3, the song became the best-selling single in UK history at the time and generated about $13 million for Ethiopian famine relief.

In the summer of 1985 Geldof and Ure organized Live Aid, a worldwide concert with venues in London, Philadelphia, Sydney, and Moscow that featured some of best-known pop musicians of the time and was broadcast in 100 countries to an estimated 1.5 billion viewers. The concerts raised approximately $245 million for famine relief and ushered in a new era of charity events with celebrity participants that continues into the twenty-first century. For his efforts, Geldof was knighted in England and has been nominated for the Nobel Peace Prize. The song "Do They Know It's Christmas?" was re-recorded by different sets of popular singers once in 1985 (Band Aid II) and again in 2004 (Band Aid 20), with the proceeds going to poverty relief through Geldof's organization, Band Aid Trust.

ONE FAMINE ENDS, ANOTHER BEGINS. In early 2006 the entire Horn of Africa region, which includes Ethiopia, Kenya, Somalia, and Djibouti, was in danger of experiencing another food crisis. According the United Nations Food and Agriculture Organization (FAO), as of January 2006 an estimated eleven million people in these countries were at risk of starvation because of drought and ongoing violent conflict. The FAO reported that at least eight million people in Ethiopia, 2.5 million in Kenya, two million in Somalia,

and 150,000 in Djibouti were expected to be dependent on food aid at least through the summer of 2006 ("Millions of People Are on the Brink of Starvation in the Horn of Africa," January 6, 2006, http://www.fao.org/newsroom/en/news/2006/1000206/index.html).

NATURAL DISASTERS OF 2004–05

The years 2004 and 2005 saw three natural disasters so devastating that they shocked the world. All of them had an especially powerful impact on the poor. One was in a high-poverty area that was also a popular tourist destination for the wealthy; the second was in a desperately impoverished zone with treacherous terrain and little outside contact; and the third, in one of the world's richest nations, exposed a long-ignored underclass. These disasters and their impact demonstrate how natural catastrophes tend to push those who are already struggling to get by deeper into poverty.

Asian Tsunami

On December 26, 2004, an undersea earthquake with a magnitude of more than 9.0 on the Richter scale (a measure of an earthquake's magnitude) occurred in the Indian Ocean, off the coast of Sumatra, Indonesia. Unlike most earthquakes, which last several seconds, the Sumatra earthquake lasted nearly ten minutes and briefly shook the entire planet, triggering other, less powerful, earthquakes around the world and a massive tsunami (a series of rolling tidal waves) that devastated twelve countries in and along the Indian Ocean and caused deaths as far away as South Africa. The earthquake was so powerful that scientists say it caused the Earth to shake on its axis and slightly altered its rotation. The exact number of dead will never be known, but some estimates put the death toll at nearly 300,000. The countries directly affected include Indonesia, Sri Lanka, India, Thailand, Somalia, Myanmar, Maldives, Malaysia, Tanzania, Seychelles, Bangladesh, South Africa, Yemen, Kenya, and Madagascar. (See Figure 8.1.) Thousands of tourists, enjoying the region's spectacular beaches, were among those killed. In all, the earthquake and tsunami together are believed to be one of the deadliest and costliest natural disasters on record.

The affected areas included some of the poorest in the world. In the Indonesian provinces of Aceh and Nias, one-third of the population lived in poverty before the disaster struck, and a year later, nearly 50% of those who had survived the disaster were dependent on food aid. Aceh also has a history of violent conflict, with Acehnese separatists periodically rebelling against the Indonesian government in uprisings that intensified the poverty and general instability that prevailed in the region before the tsunami occurred. Indonesia suffered the most casualties in the tsunami, with more than 100,000 people dead, another 100,000 injured, and as many as 700,000

FIGURE 8.1

Areas most affected by Asian tsunami, 2005

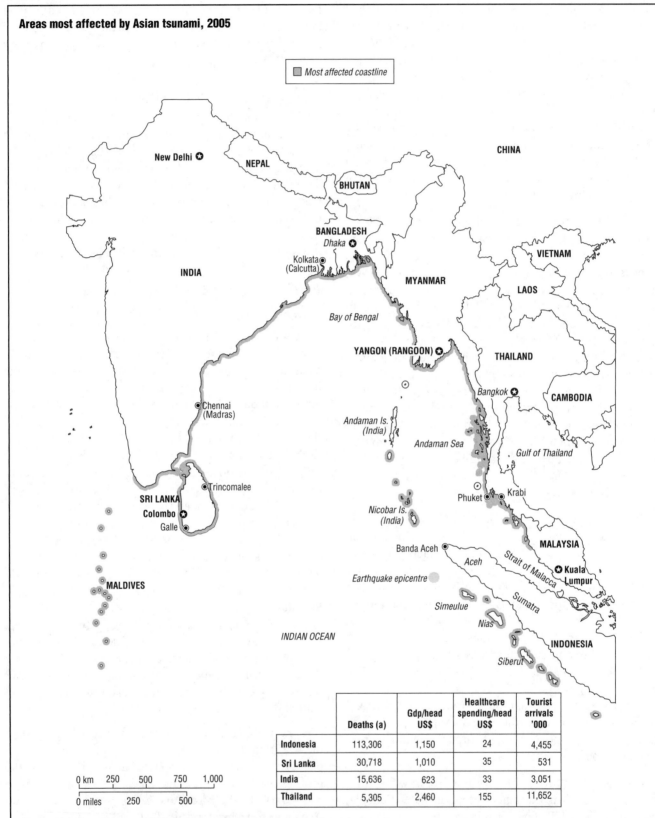

☐ *Most affected coastline*

	Deaths (a)	Gdp/head US$	Healthcare spending/head US$	Tourist arrivals '000
Indonesia	113,306	1,150	24	4,455
Sri Lanka	30,718	1,010	35	531
India	15,636	623	33	3,051
Thailand	5,305	2,460	155	11,652

*Confirmed deaths as of January 9, 2005. Totals are expected to rise.
Notes: All other data are Economist Intelligence Unit estimates, 2004.

SOURCE: "Areas Most Affected by Asian Tsunami," in *Asia's Tsunami: The Impact*, The Economist Intelligence Unit, January 2005, http//72.14.203.104/
search?q=cache:1EVDy4JYaYwJ:www.pppl.gov/library/tsunami_special.pdf+&hl=en&gl=us&ct=clnk&cd=1 (accessed March 28, 2006)

displaced. Sri Lanka, where the tsunami killed an estimated 38,000 people, injured 15,000, and displaced 500,000, has also been engaged in a twenty-year civil war, in which more than 64,000 people have been killed and 800,000 displaced (World Bank, "Sri Lanka Country Fact Sheet," July 2005). According to the World Bank report, nearly one-quarter of Sri Lankans lived in poverty in 2005.

In *After the Tsunami: Rapid Environmental Assessment* (2005, http://www.unep.org/tsunami/tsunami_rpt.asp), the United Nations Environmental Program (UNEP) estimated damage to the region at more than $10 billion. Every living creature was affected, including the wildlife in ecosystems that were destroyed. Many mangrove forests, coral reefs, sand dunes, and sea grasses were devastated, even while serving as a buffer against the strongest impact of the waves and preventing even more destruction. Fishermen lost their boats, fishing equipment, and livelihoods. Farmers lost the farm animals necessary to their survival and lost rice, fruit, and vegetable crops to saltwater contamination.

Many more women than men were killed, as many men were out fishing on the sea, where their boats managed to survive the waves, or were working in the fields or selling crops at inland markets. The women and children, by contrast, were either at home or on the beach awaiting the fishermen's return. An Oxfam survey in Indonesia found that in the four villages surveyed in the Aceh Besar district, male survivors outnumbered females three to one. In the North Aceh district, women made up 77% of the dead. Oxfam has noted that this disproportion of men to women could have significant socioeconomic consequences in these societies, causing long-term demographic changes and potentially altering women's home, work, marriage, childbearing, property ownership, and education patterns, possibly over the course of generations.

Northern Pakistan Earthquake

On October 8, 2005, an earthquake with a magnitude of about 7.6 on the Richter scale hit South Asia. Damage and casualties were recorded over an area of 11,500 square miles. According to the ReliefWeb organization in *Pakistan: A Summary Report on Muzaffarabad Earthquake* (November 7, 2005), more than 80,000 people were killed, 200,000 were injured, and four million were left homeless. The earthquake set off a series of landslides that buried entire villages and blocked roadways in the mountains, impeding rescue efforts. Damages were estimated at $5 billion. Afghanistan and northern India suffered some damage from the earthquake, but Pakistan by far sustained the most, particularly the Pakistan-controlled portion of Kashmir, whose capital city, Muzaffarabad, was completely destroyed.

According to the UNDP's *Pakistan National Human Development Report 2003* (2003, http://www.un.org.pk/nhdr/nhdr-pak-2003.pdf) Pakistan fares worse than other South Asian countries in human development indicators. In 1998 Pakistan's rate of infant mortality was ninety-one per 1,000 lives births, and its child mortality was 120 per 1,000. Between 1990 and 1996, 30% of Pakistanis had access to sanitation. In 1997 primary school enrollment was 62%. (See Table 8.1.) In 1999 the literacy rate was 46.4%. Sixty percent of Pakistan's health problems in 2003 were attributable to three factors: communicable infectious diseases, reproductive disorders, and malnutrition—all directly related to high levels of poverty.

Stockpiles of food that had been stored for the winter were destroyed in the rubble, and because of the postquake landslides, the remote Himalayan villages became even more isolated. Relief efforts were complicated further because certain areas of the northwestern frontier province in the Pakistani-controlled region of Kashmir are part of the "forbidden tribal belt" (Reuters Foundation's AlertNet, "World Vision Aids Pakistan Victims in Forbidden Quake Zone," March 1, 2006). These areas are ruled by tribal leaders, who forbid outsiders to visit; in fact, the only maps of the region were created by a British army officer in 1888. With more than 13,000 families in these villages in desperate need of help after the earthquake, tribal leaders contacted a trusted Pakistani aid organization which managed to send help to the area. Other aid organizations were warned not to enter the area because of the possibility of armed attack.

By March 2006 millions of people in the mountains were still living in tents, with no water, electricity, or communications systems. Snow in the high elevations and heavy rains in the valleys hampered relief efforts, as helicopters were grounded and roadways blocked. The U.S. military organized a 1,000-person relief effort in and around the city of Balakot, which had been largely destroyed. In February 2006 the World Health Organization reported that the region was seeing many cases of acute respiratory infection, acute diarrhea, fevers, and earthquake-related injuries ("Health Situation Report #34," February 14–28, 2006). There have also been reported cases of measles, meningitis, and acute hepatitis.

Hurricane Katrina: Exposing the Worst in the World's Richest Nation

On August 29, 2005, one of the strongest, costliest, and deadliest hurricanes in U.S. history made landfall on the Gulf Coast states of Louisiana, Mississippi, and Alabama. More than 1,800 people were killed, the Gulf Coast was devastated, and nearly 90,000 square miles of land were declared a federal disaster area. The damage was estimated

TABLE 8.1

Pakistan's human development compared with India and Sri Lanka, by selected characteristics, selected years 1992–99

		Pakistan	India	Sri Lanka	Low income countries
Health					
Infant mortality rate (per 1,000 live births)	Year 1998	91	70	16	68
Child (under 5) mortality rate (per 1,000)	Year 1998	120	83	18	107
Prevalence of child malnutrition (% of children under 5)	Years 1992–98	38		38	
	Male	61	62	71	59
Life expectancy at birth (years)	Year 1998				
	Female	63	64	76	61
Access to sanitation (% of population)	Years 1990–96	30	16	52	24
Education					
Net enrollment ratio at primary level (% of relevant age group)	Year 1997	62[b]	77	100	76
Public expenditure on education (% of GNP[a])	Year 1997	2.7	3.2	3.4	3.3
Population					
Average annual population growth rate (%)	Years 1990–99	2.5	1.8	1.2	2.0
Total fertility rate (births per woman)	Year 1998	4.9	3.2	2.1	3.1
Contraceptive prevalence rate (% of women ages 15–49)	Years 1990–98	24	41		24
Human development index (HDI)[c]					
Human development index	Year 2002	0.499	0.577	0.741	

[a]GNP is Gross National Product.
[b]For the year 1996.
[c]Human development index (HDI) is a summary measure of human development. It measures the average achievements in a country in three basic dimensions of human development: (1) a long and healthy life, as measured by life expectancy at birth, (2) knowledge, as measured by the adult literacy rate (with two-thirds weight) and the combined primary, secondary and tertiary gross enrollment ratio (with one-third weight), and (3) A decent standard of living, as measured by Gross Domestic Product (GDP) per capita. Calculation of HDI is an evolving methodology, and comparisons should not be made between years (when methods might have varied) but can be made between countries.

SOURCE: Akmal Hussain, with A.R. Kemal, A.I. Hamid, Imran Ali, Khawar Mumtaz, and Ayub Qutub, "Table 5. Pakistan's Human Development Compared with India and Sri Lanka," in *Pakistan National Human Development Report 2003: Poverty, Growth, and Governance*, United Nations Development Programme, 2003, http://hdr.undp.org/docs/reports/national/PAK_Pakistan/Pakistan_2003_en.pdf (accessed April 10, 2006). Data from World Bank, *World Development Report 2000/2001: Attacking Poverty*, and from United Nations Development Programme (UNDP), *Human Development Report 2002*.

---

at $75 billion. Much of the city of New Orleans lies below sea level and is protected by a system of levees, which were breached by the rising water, and more than 80% of the city was flooded. Residents trapped in their homes climbed to their attics, then to their roofs, but many drowned.

In the aftermath of the storm, much of the world's attention was focused on two factors. First, the administration of President George W. Bush and the Federal Emergency Management Agency (FEMA) came under scathing criticism for their handling of the crisis. Critics charged that the preparations for the storm were inadequate, that warnings about its danger were ignored or came too late, and that rescue efforts were uncoordinated and often ineffective. Second, the catastrophe highlighted the extreme poverty of many of the residents in the areas hardest hit by the storm, many of whom did not own cars with which to escape or even have telephone service. Because many of the residents of the devastated areas were African-American, the exposure of their poverty and the feeble response by FEMA engendered charges of racism and brought to light issues of racial inequality that still persist in the United States.

POVERTY BEFORE THE HURRICANE. Arloc Sherman and Isaac Shapiro report in *Essential Facts about the Victims of Hurricane Katrina* (September 19, 2005, http://www.cbpp.org/9-19-05pov.htm) that the hurricane-

TABLE 8.2

Poverty and income in U.S. states hit by Hurricane Katrina, 2005

[2004 data]

	Poverty rate	Rank	Median household income	Rank
Alabama	16.1%	8th worst	$36,709	9th lowest
Louisiana	19.4%	2nd worst	$35,110	5th lowest
Mississippi	21.6%	Worst	$31,642	2nd lowest
U.S.	13%		$44,684	

Notes: According to the Census Bureau, American Community Survey (which the government uses for ranking states by poverty), the national poverty rate was 13.1 percent in 2004. According to another government survey, the Current Population Survey, it was 12.7 percent. In the 2000 census data, Alabama is ranked the fifth poorest state, while the ranks for Mississippi and Louisiana do not change. These state ranks exclude the District of Columbia.

SOURCE: Arloc Sherman and Isaac Shapiro, "Table 1. Poverty Especially High, and Incomes Especially Low, in States Hit Hardest by Katrina," in *Essential Facts about the Victims of Hurricane Katrina*, Center on Budget and Policy Priorities, September 19, 2005, http://www.cbpp.org/9-1905pov.pdf (accessed April 10, 2006)

affected states of Mississippi, Louisiana, and Alabama were in 2005 the first, second, and eighth poorest states in the country, respectively. More than one million of the 5.8 million people affected by Hurricane Katrina were poor before the disaster. Mississippi's poverty rate in 2004 was 21.6%; Louisiana's was 19.4%; and Alabama's was 16.1%. (See Table 8.2.)

TABLE 8.3

Population and poverty data for areas affected by Hurricane Katrina

[Numbers in thousands; census data from 2000]

	All races				Black or African-American[a]			
	All persons	Number poor	Percent poor[b]	Number below 50% of poverty line	All persons	Number poor	Percent poor[b]	Number below 50% of poverty line
U.S.	281,422	33,900	12.4%	15,337	36,213	8,535	24.7%	4,279
Hardest-hit states: AL, LA, MS	**11,761**	**2,097**	**18.4%**	**973**	**3,671**	**1,208**	**34.4%**	**589**
Alabama	4,447	698	16.1%	315	1,167	350	31.2%	168
Louisiana	4,469	851	19.6%	408	1,462	511	36.6%	256
Mississippi	2,845	548	19.9%	250	1,042	348	34.9%	165
Federal disaster areas:								
Counties eligible for any FEMA assistance[c]	**14,194**	**2,417**	**17.5%**	**1,124**	**4,065**	**1,278**	**32.7%**	**624**
Alabama	1,877	307	16.7%	142	588	179	31.2%	86
Florida	5,003	711	14.5%	324	973	241	25.6%	117
Louisiana	4,469	851	19.6%	408	1,462	511	36.6%	256
Mississippi	2,845	548	19.9%	250	1,042	348	34.9%	165
Hardest hit-counties: eligible for aid to individuals	**5,780**	**1,043**	**18.6%**	**493**	**1,909**	**625**	**34.0%**	**305**
Alabama	771	130	17.2%	60	231	75	33.5%	35
Florida	0	0	0.0%	0	0	0	0.0%	0
Louisiana	3,110	559	18.4%	272	998	331	34.5%	167
Mississippi	1,899	355	19.3%	161	680	219	33.6%	103
New Orleans metropolitan area	1,317	237	18.3%	120	496	159	32.9%	83
New Orleans city	**485**	**131**	**27.9%**	**70**	**328**	**111**	**34.9%**	**59**

[a]"Black or African American" includes some individuals who specified more than one race.

[b]Percentage poor equals column 2 divided by the population for whom poverty status is determined. This may not equal column 2 divided by column 1.

[c]Includes counties eligible for assistance to individuals as well as a broader group of counties eligible only for assistance to public agencies. For Louisiana and Mississippi, this includes all counties in the state. For Alabama and Florida, only selected counties are included. FEMA is Federal Emergency Management Agency.

SOURCE: Arloc Sherman and Isaac Shapiro, "Population and Poverty Data for Areas Affected by Hurricane Katrina, from the 2000 Census," in *Essential Facts about the Victims of Hurricane Katrina*, Center on Budget and Policy Priorities, September 19, 2005, http://www.cbpp.org/9-19-05pov.pdf (accessed April 10, 2006)

In New Orleans, 131,000 (27.9%) of the total population of 485,000 residents—and 111,000 (34.9%) of the city's 328,000 African-Americans—lived in poverty before Hurricane Katrina. (See Table 8.3.) As is shown in Table 8.4, the population of the flooded areas of the New Orleans metropolitan area tended to be nonwhite, poorer, and more likely to be renters than those in the areas that remained dry, and more than 200,000 households, or approximately 40% of the total, had no access to a car. In addition, 8% of households in New Orleans had no phone service (National Center for Children in Poverty [NCCP] at Columbia University, *Child Poverty in States Hit by Hurricane Katrina*, September 2005, http://www.nccp.org/media/cpt05a_text.pdf).

The NCCP further reported that in 2004, 38% of children in New Orleans lived in poverty (see Figure 8.2), as did 23% of children in Louisiana as a whole, 24% of children in Mississippi, and 21% in Alabama. (See Figure 8.3.) For African-American children in these states the situation was even worse: 44% of African-American children in Louisiana lived in poor families,

as did 41% in Mississippi and 42% in Alabama. (See Figure 8.4.)

POVERTY IN THE HURRICANE ZONE SIX MONTHS LATER. In February 2006 Oxfam America declared in *Recovering States? The Gulf Coast Six Months after the Storms* (http://www.oxfamamerica.org/newsandpublications/publications/briefing_papers/recovering_states):

Six months after Hurricane Katrina laid bare the stark social and economic inequities present in the United States, little has changed. Despite the commitments of elected officials to confront deep and persistent poverty with bold action, and despite the investigative reports of the federal systems failure, the same people neglected prior to Hurricane Katrina and abandoned in its aftermath continue to be left behind today.

Oxfam reports that the most serious issue is the housing crisis caused by the disaster's displacement of between 700,000 and 800,000 people. Eric Lipton in "Trailer Dispute May Mean Thousands Will Go Unused" (February 14, 2006, http://www.civilrights.org/issues/housing/details.cfm?id=40496) stated that of the 25,000

TABLE 8.4

Households affected by Hurricane Katrina flooding, by geographic, economic, and demographic characteristics, 2005

Area	Total households	Average household income	Percent owner-occupied housing units	Percent renter-occupied housing units	Percent non-white population	Poverty rate	Estimated population with no access to a car
New Orleans metro	498,587	$49,167	61.5%	38.5%	45.2%	18.3%	201,176
Dry areas of metro	270,908	$53,108	68.9%	31.1%	35.1%	15.3%	77,505
Flooded areas of metro	227,679	$44,479	52.7%	47.3%	58.0%	22.1%	123,671
Dry areas of Orleans Parish	54,519	$55,316	46.7%	53.3%	55.0%	23.8%	28,019
Flooded areas of Orleans Parish	133,732	$38,263	46.4%	53.6%	80.3%	29.5%	105,152
Dry areas of Jefferson Parish	106,127	$47,698	68.4%	31.6%	39.4%	15.7%	30,963
Flooded areas of Jefferson Parish	70,107	$56,297	57.0%	43.0%	26.2%	10.1%	11,924
Dry areas of St. Bernard Parish	3,842	$42,917	78.1%	21.9%	18.1%	13.9%	1,225
Flooded areas of St. Bernard Parish	21,281	$44,867	74.1%	25.9%	15.2%	13.0%	5,725
Dry areas of Plaquemines Parish	6,462	$48,583	76.5%	23.5%	27.9%	16.8%	1,692
Flooded areas of Plaquemines Parish	2,559	$42,298	84.8%	15.2%	39.5%	21.0%	869
St. Charles Parish (no major flooding)	16,422	$55,247	81.4%	18.6%	29.5%	11.4%	3,071
St. John the Baptist Parish (no major flooding)	14,283	$46,075	81.0%	19.0%	49.0%	16.7%	4,080
St. Tammany (no major flooding)	69,253	$61,590	80.5%	19.5%	14.7%	9.7%	8,454

SOURCE: "Flooded Areas of the Metropolitan Region Tended to be Poorer, Have More Renters, and Be Predominantly Non-White," in *New Orleans after the Storm: Lessons from the Past, a Plan for the Future*, The Brookings Institute, October 2005, http://www.brookings.edu/metro (accessed April 10, 2006)

FIGURE 8.2

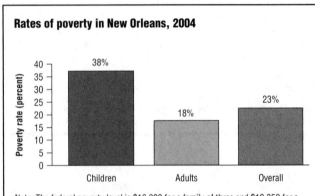

Rates of poverty in New Orleans, 2004

Note: The federal poverty level is $16,090 for a family of three and $19,350 for a family of four.

SOURCE: Sarah Fass and Nancy K. Cauthen, "Rates of Poverty in New Orleans, 2004," in *Child Poverty in States Hit by Hurricane Katrina*, Fact Sheet No. 1, National Center for Children in Poverty, Columbia University, Mailman School of Public Health, September 2005, http://www.nccp.org/media/cpt05a_text.pdf (accessed April 10, 2006)

FIGURE 8.3

Percent of children in poor and extremely poor families, in U.S. states hit by Hurricane Katrina, 2005

[2004 data]

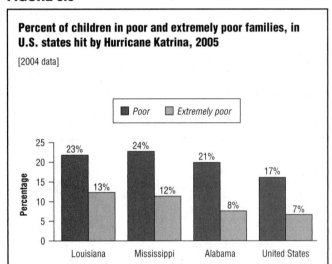

SOURCE: Sarah Fass and Nancy K. Cauthen, "Percent of Children in Poor and Extremely Poor Families, 2004," in *Child Poverty in States Hit by Hurricane Katrina*, Fact Sheet No. 1, National Center for Children in Poverty, Columbia University, Mailman School of Public Health, September 2005, http://www.nccp.org/media/cpt05a_text.pdf (accessed April 10, 2006)

furnished mobile homes FEMA ordered, at a cost of $850 million, only 2,700 of them had been installed for use, while 55,000 families displaced from Louisiana alone remained homeless. More than 10,000 of the trailers had been shipped to a cow pasture in Hope, Arkansas, where they were reportedly sinking into the mud and some had been dismantled by thieves, because of a federal regulation stipulating that government-purchased temporary housing units not be allowed in the region of flood plains. Meanwhile, the Oxfam study found that low-income households had been largely left out of state and national plans for housing reconstruction: the federally run Small Business Association was not making loans for rebuilding available to low-income families, and the plans presented by the Mississippi governor Haley Barbour had placed restrictions on funds available for low-income senior citizens and families, as well as for the disabled.

FIGURE 8.4

Child poverty by race in U.S. states hit by Hurricane Katrina, 2005

[2004 data]

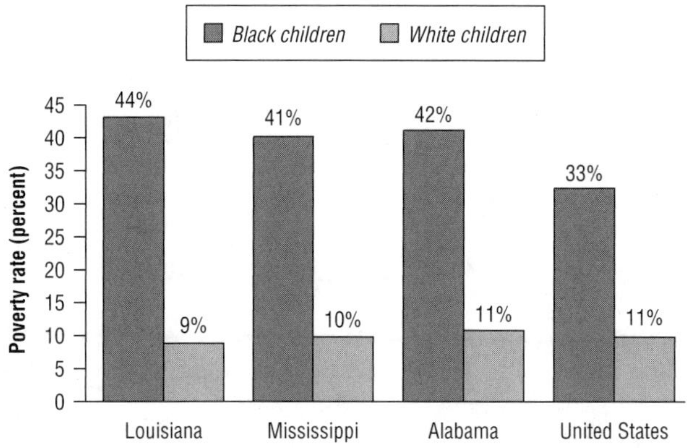

SOURCE: Sarah Fass and Nancy K. Cauthen, "Child Poverty by Race, 2004," in *Child Poverty in States Hit by Hurricane Katrina*, Fact Sheet No. 1, National Center for Children in Poverty, Columbia University, Mailman School of Public Health, September 2005, http://www.nccp .org/media/cpt05a_text.pdf (accessed April 10, 2006)

CHAPTER 9
POVERTY AND VIOLENT CONFLICT

The populations of countries engaged in conflict or warfare almost always experience some degree of economic hardship. During World War II (1939–45) much of Europe was reduced to near starvation, and even the United States—which saw no military action on its own soil—imposed strict rationing of goods on its citizens. This is because during times of war financial resources that could be used to meet human needs are diverted instead to military efforts. For example, Figure 9.1 displays the great disparity between spending on health issues and spending on military concerns in Eritrea, Yemen, Burundi, Angola, and Ethiopia, all countries with low human development that were experiencing military conflict during 2003. However, poverty can also be used as a tool of war, especially in internal conflict situations. Economic oppression and the withholding of aid for development are frequently used as a form of violence against those perceived as enemies. Refugees of war or conflict who are displaced from their homes must live in camps with squalid conditions, with little hope of earning a living or returning home.

In *Violent Conflict, Poverty, and Chronic Poverty* (Chronic Poverty Research Centre, May 2001, http://www.chronicpoverty.org/pdfs/06Goodhand.pdf), Jonathan Goodhand estimated that between 1989 and 2001 more than four million people worldwide had been killed in regional and internal warfare, mostly in poor and low-income countries. According to the United Nations Development Program's (UNDP) *Human Development Report 2005* (2005, http://hdr.undp.org/reports/global/2005/pdf/HDR05_complete.pdf), the overall number of violent conflicts decreased between 1991 and 2003, from fifty-one to twenty-nine, "but the share of those conflicts occurring in poor countries has increased."

Goodhand's estimate includes only those people directly killed in conflict, not those who died as an indirect result of warfare. The indirect casualties of war can greatly outnumber those killed in actual fighting. In 2006 a mortality survey that included both direct and indirect war fatalities was conducted by the International Rescue Committee in the Democratic Republic of Congo, a country that had been in a state of conflict since 1998. The survey found that nearly four million people had died as a result the conflict and that most of the deaths were attributable to preventable disease and malnutrition. In the eastern part of the country only 2% of deaths were a direct result of armed violence. Displacement is another result of conflict. As of 2005 at least twenty-five million people globally had fled from their homes and countries because of warfare.

Violent conflict—especially drawn out over a number of years or decades—does not cause just a state of immediate chaos and death; it has long-term consequences for social, political, and economic development. For years after the conflict ends, a country might suffer the effects of war in the forms of damaged or nonexistent infrastructure, environmental degradation, an unbalanced population in terms of gender, a shortage of teachers and schools, war-related physical and psychological issues, widespread hunger, and other problems associated with poverty. Because education is interrupted during and in the aftermath of armed conflict, countries that have experienced such violence typically show diminished rates of adult literacy.

CATEGORIES OF VIOLENT CONFLICT

There are four different types of violent conflict:

- *Internal conflict* occurs within a single country, such as a civil war or a conflict over the use and ownership of natural resources. Table 9.1 lists examples of such conflicts dating from 1949, including wars fought over control of oil, timber, crops, and gems.

- *Internationalized internal conflict* is characterized by the intervention of foreign nations in a dispute between

FIGURE 9.1

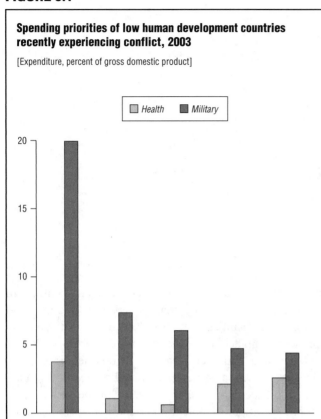

Spending priorities of low human development countries recently experiencing conflict, 2003

[Expenditure, percent of gross domestic product]

SOURCE: "Figure 5.3. Spending Priorities of Low Human Development Countries Recently Experiencing Conflict," in *Human Development Report 2005*, United Nations Development Programme, 2005, http://hdr.undp.org/reports/global/2005/pdf/HDR05_complete.pdf (accessed April 10, 2006)

TABLE 9.1

Countries experiencing internal conflicts over natural resources, 1949–2006

Country	Duration of conflict	Resources
Afghanistan	1978–2001	Gems, opium
Angola	1975–2002	Oil, diamonds
Angola, Cabinda	1975–	Oil
Cambodia	1978–97	Timber, gems
Colombia	1984–	Oil, gold, coca
Congo	1997	Oil
Congo, Dem. Rep. of the	1996–97, 1998–2002	Copper, coltan, diamonds, gold, cobalt
Indonesia, Aceh	1975–	Natural gas
Indonesia, West Papua	1969–	Copper, gold
Liberia	1989–96	Timber, diamonds, iron, palm oil, cocoa, coffee, marijuana, rubber, gold
Morocco	1975–	Phosphates, oil
Myanmar	1949–	Timber, tin, gems, opium
Papua New Guinea	1988–98	Copper, gold
Peru	1980–95	Coca
Sierra Leone	1991–2000	Diamonds
Sudan	1983–2005	Oil

SOURCE: "Table 5.2. Natural Resources Have Helped Fuel Conflicts in Many Countries," in *Human Development Report 2005*, United Nations Development Programme, 2005, http://hdr.undp.org/reports/global/2005/pdf/HDR05_complete.pdf (accessed April 10, 2006). Data adapted from Bannon and Collier 2003.

warring factions within another country. The war in Bosnia in the 1990s is an example of this type of conflict.

- *Interstate conflict* is war between or among nations.

- *Extrasystemic conflict* occurs between the government of one nation and a nongovernment group in another nation.

Some researchers distinguish between war and conflict by saying that more than 1,000 people per year die in a true war. For example, in *Armed Conflict 1946–99: A New Dataset* (February 2001, http://www.isanet.org/archive/npg.html), Nils Petter Gleditsch and his colleagues state that the violence in Northern Ireland that began in 1969 qualifies as a conflict rather than as a war because there were more than 1,000 "battle deaths" throughout the events but not more than 1,000 per year. In addition, situations that have or can become violent, such as a regime change or oppression of a minority group, are also considered conflict.

VIOLENT CONFLICT AND HUMAN DEVELOPMENT

The countries that have experienced violent conflict and those that have ongoing conflicts typically have some

of the lowest rankings on the UNDP's Human Development Index (HDI). Nine of the ten countries with the lowest HDI rankings—Burundi, Central African Republic, Chad, Ethiopia, Guinea-Bissau, Mali, Mozambique, Niger, and Sierra Leone—have undergone a period of violent conflict since 1990; the tenth nation, Burkina Faso, has remained at peace since 1990, but conflicts in neighboring Côte d'Ivoire and Ghana have contributed to its impoverishment by curtailing regional economic opportunities.

Achievement of the UN's Millennium Development Goals is also off track for the most part in countries that have experienced violent conflict. High child mortality, low primary school enrollment, and low overall life expectancy are common. As shown in Figure 9.2, only three out of the twelve countries that have a child mortality rate higher than 20% have not experienced armed conflict since 1999. Economic growth also slows considerably during a conflict. According to figures from the World Bank cited in the *Human Development Report 2005*, civil wars typically last seven years, and each year economic growth drops by an average of 2.2%. Refugees fleeing to neighboring countries, and the possibility of those countries being drawn into the fighting, can strain the entire region in which a conflict takes place.

The unbalanced gender ratio that usually results from violent conflict also affects a region's human development. With large numbers of men killed in fighting, women are left to support and protect their families by themselves. This leaves them vulnerable to attack and

FIGURE 9.2

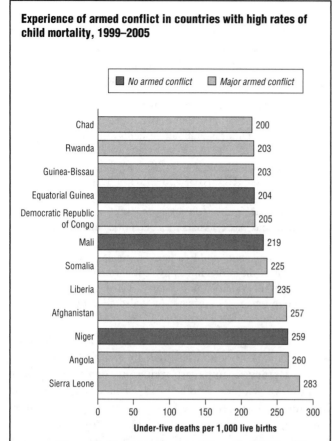

Experience of armed conflict in countries with high rates of child mortality, 1999–2005

■ No armed conflict ■ Major armed conflict

Country	Under-five deaths per 1,000 live births
Chad	200
Rwanda	203
Guinea-Bissau	203
Equatorial Guinea	204
Democratic Republic of Congo	205
Mali	219
Somalia	225
Liberia	235
Afghanistan	257
Niger	259
Angola	260
Sierra Leone	283

SOURCE: "Figure 2.3. Most of the Countries Where 1 in 5 Children Die Before Five Have Experienced Major Armed Conflict Since 1999," in *The State of the World's Children 2006*, United Nations Children's Fund, 2005, http://www.unicef.org/sowc06/pdfs/sowc0506_eps_charts .pdf (accessed April 8, 2006). Data on child mortality from: UNICEF, United Nations Population Division and United Nations Statistics Division; data on major armed conflicts from: Stockholm International Peace Research Institute and The Uppsala Conflict Data Program, *SIPRI Yearbook 2005: Armaments, Disarmament and International Security* (Oxford University Press; Oxford, 2005)

rape during conflict and to poverty and lowered levels of education and health care for themselves, their children, and future generations. In some cases the loss of an excessively large number of young men in fighting can bring about massive demographic changes and set back the security, education, and health of women for years. With fewer marriageable young men in the population, young women might become betrothed to elderly men or in some cases to relatives.

In addition, violent conflict increases the risk of a food crisis—especially in rural areas—because livestock, crops, and arable land might be destroyed. However, it is not just the physical destruction of farms during war that leaves societies vulnerable to hunger. The displacement of farmers as refugees causes just as much harm to agricultural production. According to *Human Development Report 2005*, for example, Sierra Leone's decade-long civil war from 1991 to 2000 left about 500,000 farm families displaced from their homes, causing rice production to drop to just 20% of its prewar level.

The health of a population engaged in conflict or warfare decreases dramatically. The UNDP report explains that more people die because of the consequences of war than because of the immediate violence. Infectious diseases spread rapidly among refugees and quickly spill over from refugee camps into the populations surrounding them. In a survey conducted in Africa during the 1990s mortality rates among refugees were found to be eighty times higher than those of nonrefugees (http://www.sas.upenn.edu/~dludden/ RefugeePublicHealth.pdf). Medical facilities often serve as targets for opposition fighters because of the supplies they contain and because their destruction further weakens the population. With hospitals and health centers destroyed, citizens have no source of medical care, sometimes permanently.

Land Mines

One of the most brutal tools of conflict affecting human health and security is the presence of land mines, which can damage and terrorize a population physically and psychologically for decades. Land mines are explosive devices that are usually buried underground or laid just above ground and triggered by vehicles or footsteps. Antitank land mines are, as their name suggests, designed to blow up tanks and large vehicles. Antipersonnel land mines (APLs) are designed so that they are triggered by even the lightest of footsteps. APLs are by far the more devastating kind of land mine for two reasons: first, they are indiscriminate in blowing up both soldiers and civilians; second, they exist in regions indefinitely after a war or conflict ends. APLs are also designed to look like small, colorful toys, candy, stones, or even butterflies, making them extremely dangerous to children (United Nations Children's Fund in *State of the World's Children 1996: Children in War* (1996, http://www.unicef.org/sowc96/contents.htm?468,235).

The continuing presence of land mines after a conflict ends limits development and increases poverty in affected regions. Areas known to contain land mines are unusable for farming, building, living, or commerce of any kind. From 2004 to 2005 at least fifty-eight countries in Africa, Europe, the Middle East, Asia and the Pacific, and Central and South America experienced 15,000 to 20,000 land mine-related deaths or injuries, according to the *Landmine Monitor Report 2005* (http://www.icbl.org/lm/2005/). An analysis of land mine casualties in Afghanistan, Angola, Azerbaijan, Bosnia and Herzegovina, Cambodia, Chad, Eritrea, Ethiopia, Lebanon, Mozambique, Somalia, Thailand and Yemen (Survey Action Center, September 2005) found that reported casualties during the previous twenty-four months were 96% civilian, 88% male, and

24% children under age fifteen. Besides the human casualties, livestock and wild animals are frequently injured or killed by land mines. This not only harms regional environments but it also destroys farming economies. The people in affected regions must live as virtual prisoners in their own lands. Cambodia (898), Afghanistan (878), and Colombia (863) had the highest number of reported land mine casualties in 2004–05.

Refugees

In 1950 the position of United Nations High Commissioner for Refugees (UNHCR) was created, and the UN Convention on the Status of Refugees was adopted. The two main tenets of the convention are that refugees are not to be returned to an area where they face persecution and that refugees are not to face discrimination in the country that accepts them. However, according to the UNHCR in *State of the World's Refugees: Human Displacement in the New Millennium* (2006, http://www.unhcr.org/cgi-bin/texis/vtx/template?page=publ&src=static/sowr2006/toceng.htm), people seeking asylum as refugees are increasingly becoming the targets of xenophobia and accusations of terrorist activity, even though there were fewer refugees in 2006 than at any time since 1980.

In "Refugees by Numbers" (2005; http://www.unhcr.org/cgi-bin/texis/vtx/basics/opendoc.htm?tbl=BASICS&id=3b028097c#Refugees), the UNHCR reports that as of January 2005 they were assisting more than nine million refugees in the world: 3.4 million were in Asia, three million in Africa, two million in Europe, 562,000 in North America, 76,000 in Oceania, and 36,000 in Latin America and the Caribbean. More than 800,000 of these refugees were classed as "asylum seekers," that is, they had applied for legal recognition in the country to which they had fled. At the beginning of 2005 another 5.4 million people were considered internally displaced persons (IDPs) within their home nations. These numbers reflect only those who receive aid from the UNHCR. Among those not included in the above figures are the estimated four million displaced Palestinians, who are counted by a related organization, the UN Relief and Works Agency for Palestine Refugees in the Near East (UNRWA). An unknown number of refugees and IDPs do not receive aid and therefore cannot be accurately counted.

Some people are forced to leave their homes and seek refuge in other countries because of natural disasters, but most refugees leave because their homelands are torn by violent conflict or because human rights abuses are rampant. In situations of long-term conflict, groups of people may endure recurring periods of short-term displacement, or they may be displaced indefinitely. According to *State of the World's Refugees*, while conditions for refugees are typically substandard in terms of housing, food, and other necessities, it is those who cannot leave conflict regions because of extreme poverty or ill health who are often the most vulnerable.

State of the World's Refugees notes that of the 7.5 million "persons of concern" in 2003, about 50% were younger than eighteen years old, and 13% were children under age five. According to the UNHCR report:

> The large number of young people among displaced populations has important implications for protection. Displaced children and adolescents are particularly vulnerable to threats to their safety and wellbeing. These include separation from families, sexual exploitation, HIV/AIDS infection, forced labour or slavery, abuse and violence, forcible recruitment into armed groups, trafficking, lack of access to education and basic assistance, detention and denial of access to asylum or family-reunification procedures. Unaccompanied children are at greatest risk, since they lack the protection, physical care and emotional support provided by the family. Those accompanied by only one parent or carer may also be at higher risk than other children.

Many refugees find themselves relocated—by force or by choice—to countries that are hostile to their presence. Refugee camps are generally dangerous places because of violence both inside and outside of their boundaries. Refugees may be denied basic human rights, including the right to seek legal employment, which exacerbates their impoverished condition. Even when refugees are returned to their homelands, they sometimes encounter an unwelcoming environment: their houses, workplaces, farms, and possessions may have been destroyed, and the regime in control may react violently to their return.

POVERTY IN THE MOST DANGEROUS PLACES ON EARTH

Although both poverty and violent conflict exist on almost every continent, there are some regions that, for one reason or another, were particularly dangerous as of 2006.

Darfur

Darfur is a region in western Sudan, a nation in northeast Africa. (See Figure 9.3.) It has an area of about 196,000 square miles and a population of about eight million people, most of whom are either subsistence farmers or nomadic herdsmen. The two main ethnic groups in the region are the Arabic Baggara (who are nomads) and the non-Arabic Fur (who are farmers). These groups are further divided into smaller ethnic groups. Tensions between the Baggara and the Fur range back over centuries. The region was a center of commercial activity during the slave trade, when native Africans were exported to Arabic countries. Since the mid-1950s the government of Sudan has been under Muslim control

FIGURE 9.3

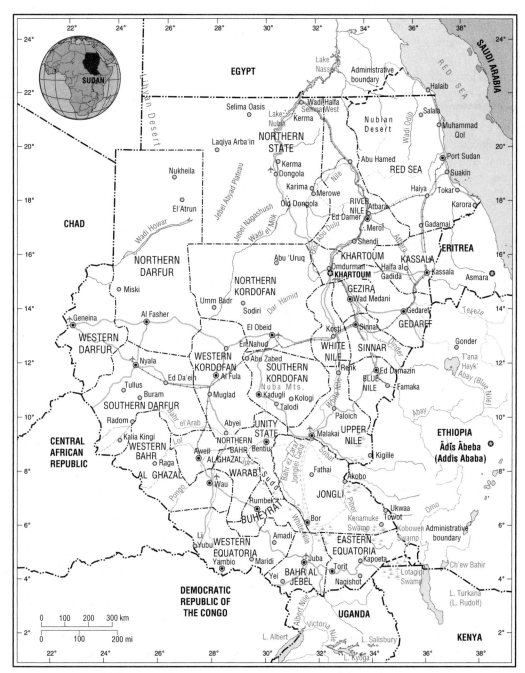

Note: The boundaries and names shown and the designations used on this map do not imply official endorsement or acceptance by the United Nations.

SOURCE: William G. O'Neill and Violette Cassis, "Map of Sudan," in *Protecting Two Million Internally Displaced: The Successes and Shortcomings of the African Union in Darfur*, The Brookings Institute–University of Bern Project on Internal Displacement, November 2005, http://www.brookings.edu/fp/projects/idp/200511_au_darfur.pdf (accessed April 10, 2006).

and in near constant conflict with non-Muslim opposition within the country. A combination of domination by ruling Muslims and competition for scarce resources caused tensions in Darfur to escalate in 2003, creating an immense humanitarian crisis in the region.

Early in 2003, Arabic Janjaweed militias began a campaign against the black African rebel groups Sudanese Liberation Army (SLA) and Justice and Equality Movement (JEM), who had taken up arms against the government. A major factor was the competition for water and land between the Arabic nomads and non-Arabic farmers. However, the situation quickly degenerated into indiscriminate Janjaweed attacks on civilians. According to the *Darfur Daily News* (November 11, 2005, http://darfurdaily.blogspot.com/2005_11_06_darfurdaily_archive.html) the result was mass murder, rape, and the displacement of as many as two million people from their homes to refugee camps within Darfur and the neighboring country of Chad. All of this provoked international attention, and led to the deployment in October 2005 of 7,000 African Union (AU) troops in an attempt to restore order, but the poorly funded and organized mission could do little to stop the atrocities. A number of temporary cease-fires were attempted, with no lasting success.

The Sudanese government is widely seen as supporting the actions of the Janjaweed, although it maintains that this is not the case. On September 8, 2004, U.S. Secretary of State Colin Powell accused the government of Sudan and the Janjaweed militias of being responsible for a campaign of genocide in Darfur. According to the Human Rights Watch *World Report 2006* (2006, http://www.hrw.org/wr2k6/), the Sudanese government blocked the attempts of AU troops to enforce a cease-fire agreement in April 2004 and supported Janjaweed attacks on AU forces and international aid workers. In addition, Human Rights Watch reported that people living in internal displacement camps were subjected to many abuses, including arrests and detentions; women reporting rape were humiliated and tried for adultery. Outside the camps, civilians—particularly women and girls—were abducted, the livestock of the Fur farmers were stolen, and children were kidnapped or recruited to serve as soldiers.

The International Crisis Group (ICG) reported in *To Save Darfur* (March 17, 2006, http://www.liberationafrique.org/IMG/pdf/To_save_darfur.pdf) that in 2005 an estimated 3.5 million people in the region were dependent on humanitarian aid for survival, although in some areas nongovernmental organizations (NGOs) were able to access only 45% to 70% of them. In West Darfur, where fighting was most heavily concentrated, at least 140,000 people were left with no assistance at all because NGOs were forced to withdraw.

On May 5, 2006, a peace agreement was signed by the Sudanese government and the Sudan Liberation Movement. The treaty called for complete disarmament and demobilization of the Janjaweed militia by mid-October 2006 and established size and movement restrictions for the government-backed Popular Defense Forces. The agreement also outlined democratic processes that called for an election in 2010 to determine the region's administrative status. Provisions in the treaty furnish humanitarian assistance to those displaced by the violence, including helping refugees and displaced people return to their homes. As part of the agreement the Sudanese government pledged $30 million in compensation to victims of the conflict and increased representation of the rebel constituents in the government.

Because the treaty was not signed by all warring rebel factions, the International Crisis Group was not optimistic about the agreement's chances for success. In a June 2006 policy briefing ("Darfur's Fragile Peace Agreement" June 20, 2006), the organization warned that without deployment of a "robust" UN peacekeeping force, sanctions against anyone who breaks the cease-fire, and increased assistance to victims of the violence, the agreement had little chance of providing ongoing stability in the region.

LIVING CONDITIONS IN DARFUR. Since the conflict began, the people of Darfur have been living in a state of constant threat to their lives, with no legal or political recourse. According to the ICG in *To Save Darfur*:

> A tribal militia can wipe out an entire village, such as Mershing in South Darfur on 2 February 2006, and the government can plead innocence, even as it creates the conditions for the militias to operate by giving impunity, supplying weapons and ammunition, deploying police who do nothing to stop attacks and coordinating between the militias and the state government.

According to Human Rights First in *About the Crisis* (2006;http://www.humanrightsfirst.org/international_justice/darfur/about/background.asp), official estimates of how many people in Darfur were killed between 2003 and 2006 vary from 180,000 to 400,000. Many have died not directly from Janjaweed violence but from the disease and starvation that accompany situations of conflict and war. At least two to three million people are IDPs and are living in refugee camps set up within Darfur. Most at risk are women and children, who make up approximately 80% of those living in internal refugee camps, according to IRINnews.org ("Sudan: Helping Reduce Women's Vulnerability," March 3, 2006, http://www.irinnews.org/report.asp?ReportID=51993). Janjaweed militia members commonly use rape as a tool of war to terrorize and inflict long-term psychological damage. Because women and girls must leave the refugee camps regularly to collect firewood and forage for food, they are daily targets of gang rape and torture. Frequently, rapes result in unwanted pregnancies; as many as 25% of women and girls in Darfur's refugee camps are pregnant at any given time, according to the article from IRINnew.org. This has led to a grave cultural conflict, as sexual relations outside of marriage are strictly forbidden in Sudan and much of the rest of Africa. Women who become pregnant outside of marriage—even as a result Janjaweed attacks—may be arrested and charged with adultery in Sudan. Police and AU officials in Darfur have, however, agreed to bypass the law if a woman reports a rape immediately.

Civilians in the region are further terrorized by Janjaweed tactics that even practiced military experts find it difficult to witness or comprehend: large-scale arson, in which entire families are locked inside houses and burned alive, and the killing of children and babies either by stabbing them with bayonets or throwing them into bonfires. Brian Steidle, a former Marine captain sent to Darfur as a military observer with AU troops from September 2004 to February 2005, recorded in photographs much of what he saw. In "In Darfur, My Camera Was Not Nearly Enough" (March 20, 2005, http://www.ushmm.org/conscience/alert/darfur/steidle/), Steidle wrote of his experience:

> Every day we surveyed evidence of killings: men castrated and left to bleed to death, huts set on fire with people locked inside, children with their faces smashed in, men with their ears cut off and eyes plucked out, and the corpses of people who had been executed with gunshots to the head. We spoke with thousands of witnesses—women who had been gang-raped and families that had lost fathers, people who plainly and soberly gave us their accounts of the slaughter.

Steidle cites a common tactic used by the Sudanese government to leave IDPs vulnerable to Janjaweed attack. Announcing that an IDP camp is to be closed, the government forces the displaced to move to a smaller camp and bulldozes the larger one. The people unable to fit into the smaller camp are left without shelter and are virtually guaranteed to be killed by the Janjaweed.

The ongoing conflict in Darfur, in combination with the many other conflicts that have plagued Sudan for decades, leave it among the world's poorest countries. The World Health Organization (2006, http://www.who.int/countries/sdn/en/) notes that the gross domestic product (GDP) per capita in Sudan was $1,361 in 2004. The average life expectancy at birth was fifty-eight years. The infant mortality rate was ninety-one deaths out of every 1,000 live births. In "Country Sheet: Sudan" (2006, http://hdr.undp.org/statistics/data/countries.cfm?c=SDN), the UNDP reports that 41% of Sudanese over age fifteen were literate, and primary school enrollment was 38%. These numbers are averages for all of Sudan; separate figures for Darfur are unavailable but would most likely be considerably worse.

The Middle East

The Middle East is a geographic and political region encompassing countries in Central and Southwest Asia as well as Northeast Africa. For the most part these countries are historically Arabic and share many cultural similarities. The region is also the birthplace of three of the world's most prominent religions: Judaism, Christianity, and Islam. For many Westerners, the Middle East is associated with wealth because of the massive oil reserves located within the region. Nevertheless, according to Farrukh Iqbal in *Sustaining Gains in Poverty Reduction and Human Development in the Middle East and North Africa* (2006, http://siteresources.worldbank.org/INTMENA/Resources/Poverty_complete_06_web.pdf), one in five people in the region lives on less than two dollars a day. During the final decades of the twentieth century the Middle East saw significant progress in its human development indicators. Overall, literacy for those aged fifteen years and older increased from 24% in 1965 to 69% in 2000; deaths among children under age five fell from 233 per 1,000 live births in 1965 to forty-six per 1,000 in 2000; life expectancy rose from fifty to sixty-eight years; and the average level of education completed for those aged fifteen years and older rose from 0.8 to 5.2 years during the same period.

Overall, the Middle East, together with the rest of North Africa, has the least poverty of all developing regions. While the increases since the 1960s are impressive, the region's ongoing violent conflicts have left millions of people in dire poverty.

A HALF-CENTURY OF CONFLICT. The Middle East is at the heart of some of the worst tension and violence in the world, much of it in the form of terrorism. Some of this tension stems from ethnic and religious differences. Since the end of World War II there have been several major interstate conflicts—including the Arab-Israeli conflict, the Iran-Iraq War, and the Gulf War of 1991—civil wars in Jordan and Lebanon, and continuing tensions between various factions throughout the region. The Arab-Israeli conflict alone has erupted into war six times since 1948. Iraq has been involved in six skirmishes, including the ongoing war with the U.S.-led coalition that began in 2003. Afghanistan is not always included as a Middle Eastern country, but its history, language, and culture are closely linked to those of Iran, so the U.S. invasion there, which began in late 2001, may also be considered a Middle Eastern conflict.

THE PALESTINIANS. The Israeli victory in the 1948 Arab-Israeli War resulted in the formation of the state of Israel on land that had been in the possession of Palestinians. The war's other outcome was that at least 500,000 to 700,000 Palestinians were forced off their land and into neighboring areas, including Jordan,

Syria, Lebanon, and Egypt, where they were placed into refugee camps. Following the 1967 Six-Day War between the Israelis and Palestinians, Israel's territory expanded to include the regions known as the West Bank and the Gaza Strip, both of which were populated primarily by Palestinians. After this war 300,000 Palestinians—many of them displaced for the second time after they had returned to their homes after the Arab-Israeli War—left the West Bank and Gaza Strip for Syria, Lebanon, and Egypt. Most refugees were not permitted to return to their homes, even after the wars ended. This "Palestinian exodus," called the Nakba ("catastrophe") by Palestinians, resulted in generations of displaced people who numbered approximately four million by the early twenty-first century, according to the UNRWA.

The Palestinian refugees are stateless individuals. Most of them have not been granted citizenship in the countries in which they reside, nor are they allowed to return to Israel. Because so many of them are unable to work legally in their host countries, poverty is high among the refugees. Those who register with the UNRWA are dependent on the agency for health care, education, and humanitarian services. According to Willy Egset, Penny Johnson, and Lee O'Brien in *UNRWA's Financial Crisis and Socio-economic Conditions of Palestinian Refugees In Lebanon, Jordan, Syria, and the West Bank and Gaza, vol. 2: The Persistence of Poverty* (2003, http://www.fafo.no/pub/rapp/427/427-vol2.pdf), the living conditions of Palestinian refugees vary greatly according to where they reside. In Jordan, for example, refugees were granted citizenship in 1954 and have full employment rights and social services access. In Lebanon, by contrast, Palestinians have never been allowed to become citizens, and their employment opportunities are limited and strictly regulated. Syria did not grant refugees citizenship, but it has allowed them to work with few restrictions. Palestinians still living in refugee camps in the West Bank and Gaza Strip face greater social and economic challenges than those living outside the camps.

Egset, Johnson, and O'Brien write that in 2003, 23% of Palestinian households living in camps in Syria were poor (having income less than two dollars a day per person), and 5% were extremely poor (income less than one dollar per day per person); in Lebanon 35% were poor, and 15% were extremely poor; and in Jordan 31% were poor, and 9% were extremely poor. In Jordan the average household income of refugees living in poverty was less than half (44%) the average of non-Palestinian Jordanians; for refugees living in extreme poverty in Jordan, the average annual income was only about one-fifth (21%) of the average income for non-Palestinian Jordanians. In Lebanon, where Palestinians have not been allowed to integrate, the median income of poor Palestinian households was 43% that of nonpoor households. Median incomes of extremely poor households were less than 25% that of nonpoor households. In the West Bank and Gaza Strip poverty was particularly high within refugee camps compared with outside the camps, although the rate of poverty in the Gaza Strip—33%—was more than double that of the West Bank's 15%.

The refugees and camps have been a source of controversy for decades. Some Israelis claim the UNRWA's financial aid in reality supports terrorist training within the camps and have called for the organization to be dissolved and the refugees to be aided by the UNHCR, like all other refugees around the world. Another key issue in the effort to secure peace between the Israelis and Palestinians is the insistence by many refugees that they be allowed to return to Israel and regain their property, the so-called right of return. The permanent refugee status of Palestinians has impinged on their sense of self-identity, according to Hillel Cohen, who writes in "Land, Memory, and Identity: The Palestinian Internal Refugees in Israel" (*Refuge*, February 2003) that the less identity the refugees have as a people and as individuals, the less likely they are to continue fighting to return to their land.

In elections held in January 2006 the political group Hamas—which many international governments, including that of the United States, consider a terrorist organization—won control of the Palestinian National Authority (PNA), the transitional administrative organization for Palestinian territories in the West Bank and Gaza Strip. In April 2006 the governments of Canada, the United States, and the European Union suspended all direct aid to the PNA because of the Hamas election victory, demanding that Hamas renounce terrorism. Furthermore, Israel decided to stop its monthly transfer of $50 million in tax revenue to the PNA, according to Matthew Gutman in "Palestinians Fear Poverty if Foreign Aid Lifeline Is Severed" (February 28, 2006, http://www.usatoday.com/news/world/2006-02-27-palestinian-aid_x.htm?csp=N009). Altogether, Gutman reports that the Palestinians stand to lose more than $1 billion annually in direct aid.

With 90% of its budget spent on the salaries of its employees, who represent one-third of all Palestinians living in the West Bank and Gaza Strip, the PNA most likely would not be able to continue operating without the money. Many of the Palestinians who depend on the group for work and income are at risk of falling below the poverty line without it. The PNA is also responsible for funding, building, and maintaining the area's infrastructure; its financial troubles could leave Palestinians in the West Bank and Gaza with less access to utilities and other basic quality-of-life public services. Interviewed by Gutman, a Palestinian street vendor commented that, while he does not work directly for the PNA, he and others depend on PNA employees for their livelihood. "When the civil servants don't get their paychecks, none of us will." If the financial impact on Palestinians is as great as expected, authorities warn that chaos and violence could break out.

Iraq

SANCTIONS WORSEN LIVING CONDITIONS. Under the rule of dictator Saddam Hussein, Iraq invaded neighboring Kuwait in 1990, prompting the imposition of sanctions. An international coalition led by the United States drove Iraq out of Kuwait in 1991. Sanctions and other restrictions on Iraq remained in place after the war ended. Because they had little effect on disarming Iraq—which was their stated goal—but instead caused a humanitarian crisis for Iraqi civilians, the sanctions were widely criticized. The United States and the United Kingdom, however, maintained that they would block any attempts to lift or soften the sanctions as long as the President Saddam Hussein remained in power.

David Cortright in "A Hard Look at Iraq Sanctions" (December 3, 2001, http://www.thenation.com/doc/20011203/cortright) estimated the total number of deaths in Iraq to be about 350,000 from 1990 to 2000—most because of the sanctions but some resulting from bombing during the Gulf War. Bombs destroyed essential infrastructure such as sanitation systems, and raw sewage then contaminated the sources of drinking water leading to the spread of infectious disease among the civilian population. According to Cortright, sanctions compounded the suffering by causing hunger and malnutrition, as well as making it nearly impossible to treat disease. Critics of Saddam Hussein, however, including Dr. Amer Abdul al-Jalil of Ibn al-Baladi hospital in Baghdad contend that Hussein's own internal policies were more detrimental to the poor than international sanctions. Abdul al-Jalil told the *Telegraph* in May 2003: "Over the past ten years the government in Iraq poured money into the military and the construction of palaces for Saddam to the detriment of the health sector. Those babies or small children who died because they could not access the right drugs, died because Saddam's government failed to distribute the drugs. The poorer areas were most vulnerable."

In 1991 the UN Security Council proposed an oil-for-food program in which Iraq would be allowed to sell limited amounts of oil on the open market in exchange for food and medicine for its impoverished citizens. Hussein rejected the plan on the grounds that it violated the country's sovereignty. In 1995 the UN countered with a plan that would increase Iraq's autonomy in distributing aid, but the Iraqi government again refused to participate. In the meantime, a full-scale humanitarian disaster was at hand, and the United States was criticized for refusing to loosen sanctions. The Iraqi government and Hussein were, however, at least equally at fault. The UN continued negotiating a relief plan with Iraq; a deal was finally forged in 1996, and the first shipments of aid reached the people in 1997. With Hussein's government allowed to administer aid in the south and central regions of Iraq, while the UN oversaw relief in the north, the results of the oil-for-food program were uneven. Child mortality, for example, decreased in the north, from eighty per 1,000 live births to seventy-two per 1,000 births, according to research conducted by Mohamed Ali of the London School of Hygiene and Tropical Medicine and Iqbal Shah of the World Health Organization ("Sanctions and Childhood Mortality in Iraq," *The Lancet*, May 2000). In south and central Iraq, however, rates increased from fifty-six per 1,000 live births between 1984 and 1989 to 131 per 1,000 between 1994 and 1999, indicating a failure on the part of Iraqi officials to successfully provide humanitarian relief to their people.

Tarek El-Guindi, Hazem Al Mahdy, and John McHarris report in *The Extent and Distribution of Chronic Poverty in Iraq's Center/South Region* (May 2003, http://www.wfp.org/newsroom/in_depth/Middle_East/Iraq/0306_Poverty_Survey.pdf) that by 2003 approximately 21% of Iraqis in districts in southern and central regions were chronically poor ("unable to meet their basic needs over long periods of time"). Significantly, districts where a government administrative center was located experienced considerably lower average poverty rates (17%) than districts without administrative centers (27%). Overall, the report found that about one-fifth of the population in the southern and central regions of Iraq were chronically poor (4.6 million out of 22.3 million people). Figure 9.4 and Figure 9.5 show chronic poverty numbers and rates in administrative districts of southern and central Iraq just after the start of the war.

POVERTY DURING AND AFTER THE U.S.-LED INVASION. A new coalition, once again led by the United States, invaded Iraq in 2003 and toppled Hussein's government. Sanctions were ended and the U.S. pledged to work to restore Iraq's infrastructure and economy. Iraq's education and health care systems had been among the best in the region in the 1970s and 1980s. While economic and living conditions had severely deteriorated since the beginning of the sanctions, hopes were high that the situation would now improve. When the UNDP released its *Iraq Living Conditions Survey 2004* (2005, http://www.iq.undp.org/ILCS/overview.htm), one year after the invasion began, 54% of families had access to drinking water, with 80% of families in rural areas using unsafe water, and only 37% of households connected to sewer networks. Twelve percent of Iraqi children aged six months to five years were suffering from malnutrition, 8% of them in an acute condition (low

FIGURE 9.4

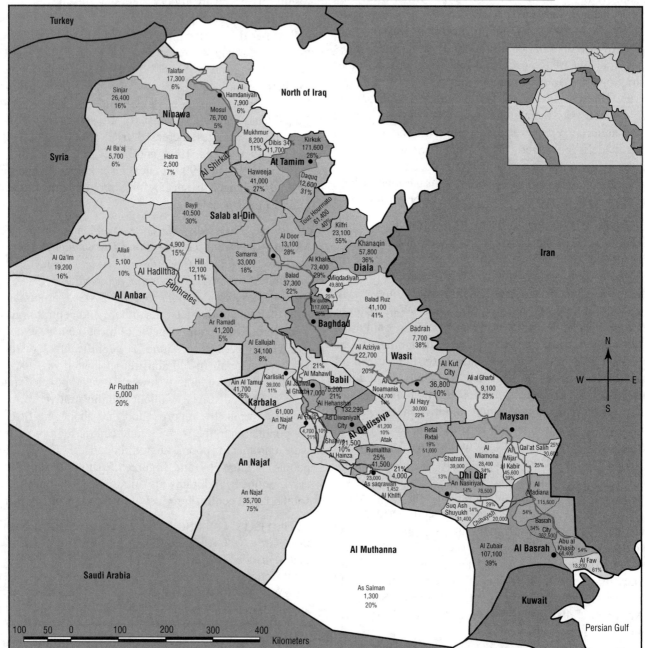

Chronically poor population in center south Iraq, 2003

Notes: Number of poor was estimated using "key informant" approach. The boundaries and names shown on this map do not imply official endorsement or acceptance by United Nations.

SOURCE: Tarek El-Guindi, Hazem Al Mahdy, and John McHarris, "Figure 1. Chronically Poor Population in Center South Iraq," in *The Extent and Geographic Distribution of Chronic Poverty in Iraq's Center/South Region*, United Nations World Food Programme, May 2003, http://www.wfp.org/newsroom/in_depth/Middle_East/Iraq/0306_Poverty_Survey.pdf (accessed April 10, 2006)

FIGURE 9.5

Chronic poverty rates in center south Iraq, 2003

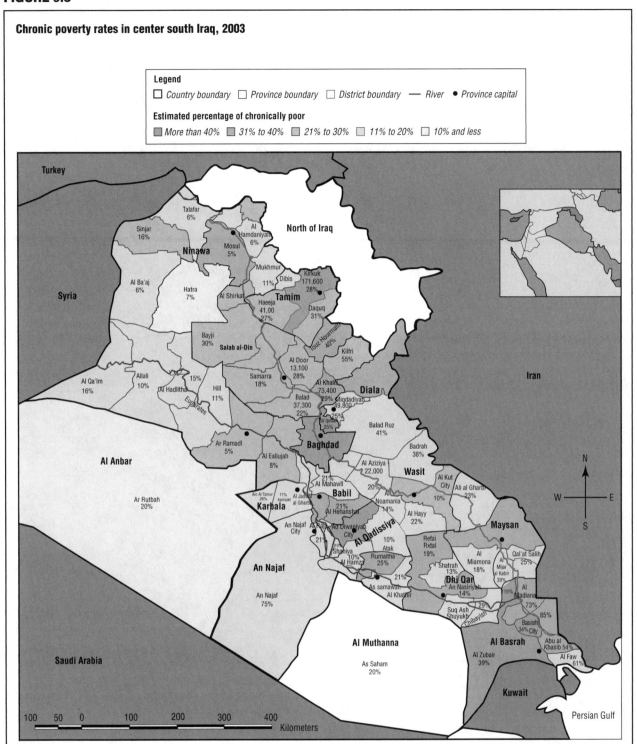

Notes: Number of poor was estimated using "key informant" approach. The boundaries and names shown on this map do not imply official endorsement or acceptance by United Nations.

SOURCE: Tarek El-Guindi, Hazem Al Mahdy, and John McHarris, "Figure 3. Chronic Poverty Rates in Center South Iraq," in *The Extent and Geographic Distribution of Chronic Poverty in Iraq's Center/South Region*, United Nations World Food Programme, May 2003, http://www.wfp .org/newsroom/in_depth/Middle_East/Iraq/0306_Poverty_Survey.pdf (accessed April 10, 2006).

weight for height) and 23% suffering a chronic condition (low weight for age). School enrollment of those aged six to twenty-four years was 55% in 2005, compared with a 62% average for Arab states overall during 2003, according to the UNDP. The literacy rate of young people aged fifteen to twenty-five years was 74%, compared with 81.3% in Arab states overall. In 2003 the average per capita annual income was $255; by the first half of 2004 it had fallen to $144.

Conflict in Iraq continued for years after the invasion defeated Hussein's government and conventional military. By 2006 the war in Iraq was characterized by sectarian and insurgent violence that impeded human development and infrastructure improvements in the country. As of June 2006 an estimated 38,000 to 42,000 Iraqi civilians had been killed since the invasion began, according to the organization Iraqi Body Count (http://www.iraqbodycount.org/). While escalating violence and the uncertain environment since the fall of Hussein's government has prevented the UN from gathering accurate data on progress toward the Millennium Development Goals in Iraq, a report from the Iraqi Labor Ministry in January 2006 found an increase in overall poverty since 2003, with two million families living below the international poverty measure of one dollar per person per day. The report blamed development losses on the collapse of the public sector, the lack of education, and the continuing violence. In response, the Labor Ministry was set to widen its social welfare program to people who were not covered during Hussein's regime, such as the unemployed, the elderly, those suffering from chronic illness, and low-income groups.

CHAPTER 10
COMBATING POVERTY: HOPE FOR THE FUTURE?

We will spare no effort to free our fellow men, women, and children from the abject and dehumanizing conditions of extreme poverty.

—UN Millennium Declaration, New York, September 2000

How effective has the international community been in combating global poverty throughout and since the twentieth century? The answers—for there are many—are varied and surprising. Some experts estimate that society is well on its way to achieving the United Nations' Millennium Development Goals, which, among other things, strive to cut extreme poverty rates in half by the year 2015. Others say those estimates are overblown and the reality is far more grim. In the early twenty-first century certain natural and man-made events—including earthquakes, hurricanes, and wars—have put poverty at the forefront of international consciousness, while television and the Internet have allowed everyone to witness the experiences of the poor like never before. New anti-poverty campaigns have been developed, some headed by renowned business people or celebrities. Charitable giving reached record highs, especially in the wake of the natural disasters of 2005. Nevertheless, poverty persists in every country in the world. As explained in Chapter 2 of this book, the reasons are complex and the questions are at times unanswerable. However, to fully understand the problem of poverty, we must see where we have been to determine where we are going.

POVERTY IMPROVES . . . OR DOES IT?

Overall rates of global poverty dropped in the last few decades of the twentieth century. Notably, the rate between 1990 and 2001 fell from 28% to 21%, according to the World Bank in its overview "Understanding Poverty" (http://web.worldbank.org/WBSITE/EXTERNAL/TOPICS/EXTPOVERTY/0,,contentMDK:20153855~menuPK: 3737 57~pagePK:148956~piPK:216618~theSitePK:336992,00. html). The World Bank also notes that human development indicators (which seek to gauge the health, income, education, and security of a population) have also generally improved in low- and middle-income countries. In 1980 the overall rate of infant mortality was eighty-six per 1,000 live births; in 2002 it was sixty per 1,000 live births. Average life expectancy rose from sixty to sixty-five years. In addition, literacy rates improved between 1990 and 2002, from 78% to 83% for adult males and from 62% to 70% for adult females.

All of this has come as good news to those who work to fight poverty. More and more international efforts have been organized in recent decades to address the problems of the poorest among us. Individuals with widely varying backgrounds and interests have joined together in support of both governmental and nongovernmental actions that may improve the living conditions of the poor and, indeed, eventually eradicate poverty altogether. However, while the world certainly has seen an overall improvement in rates of poverty and poverty-related issues, success has been uneven and hampered by serious setbacks. One devastating disease, such as AIDS, can obliterate the economy of a low-income country. One violent conflict can crush any human development advances that might have been achieved. Even in the United States, one catastrophic event, such as Hurricane Katrina, can bring social and economic devastation to an entire region for years or even decades.

In his 1964 State of the Union address, President Lyndon B. Johnson declared war on poverty in the United States. At the time, the U.S. poverty rate was about 25%. Johnson hoped to introduce a massive social welfare program that would be the hallmark of his administration's "Great Society." Congress passed the Economic Opportunity Act (EOA) later in 1964, one the few remaining legacies of which is the early childhood development program Head Start. By the 1980s public resentment against those who received the welfare benefits created by

Johnson was beginning to rise, and the EOA was slowly being dismantled. In the 1990s President Bill Clinton declared an end to "welfare as we know it" when he signed into law the Personal Responsibility and Work Opportunity Reconciliation Act of 1996 (also known as "welfare to work"), which critics argued signaled the official abandonment of the war on poverty and the beginning of the war on the poor in the United States.

Internationally, the adoption in 2000 of the Millennium Development Goals by the United Nations (UN) as a way both to track progress and to set expectations on poverty and human development appeared to mark another shift in thinking on the subject. With their clearly outlined goals and target date of 2015, the Millennium Development Goals were viewed as a commitment to improving the lives of the poor and marginalized around the world. According to some observers, if poverty rates continue to decline at the pace they have since 1990, the Millennium Development Goal of halving extreme poverty and hunger by 2015 will have been achieved.

Others disagree, however. Jan Vandemoortele argues in *Are We Really Reducing Global Poverty?* (July 2002, http://www.undp.org/poverty/docs/arewereally-reducing-gobal-poverty.pdf) that the apparent decline is deceptive because of the dramatic drop in poverty rates in China and India, which skew the numbers for the entire developing world. Vandemoortele points out that poverty rates have not declined in the regions of sub-Saharan Africa, Latin America, and the Caribbean or in the Middle East and North Africa. Vandemoortele states that "when excluding East Asia, the average proportion of income-poor in developing countries declined less dramatically—to 33 per cent in 1998, down from 35 per cent in 1990. At this pace, poverty will not be halved by 2015; it will only be one-quarter below its level in 1990."

Other researchers concur. Revisiting some of the issues covered in Chapter 1 of this book, Sanjay G. Reddy and Thomas W. Pogge of Columbia University write in their unpublished paper "How Not to Count the Poor" (October 29, 2005, http://papers.ssrn.com/sol3/papers.cfm?abstract_id=893159), "The World Bank's approach to estimating the extent, distribution and trend of global income poverty is neither meaningful nor reliable." One of the greatest controversies over the question of whether rates of poverty have actually dropped since 1990 is about the widely accepted method of counting the poor using one dollar a day as the basis. Reddy and Pogge's main argument involves the World Bank's revision of the one dollar a day measurement to $1.08 a day at 1993 purchasing power parity (PPP; see Chapter 1 for further explanation of purchasing power parity). They explain:

> In 1999, applying its method with the old ($1/day PPP 1985) IPL [international poverty line], the Bank

reported very similar poverty rates for Nigeria and Mauritania of 31.1% and 31.4% respectively. In 2000, applying its method with the new ($1.08/day PPP 1993) IPL, the Bank reported poverty rates for Nigeria and Mauritania of 70.2% and 3.8% respectively. Depending on which PPP base year is used, Nigeria's poverty rate is either slightly lower or 18 times higher than Mauritania's!

The World Bank concedes that there are problems with existing measurements but dismisses the idea that its methodology distorts the number of people living in poverty over time. For their part, Reddy and Pogge maintain that there are better, more accurate ways to decide who is poor and what constitutes poverty, as well as to see trends in poverty over time.

Another trend is highlighted in *A Compendium of Inequality: The Human Development Report 2005* (October 2005, http://www.globalpolicy.org/socecon/inequal/2005/10compendium.pdf), in which Jens Martens examines the purpose and impact of the United Nations Development Program's 2005 *Human Development Report*. Martens discusses a significant finding of the 2005 report: since 1985 fifty-three out of seventy-three countries for which statistics exist have seen an increase in social and income inequality. This phenomenon is occurring in countries of all economic levels, including the United States. Only nine countries, representing just 4% of the world's population, have experienced a narrowing of the gap between rich and poor. The poorest 40% of the global population earns 5% of overall income, while the richest 10% earns 54% of overall income.

In its report *Growth Isn't Working: The Unbalanced Distribution of Benefits and Costs from Economic Growth* (January 2006, http://www.neweconomics.org/gen/uploads/hrfu5w555mzd3f55m2vqwty5020220061129 29.pdf), the New Economic Foundation (NEF) argues that the world's poorest people in the lowest-income countries bear a disproportionate financial burden for the consumption patterns of the wealthy. In a practical sense this means that global economic growth actually causes environmental degradation, promotes social inequality, and skews the distribution of wealth toward those who need it the least, particularly within low-income countries. Regarding the importance of money distribution, the NEF writes:

> Growth calculations take no account of the distribution of income. National accounts treat one dollar of income identically, whoever receives it. This is clearly unrealistic and counter-intuitive: the effect of an additional $100 on the well-being of a household with an income of $100 is clearly far greater than for a household with an income of $1 million. As a result, the effect of a given change in aggregate income on well-being is critically dependent on *whose* income is increased. This means that from a well-being perspective, the

incomes of the rich are systematically over-valued at the expense of the incomes of the poor.

Furthermore, the NEF reports, from 1981 to 1990 the share in global per capita growth of those living on less than one dollar per day was just 2.2%; by the period 1990–2001 the proportion had shrunk to less than 1%. From 1981 to 1990 the share in global per capita growth of those living on less than two dollars per day—nearly half the earth's population—was 5.5%; from 1990 to 2001 it was down to just 3.1%. The NEF explains that for every $166 of world economic growth in the 1990s, just one dollar went toward the first Millennium Development Goal of cutting extreme poverty and hunger in half by 2015.

In *The Scorecard on Development: Twenty-five Years of Diminished Development* (September 2005, http://www.cepr.net/publications/development_2005_09. pdf), Mark Weisbrot, Dean Baker, and David Rosnick of the Center for Economic and Policy Research contend that low- and middle-income countries have experienced an overall decline in both economic growth and human development since the 1980s. The report examines progress in five income quintiles (categories) of low- and middle-income countries in two time periods: 1960–80 and 1980–2005. Overall growth in gross domestic product (GPD) declined for all quintiles except for the bottom one (with average annual per capita income of $355 to $1,225), which saw a slight average annual growth, from 1.7% to 1.8%. Weisbrot, Baker, and Rosnick note, however, that the presence of China and India in this bottom quintile weights the results toward growth; without the growth of those two countries, the entire quintile would have experienced overall decline. The fourth quintile experienced the most dramatic decline in economic growth, from 2.4% annually in the period 1960 to 1980 to just 0.7% from 1980 to 2005.

Whether caused by or the cause of the economic decline among poor countries, a parallel decline in development indicators, such as life expectancy and infant mortality, was experienced by most countries. The bottom four quintiles all saw a decline in the rate of increase of life expectancy. In the poorest group, which has an average life expectancy of thirty-one to forty-four years, life expectancy increased an average of 0.4% per year from 1960 to 1980 but dropped to an average increase of 0.24% from 1980 to 2005. The biggest drop came in the second-poorest quintile (with life expectancy averaging forty-four to fifty-three years), where average annual life expectancy increased at a rate of 0.56% from 1960 to 1980 and just 0.03% from 1980 to 2005. Similarly, infant and under-five mortality also decreased at slower rates in all quintiles in the later period, most significantly in the fourth quintile, where the rate of infant mortality fell by an average

of 2.6 per 1,000 live births in the earlier time period but was down to 1.3 per 1,000 in the later period.

The organization Social Watch International agrees that the world is not on target for achieving the Millennium Development Goals. In its *Social Watch Report 2005* the group maintains that progress is occurring at just half the pace it should to meet the goals. Social Watch states that "three out of four countries for which data are available performed worse in the last fifteen years than they did in the 1970s and 1980s" in reducing child mortality—a trend that extends to almost all human development indicators, according to Social Watch. Despite some of the successes of globalization in increasing overall global wealth, extreme poverty is actually increasing in sub-Saharan Africa, Latin America, the Middle East, eastern Europe, and Asia, although, as with all other groups reporting on poverty, Social Watch points out that the progress in India and China—as well as in Vietnam—makes the overall Asian region appear to be doing better than it actually is.

ANTIPOVERTY CAMPAIGNS CHAMPIONED BY THE RICH AND FAMOUS

In spite of the above evaluations, many people would say that there is reason for hope. While the wealthy have always taken on charitable causes to support, early in the twenty-first century the issue of poverty came to the fore when a rock star and a business couple joined together to pressure the world's wealthiest countries to take action. In December 2005 *Time* magazine named the rock singer Bono, of the band U2, and Microsoft's Bill and Melinda Gates its Persons of the Year for their work combating poverty and disease. The *Time* issue, which garnered much media attention, called the trio "the good Samaritans" and noted the unlikely juxtaposition of the three celebrities, who on the surface appear to have little in common.

Long known as the wealthiest man in the world—with a personal fortune of $46.5 billion, according to www.msnbc.msn.com ("Time Names Gateses, Bono 'Persons of 2005,'" December 18, 2005, http://www.msnbc.msn.com/id/10516674/)—Bill Gates, along with wife Melinda, created the Gates Foundation in 2000 with an endowment of $29 billion. Initially, the foundation's focus was on public health and education programs. However, a meeting in 2002 with Bono led to a partnership. Bono had been involved with poverty and AIDS campaigns since the mid-1980s, when he agreed to join Live Aid, the group of singers and musicians who performed to raise money for famine relief in Ethiopia. In a November 2005 interview in *Rolling Stone* (Jann S. Wenner, "Bono: The Rolling Stone Interview," November 3, 2005, http://www.rollingstone.com/news/story/8651280/bono/), Bono explained the experience he and his wife had when they traveled to Ethiopia after Live Aid:

> We worked in an orphanage. We lived in a little tent. The camp was surrounded by barbed wire. Woke up in the mornings as the mist lifted, and watched thousands of Africans, who had walked all night with the little belongings they had, coming toward us to beg for food and their life. We saw the everydayness of despair. People would leave their children in rags, some would be alive, some wouldn't. For a couple of kids from the suburbs, it was a very overwhelming experience. . . . You promise that you'll never forget . . . but you do. You get back to your life, to being in the band. But something in the back of my mind told me there's something here I don't fully understand—but that I will, at some point in my life, be able to help those people.

Part of the solution to ending poverty, according to Bono and others, lies in canceling the international debts of poor countries. With that end in mind, he founded the organization Debt, AIDS, Trade Africa (DATA) and joined in the international ONE: Campaign to Make Poverty History, which was founded by nongovernmental organizations including Oxfam International, DATA, CARE, Save the Children, and the International Rescue Committee. A hallmark of the ONE campaign was a 2005 public service announcement that featured celebrities and public figures as varied as Brad Pitt, Mos Def, and Pat Robertson.

In June 2006 Warren E. Buffett, founder of the Nebraska-based insurance company Berkshire Hathaway, Inc., and one of the world's wealthiest people, announced his plans to donate 85% of his $44 billion fortune—$37.4 billion—to charitable organizations. Most of the money was to be directed to the Gates Foundation. At a June 26, 2006, function at the main branch of the New York Public Library in Manhattan, where he appeared with Bill and Melinda Gates to discuss the arrangement, Buffett commented: "I'm not an enthusiast for dynastic wealth, particularly when six billion others have much poorer hands than we do in life," alluding to his own and the Gates's immense financial success in contrast to much of the rest of the world's population (Jeremy W. Peters, "Buffett Always Planned to Give Away His Billions," *New York Times*, June 26, 2006).

END OF POVERTY?

In December 2005 the renowned economist Jeffrey Sachs, the head of the Columbia University Earth Institute and the director of the UN Millennium Project, published his book *The End of Poverty: Economic Possibilities for Our Time*. Sachs, who has been described as a "rock star economist," declares that, if all parties cooperate, extreme poverty can be entirely eliminated by 2025. Using a nine-point plan, Sachs proposes that wise investment, in the form of foreign aid, in the health systems and infrastructure of low-income countries is the key to ending poverty. In particular, Sachs claims his goal can be met if wealthy countries at least double their annual aid contributions. In the case of the United States aid would quadruple, from one-eighth of 1% of annual GDP to 0.7% of GDP. This is the increase agreed to by President George W. Bush, who set up a Millennium Challenge Account in 2002 to channel funds to low-income countries. As of 2006, however, the 0.7% goal had not been met.

Critics of Sachs's ideas say that programs emphasizing foreign aid to low-income countries have been ongoing since the 1960s, with few lasting results, and they point out that Sachs does not appear to take into account the widespread government corruption in poor countries that usually prevents aid from reaching the people who need it most. Additionally, Sachs's detractors maintain that his past interventions in Poland and Russia during those countries' political upheavals in the 1990s led to economic devastation, especially in Russia, where Sachs helped to institute what has become known as the "shock therapy" solution to stabilize an economy in transition. Economic shock therapy calls for the sudden end to price supports and trade barriers, which, in the case of the former Soviet Union, was meant to convert the nation from communism to a free market society. In Russia, the sudden change caused widespread unemployment and the collapse of their public health system, among other problems, and critics faulted the therapy as being too harsh or as not having been implemented properly.

Nonetheless, despite the drawbacks of his proposed program to end poverty—some commentators have called him an overly self-confident dreamer—almost everyone agrees that things could hardly be worse for the poor. And most believe it is worth giving Sachs's ideas a try. If Sachs is correct at all, millions of lives could be saved every year. In his book Sachs sums up his hope for ending poverty: "Great social forces are the mere accumulation of individual actions. Let the future say of our generation that we sent forth mighty currents of hope, and that we worked together to heal the world."

Another noted economist, William Easterly of New York University, disagrees completely with Sachs and his admirers. In his 2006 book *The White Man's Burden: Why the West's Efforts to Aid the Rest Have Done So Much Ill and So Little Good*, Easterly argues that the global program of foreign aid does far more harm than good to poor countries because it is based on a fundamental misunderstanding of the cultures and governments it purports to help. Specifically, according to syndicated columnist David Ignatius's review of the book ("Paved with Good Intentions," May 21, 2006, http://www.washingtonpost.com/wp-dyn/content/article/2006/05/18/AR2006051801085.html), Easterly believes that the biggest mistake made by the governments of industrialized countries who continually provide foreign aid "is that they are 'Planners,' who seek to impose solutions from the top down, rather than 'Searchers,' who adapt to the real life and culture of foreign lands from the bottom up." Easterly encourages this bottom–up approach wherein low-income countries are responsible for creating and running their own self-sustaining programs to address poverty.

A former World Bank development economist, Easterly is harshly critical of that organization's programs, along with those of the International Monetary Fund and other groups that promote increased globalization along with foreign aid. Easterly points out that the most economically successful lower-income countries—China, Thailand, and South Korea—are those that have never been colonized and, therefore, have been allowed to develop political and economic programs naturally.

Still, as op-ed *New York Times* columnist Nicholas Kristof points out in "Foreign Aid Has Flaws. So What?" (June 13, 2006), many antipoverty and development programs imposed in the top–down approach that Easterly rejects have been enormously successful. "Eradicating smallpox and reducing river blindness have improved the lives of more people for less money than almost any investment imaginable. . . . So let's not shy away from a conversation about the effectiveness of aid. The problems are real, but so are the millions of people alive today who wouldn't be if not for aid."

IMPORTANT NAMES AND ADDRESSES

Amnesty International
5 Penn Plaza, 14th Fl.
New York, NY 10001
(212) 807-8400
FAX: (212) 463-9193
E-mail: admin-us@aiusa.org
URL: http://www.amnesty.org

Asian Development Bank (ADB)
6 ADB Ave.
Mandaluyong City, Philippines 1550
011-632-632-4444
FAX: 011-632-636-2444
URL: http://www.adb.org

Brookings Institution
1775 Massachusetts Ave. NW
Washington, DC 20036
(202) 797-6000
FAX: (202) 797-6004
E-mail: communications@brookings.edu
URL: http://www.brookings.edu

**Center for Economic and Policy
Research**
1611 Connecticut Ave. NW, Ste. 400
Washington, DC 20009
(202) 293-5380
FAX: (202) 588-1356
E-mail: cepr@cepr.net
URL: http://www.cepr.net

**Chronic Poverty Research Center
Institute for Development Policy and
Management
School of Environment and Development
University of Manchester**
Harold Hankins Building
Booth Street W.
Manchester, United Kingdom M13 9QH
011-44-161-275-2810
FAX: 011-44-161-273-8829
URL: http://www.chronicpoverty.org

Global Policy Forum
777 United Nations Plaza, Ste. 3D
New York, NY 10017

(212) 557-3161
FAX: (212) 557-3165
E-mail: globalpolicy@globalpolicy.org
URL: http://www.globalpolicy.org

Human Rights Watch
350 Fifth Ave., 34th Fl.
New York, NY 10118-3299
(212) 290-4700
FAX: (212) 736-1300
E-mail: hrwnyc@hrw.org
URL: http://www.hrw.org

Institute for Economic Democracy
9936 West Camden Ave.
Sun City, AZ 85351
1-888-533-1020
E-mail: ied@ied.info
URL: http://www.ied.info

**Food First/Institute for Food and
Development Policy**
398 Sixtieth St.
Oakland, CA 94618
(510) 654-4400
FAX: (510) 654-4551
URL: http://www.foodfirst.org

**International Committee of the Red
Cross**
19 Ave. de la Paix
Geneva, Switzerland CH 1202
011-41-22-734-6001
FAX: 011-41-22-733-2057
URL: http://www.icrc.org

International Crisis Group
149 Ave. Louise, Level 24
Brussels, Belgium B-1050
011-32-2-502-9038
FAX: 011-32-2-502-5038
URL: http://www.crisisgroup.org

International Forum on Globalization
1009 General Kennedy Ave., No. 2
San Francisco, CA 94129
(415) 561-7650

FAX: (415) 561-7651
E-mail: ifg@ifg.org
URL: http://www.ifg.org

International Labor Organization
4 Route des Morillons
Geneva 22, Switzerland CH-1211
011-41-22-799-6111
FAX: 011-41-22-798-8685
E-mail: ilo@ilo.org
URL: http://www.ilo.org

MADRE
121 West 27th St., No. 301
New York, NY 10001
(212) 627-0444
FAX: (212) 675-3704
E-mail: madre@madre.org
URL: http://www.MADRE.org

**National Center for Children in Poverty
Columbia University
Mailman School of Public Health**
215 West 125th St., 3rd Fl.
New York, NY 10027
(646) 284-9600
FAX: (646) 284-9623
E-mail: info@nccp.org
URL: http://www.nccp.org

New Economics Foundation
3 Jonathan St.
London, United Kingdom SE11 5NH
011-44-20-7820-6300
FAX: 011-44-20-7820-6301
E-mail: info@neweconomics.org
URL: http://www.neweconomics.org

Oxfam International
266 Banbury Rd., Ste. 20
Oxford, United Kingdom OX2 7DL
011-44-1865-339-100
FAX: 011-44-1865–339-101
E-mail:
information@oxfaminternational.org
URL: http://www.oxfam.org

Social Watch
Jackson 1136
Montevideo, Uruguay 11200
011-598-2-419-6192
FAX: 011-598-2-411-9222
E-mail: socwatch@socialwatch.org
URL: http://www.socialwatch.org

United Nations Development Fund for Women (UNIFEM)
304 East 45th St.
New York, NY 10017
(212) 906-6400
FAX: (212) 906-6705
URL: http://www.unifem.org

United Nations Development Program (UNDP)
1 United Nations Plaza
New York, NY 10017
(212) 906-5000
FAX: (212) 906-5364
URL: http://www.undp.org

United Nations Educational, Scientific, and Cultural Organization (UNESCO)
7 Pl. de Fontenoy
Paris 07 SP, France 75352
011-33-1-4568-1000
FAX: 011-33-1-4567-1690
E-mail: bpi@unesco.org
URL: http://www.unesco.org

UNICEF
3 United Nations Plaza
New York, NY 10017
(212) 326-7000
FAX: (212) 887-7465
URL: http://www.unicef.org

United Nations Population Fund (UNFPA)
220 East 42nd St.
New York, NY 10017
(212) 297-5000
URL: http://www.unfpa.org

United States Bureau of the Census
4700 Silver Hill Rd.
Washington, DC 20233-0001
URL: http://www.census.gov

United States Department of Labor, Bureau of Labor Statistics Division of Information Services
2 Massachusetts Ave. NE, Rm. 2860
Washington, DC 20212
(202) 691-5200
FAX: (202) 691-7890
E-mail: blsdata_staff@bls.gov
URL: http://www.bls.gov

United States Department of Agriculture
1400 Independence Ave. SW
Washington, DC 20250
URL: http://www.usda.gov

Women's Environment and Development Organization
355 Lexington Ave., 3rd Fl.
New York, NY 10017
(212) 973-0325
FAX: (212) 973-0335
E-mail: wedo@wedo.org
URL: http://www.wedo.org

World Bank
1818 H St. NW
Washington, DC 20433
(202) 473-1000
FAX: (202) 477-6391
URL: http://www.worldbank.org

World Food Program
Via C. G. Viola 68
Parco dei Medici
Rome, Italy 00148
011-39-06-65131
FAX: 011-39-06-6513-2840
E-mail: wfpinfo@wfp.org
URL: http://www.wfp.org

World Health Organization (WHO)
Ave. Appia 20
Geneva, 27 Switzerland 1211
011-41-22-791-2111
FAX: 011-41-22-791-3111
E-mail: info@who.int
URL: http://www.who.int

RESOURCES

The United Nations Development Program (UNDP) publishes an annual *Human Development Report*, which focuses on a different development issue each year. In addition, it publishes regional and national reports on poverty and development. The UNDP is one of the main proponents of the Millennium Development Goals; each year its *Human Development Reports* address progress toward the MDGs.

Other UN programs focus on specific facets of human development. The United Nations Children's Fund, or UNICEF, which is devoted to the rights and needs of children, publishes an annual report called *State of the World's Children*. Programs within UNICEF address children's health—most notably, children with HIV/AIDS—and education. UNICEF's Innocenti Research Center "promotes the effective implementation of the Convention on the Rights of the Child, in both developing and industrialized countries," publishing a variety of papers on such topics as child poverty, child work and labor, and conflict and displacement. UNIFEM, the United Nations Development Fund for Women, lists its primary purposes as "reducing feminized poverty; ending violence against women; reversing the spread of HIV/AIDS among women and girls; and achieving gender equality in democratic governance in times of peace as well as war." The organization publishes reports and papers related to all of these subjects. Part of the mission of UNESCO—the United Nations Educational, Scientific, and Cultural Organization—is to monitor and report on the state of education in developing countries. Through its Education for All (EFA) program, UNESCO publishes an annual *EFA Global Monitoring Report*. The Food and Agriculture Department of the United Nations publishes an annual *State of Food Insecurity in the World*, and the World Food Program publishes information about its food aid programs on its Web site (http://www.wfp.org). The International Labor Organization is the UN program dedicated to policing and reporting on human and labor rights around the world, particularly poverty-related issues such as low wages, the informal economy, and human trafficking. The United Nations Population Fund (UNFPA) focuses on improving the living conditions—especially reproductive health—of women in developing countries. The UNFPA publishes an annual *State of World Population*. The World Health Organization (WHO) is the arm of the United Nations devoted to tracking and promoting health issues, many of which particularly affect the poor, including HIV/AIDS, malaria, infectious disease, and child mortality. WHO publishes its *World Health Report* annually. IRINnews.org is an online news source run by the UN Office for the Coordination of Humanitarian Affairs; it publishes news stories on events in sub-Saharan Africa, the Middle East, and Central Asia.

Like the UNDP, the World Bank is an international organization of member countries concerned with poverty and human development. The World Bank publishes numerous reports on the economic and development status of regions and individual nations in addition to its primary function of offering low-interest loans and lines of credit to underdeveloped and developing countries. The World Bank also publishes reports on topical issues affecting the poor, such as natural disasters.

The Asian Development Bank (ADB) is similar to the World Bank in its structure and goals, but is focused exclusively on ending poverty in Asian countries. The ADB publishes an annual report as well as a report called *Asian Development Outlook*.

The U.S. Bureau of the Census publishes the most recent statistics on poverty in its report *Income, Poverty, and Insurance Coverage in the United States*. On its Web site (http://www.census.gov/hhes/www/poverty/poverty.html) it provides valuable information on how poverty is measured and defined.

The United States Department of Agriculture's Web site (http://www.usda.gov) provides links to reports on regional and local poverty—particularly in rural areas—

as well as information on food security and food assistance programs in the United States.

The United States Department of Labor's Bureau of Labor Statistics tracks historical and recent patterns of wages, unemployment, and careers. Its information is available in published reports and online.

Many nongovernmental organizations (NGOs), think tanks, and watchdog groups maintain Web sites that provide invaluable insight and information on poverty and the poor. Among them are Amnesty International; the Brookings Institution; the Chronic Poverty Research Center; Global Policy Forum; Human Rights Watch; the International Committee of the Red Cross; the International Forum on Globalization; the Institute for Economic Democracy; MADRE; the National Center for Children in Poverty; Oxfam International; Social Watch; and Women's Environment and Development Organization.

INDEX